THE *1790–1890* FEDERAL POPULATION CENSUSES

CATALOG OF

NATIONAL ARCHIVES MICROFILM

NATIONAL ARCHIVES TRUST FUND BOARD
WASHINGTON, DC
REVISED 2001

PUBLISHED FOR THE
NATIONAL ARCHIVES AND RECORDS ADMINISTRATION
BY THE NATIONAL ARCHIVES TRUST FUND BOARD
Revised 2001

Library of Congress Cataloging-in-Publication Data
United States. National Archives and Records Administration.
   The 1790–1890 federal population censuses: catalog of National Archives
microfilm.
     p. cm.
   Rev. ed. of: United States. National Archives and Records Service.
Federal population censuses, 1790–1890. 1971.
    Includes indexes.
    ISBN 0-911333-63-0: $3.50
    1. United States—Bibliography—Microform catalogs. 2. United States—
Genealogy—Bibliography—Microform catalogs. 3. United States—Census—
Bibliography—Microform catalogs. 4. United States. National Archives and
Records Administration—Microform catalogs. 5. Microforms—Catalogs.
6. United States—Census—Bibliography—Microform catalogs. I. United
States. National Archives and Records Service. Federal population censuses,
1790–1890. II. Title.
Z5313.U5U53 1993
[CS47]
016.929'373'–dc20   93-17537
                                    CIP

The paper used in this publication meets the minimum requirements of the American
National Standard for Permanence of Paper for Printed Library Materials Z39.48-
1992.

Revised text by Constance Potter and Benjamin Guterman based on an edited ver-
sion of a 1993 introduction written by Dr. Wayne B. Cook. Design by Janice Hargett.

Cover: Immigrants pose at Ellis Island in New York Harbor, ca. 1890.
(NWDNS-90-G-125-3)

FOREWORD

The National Archives and Records Administration is responsible for administering the permanently valuable noncurrent records of the Federal Government. These archival holdings, now amounting to more than 2 million cubic feet, date from the first Continental Congress and consist of records of the legislative, judicial, and executive branches. The Presidential libraries of Herbert Hoover, Franklin D. Roosevelt, Harry S. Truman, Dwight D. Eisenhower, John Fitzgerald Kennedy, Lyndon Baines Johnson, Gerald R. Ford, Jimmy Carter, and Ronald Reagan, as well as the Nixon and Bush Presidential projects, contain the papers of those Presidents and many of their associates.

These research resources document significant events in our nation's history, but most of them are preserved because of their continuing practical use in the ordinary processes of government, for the protection of private rights, and for the use of researchers and the public. Although Federal records were not created for genealogists, the holdings of the National Archives of the United States contain valuable sources of genealogical information. Perhaps the richest source for genealogists is the information contained in the Federal decennial population census schedules.

CONTENTS

LIST OF FIGURES

LIST OF TABLES

INTRODUCTION

Article I, section 2, of the U.S. Constitution requires that a decennial population census, a nationwide enumeration or count of the population, be taken every 10 years. Congress uses the census figures to apportion seats in the House of Representatives. The census also determines each state's number of votes in the electoral college, which selects the President and Vice President; and affects apportionment in state and local legislatures. Section 9 provides that "no capitation or other direct tax shall be laid, unless in proportion to the census or Enumeration herein before directed to be taken."

The population schedules, first prepared in 1790, contain a wealth of information for historians, economists, and other researchers interested in topics such as Revolutionary War pensioners, Civil War veterans, western expansion, regional and local history, immigration, and naturalization.

To ensure the privacy of individuals, Congress has provided for a 72-year restriction to access of Federal census schedules. The 1920 census was released in 1992; the 1930 census will be opened in 2002. To obtain specific nonrestricted data from post-1920 censuses, use Bureau of the Census Form BC-600, "Application for Search of Census Records." Copies of BC-600 are available from the Bureau of the Census, P.O. Box 1545, Jeffersonville, IN 47131.

This catalog lists the microfilmed copies of the original 1790–1890 schedules and the published 1790 schedules. Microfilm copies of the 1790–1920 population schedules are available for rental and sale.

Microfilmed copies of census schedules are located in the Microfilm Research Room in the National Archives Building, which is on Pennsylvania Avenue, NW, between Seventh and Ninth Streets in Washington, DC, as well as the 13 National Archives Regional Records Services facilities. See page xxi for a list of the regional facilities, their addresses, telephone numbers, and other information. Many state and local archives, libraries, and genealogical or historical societies; many of the Family History Centers of the Church of Jesus Christ of Latter-Day Saints (Mormons); and other institutions have purchased all or some of the census microfilms. Information on many of these institutions appears in Alice Eichholz, ed., *Ancestry's Red Book: American State, County, & Town Sources* (Salt Lake City: Ancestry Publishing Co., 1991) and Elizabeth Petty Bentley, *The Genealogist's Address Book* (Baltimore: Genealogical Publishing Co., 3d ed.,1995).

CENSUS SCHEDULES

The 1790–1820 population schedules were nearly all handwritten; the Government started using printed schedules in 1830.

With each census, the forms asked for additional information. See *Guide to Genealogical Research in the National Archives*, chapter 1, and *200 Years of U.S. Census Taking: Population and Housing Questions, 1790–1990* (Washington, DC: U.S. Department of Commerce, Bureau of the Census, 1989). The latter work is available at some commercial bookstores.

The 1790–1840 schedules furnish only the names of the free heads of family, not of other family members. These schedules totaled the number of other family members, without name, by free or slave status. Also, the sex and age categories that the schedules first used only for free whites from 1790 through 1810 eventually applied to other persons, and the age categories increased after 1790.

The 1820 census first asked about naturalization status. The 1840 census included a special inquiry regarding pensioners for Revolutionary or military service. This section named persons who were either family heads or members and specified the pensioner's age, not just a range of ages. The results were summarized in *Census of Pensioners: Revolutionary or Military Services . . .* (Washington, DC: Blair and Rives, 1841). Roll 3 of *First Census of the United States, 1790*, National Archives Microfilm Publication T498 reproduces this report.

The 1850 census was the first to record each person's name, specific age, occupation of those over age 15, place of birth, and value of real estate. The slave schedules, however, name only the slave owner and indicate only if a slave was black or mulatto, and his or her sex and age.

The 1860 schedules were almost identical to those for 1850, but the 1860 census was the first to inquire about the value of each free person's personal estate.

The 1870 schedule asked if a person's father or mother were foreign born. Columns 19 and 20 cover "Constitutional relations."

The enumerator checked column 19 if a male was a "citizen of the U.S. of 21 years of age and upwards." In column 20 the enumerator marked if a male citizen 21 years or older had had his "right to vote denied or abridged on other grounds than rebellion or other crime." In other words, was the person denied the right to vote in violation of the 14th amendment, which guarantees citizenship, due process, and equal protection under the law for men regardless of race.

The 1880 schedule was the first to ask about the relationship of each individual to the head of the family, specifying what could only be assumed in earlier censuses. Moreover, the 1880 census was the first to inquire about the birthplace of each person's parents, including the country of those who were foreign born. The census gives the state or country of birth, not the city or county. A fire destroyed many 1890 population and special schedules, and water used to extinguish the blaze damaged many more. As a result, the Government disposed of most schedules. The few remaining 1890 population schedules or fragments are indexed.

For information about the 1890 schedules and the fire, see Kellee Blake, "'First in the Path of Firemen': The Fate of the 1890 Population Census," *Prologue: Quarterly of the National Archives* 28 (Spring 1996): 64–81.

The 1890 *Special Schedules . . . Enumerating Union Veterans and Widows of Veterans of the Civil War* (M123), are most important for providing data about the military service of veterans, including some Confederates. The information about post office addresses and sometimes streets and house numbers can lead outside the National Archives to important non-Federal records such as deeds, tax lists, and other property records that are mostly kept at local levels.

CATALOG ARRANGEMENT

This catalog arranges the 1790–1890 schedules chronologically, and thereunder alphabetically by state and county. The counties are generally in alphabetical order. Some of the major cities, such as Philadelphia, are listed separately. The catalog also lists the enumeration districts (EDs) for the 1880 schedules.

MICROFILM PROBLEMS

The National Archives acquired the master negative microfilm rolls from the Bureau of the Census and could not correct some problems with legibility. Also, some Census Bureau volume pages at the beginning of the schedules may omit or misorder counties, MCDs, or EDs and include other errors that the National Archives did not create but which this catalog reflects. The Soundex, prepared by the Works Progress Administration, and the microfilm produced by the Bureau of the Census may include additional problems. While the National Archives did not have the staff necessary to detect and correct all these problems, researchers who identify any may report them to the Records Control and Product Management Branch (NWP), National Archives and Records Administration, Washington, DC 20408.

CENSUS INDEXES
Privately Printed Indexes

Privately printed indexes are available for most States or territories from 1790 through 1870 and for the 1890 special schedules. For each State or territory, these indexes typically alphabetize sur-

names (last names) and then given (first) names or other names and initials of heads of families and specify the county, city, and possibly an MCD. The Microfilm Research Room, regional archives, and numerous libraries or other institutions have many of these indexes, which appear in microfilmed, microfiched, or published form.

Many schedules have different kinds of page numbers. Forewards to the indexes, though, usually explain the approach used and may include helpful aids such as census maps, histories, and bibliographies. Some indexes for early censuses also transcribe most census data from the schedules.

Government Indexes

The Microfilm Research room and the 13 Regional Records Services facilities hold microfilmed indexes that the Federal Government prepared for the 1790, 1810, 1820, 1880, and 1890 censuses.

The Government Printing Office published and indexed the 1790 schedules of 11 States, along with Virginia data that was reconstructed from state enumerations from 1782 to 1785 and was intended to replace the missing 1790 schedules. National Archives Microfilm Publication T498, *First Census of the United States, 1790*, reproduces these works, which are also commercially reprinted. *List of Free Black Heads of Families in the First Census, 1790*, Special List 34, compiled by Debra L. Newman (Washington, DC: National Archives and Records Service, rev. 1974), indexes names of free black heads of families nationwide. The 1840 census of Revolutionary War pensioners is reproduced on roll 3 of T498.

Index to the 1810 Census Schedules for Virginia (T1019) alphabetizes names, references counties, and notes volume, page, and line numbers of the schedules. Volume numbers that the index notes appear within the microfilm rolls, not in this catalog. *Compilation of Tennessee Census Reports*, 1820, National Archives Microfilm Publication T911, includes alphabetized indexes, partly transcribed data, and copies of an original 1820 schedule.

Index to the Eleventh Census of the United States (M496) indexes the remaining 1890 population schedules. Roll 1 covers alphabetized surnames from A through J; roll 2, from K through Z. After the surname, the given or middle names and also initials are alphabetized. The numbers on the right-hand side for the cards refer to those stamped on the schedules.

THE SOUNDEX CODING SYSTEM

The Soundex is a coded surname (last name) index based on the way a surname sounds rather than the way it is spelled. Surnames that sound the same, but are spelled differently, like SMITH and SMYTH, have the same code and are filed together. The Soundex coding system was developed to find a surname even though it may have been recorded under various spellings. Every Soundex code consists of a letter and three numbers, such as W252 (see chart below). The letter is always the first letter of the surname whether it is a consonant or a vowel. The numbers are assigned to the remaining consonants of the surname according to the Soundex guide.

Disregard the remaining vowels (A, E, I, O, and U) as well as W, Y, and H. Assign numbers to the next three consonants of the surname according to the coding guide included in table 1. Disregard any remaining consonants. If there are not three consonants following the initial letter, use zeroes to complete the three-digit code. For example, Lee is coded L000; Jones is coded J520; Western is coded W236; and Tymczak is coded T522 representing T, M, C, and K. The names are arranged by the Soundex code and then alphabetically by the first name.

TABLE 1

SOUNDEX CODING GUIDE

After retaining the first letter of the surname and disregarding the next letters if they are A, E, I, O, U, W, Y, and H, then:

The number	Represents the letters
1	B, P, F, V
2	C, S, K, G, J, Q, X, Z
3	D, T
4	L
5	M, N
6	R

Prefixes

If the surname has a prefix, such as D', De, dela, Di, du, Le, van, or Von, code it both with and without the prefix because it might be listed under either code. The surname vanDevanter, for example, could be V-531 or D-153. Mc and Mac are not considered to be prefixes and should be coded like other surnames.

Double Letters

If the surname has any double letters, they should be treated as one letter. Thus, in the surname Lloyd, the second *l* should be crossed out. In the surname Gutierrez, the second *r* should be disregarded.

Side-By-Side Letters

A surname may have different side-by-side letters that receive the same number on the Soundex coding guide. For example, the *c*, *k*, *s* in Jackson all receive a number 2 code. These letters with the same code should be treated as only one letter. In the name Jackson, the *k* and *s* should be disregarded. This rule also applies to the first letter of a surname, even though it is not coded. For example, *Pf* in Pfister would receive a number 1 code for both the *P* and

f. Thus in this name the letter *f* should be crossed out, and the code is P-236.

American Indian and Asian Names

A phonetically spelled American Indian or Asian name was sometimes coded as if it were one name. If a distinguishable surname was given, the name may have been coded in the regular manner. For example, Dances with Wolves might have been coded as Dances (D-522) or as Wolves (W-412), or the name Shinka-Wa-Sa may have been coded as Shinka (S-520) or Sa (S-000).

Soundex Cards

The Soundex microfilm rolls for the 1880 census include four different kinds of cards: Family Cards, Other Members of Family—Continued Cards, Individual Cards, and Institution Cards. Figures 1–4 show examples of completed cards. Explanations of some key features appear within brackets.

Figures 5–8 include blank facsimiles of the four Soundex cards. Boldfaced portions identify the information needed for locating the schedule.

Below the coded surname at the top left of the card, the surname and then first name of the head of the family ordinarily appear as recorded on the schedule. The list at the end of this introduction, Abbreviations and Terms Used in Soundex Cards, is applicable to the 1880, 1900, 1910, and 1920 Soundexes. It can help researchers determine the relationships of persons to the head of the family. The most important information to record is: **State or territory; volume, ED, sheet, and line numbers; county, city, and MCD.**

Other Soundex Cards

Frequently, if families include more than six members, the Family Card is followed by a related card, shown in figure 2, Other Members of Family—Continued Card (1880 Soundex). For very large families, more than one of these cards may appear. Handwritten numbers at the bottom of the cards refer to the first card (e.g., "#2, see #1").

Although the continuation card, shown blank in figure 6, notes the name of the head of family and name, relationship, age, and birthplace of the other family member, this card excludes other personal information such as color and sex. It also omits most jurisdictional data found on the Family Card such as the county, city, MCD, and ED.

Some researchers may need to search for a third kind of Soundex card, an Individual Card (figure 3). A blank card appears in figure 7. This card contains data only on a child age 10 or under who (1) had a surname different from the head of family, or who (2) was not an immediate member of a family (e.g., stepson or nephew), or who (3) resided in an institution without a family. For the first two purposes, the Individual Card duplicates part of the information on a Family Card; it cross-references a census schedule. The Individual

FIGURE 1
FAMILY CARD (1880 SOUNDEX)

Surname codes | Surnames; other names/initials alphabetized | Information needed to find schedule

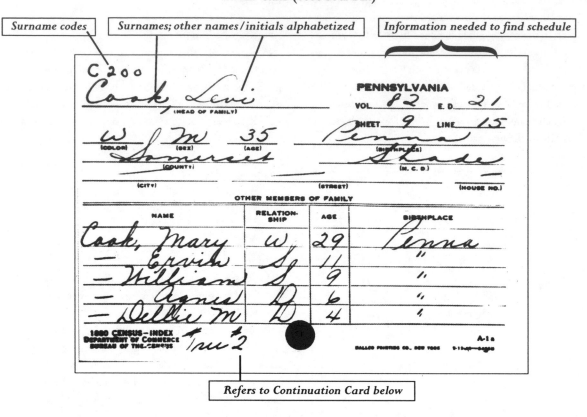

Refers to Continuation Card below

FIGURE 2
OTHER MEMBERS OF FAMILY—CONTINUED CARD
(1880 SOUNDEX)
Use the data on Family Card above to access schedule

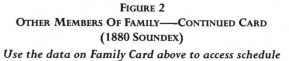

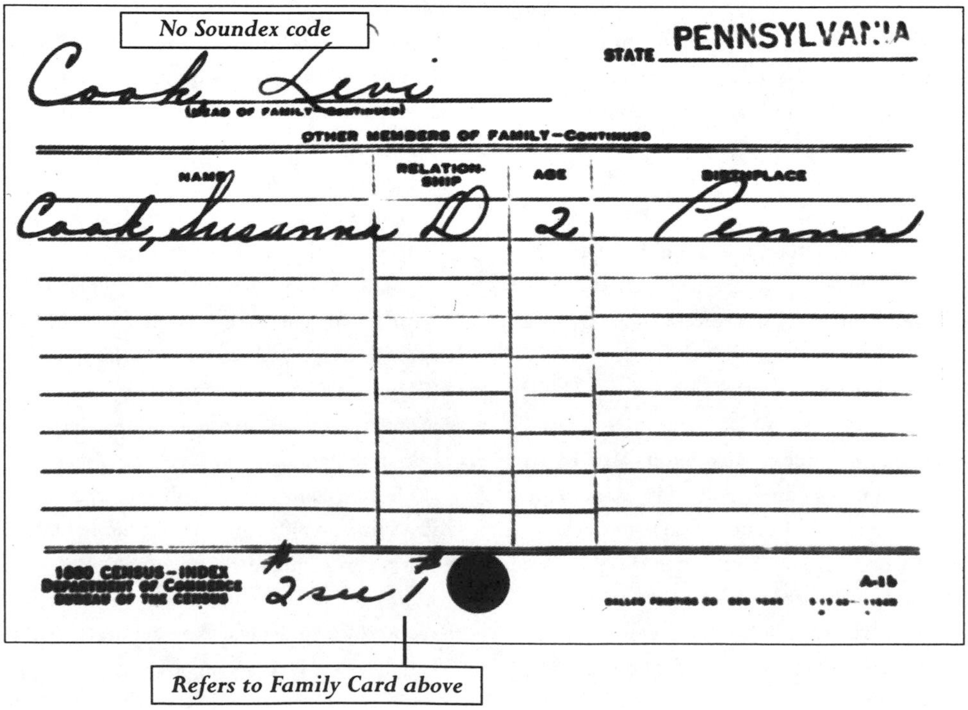

Refers to Family Card above

FIGURE 3
INDIVIDUAL CARD (1880 SOUNDEX)

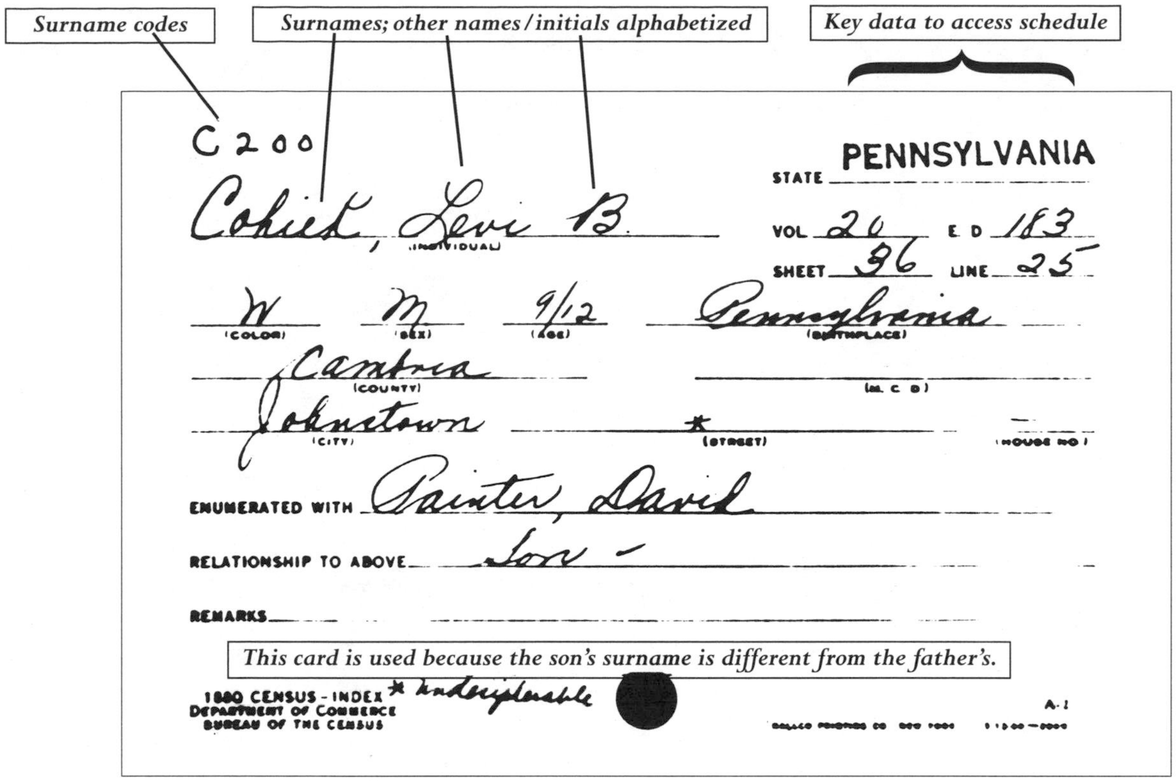

Surname codes | Surnames; other names/initials alphabetized | Key data to access schedule

C 2 0 0

Cohick, Levi B.
(INDIVIDUAL)

STATE **PENNSYLVANIA**

VOL 20   E D 183
SHEET 96   LINE 25

W   M   9/12   Pennsylvania
(COLOR)   (SEX)   (AGE)   (BIRTHPLACE)

Cambria
(COUNTY)   (M. C. D.)

Johnstown   *
(CITY)   (STREET)   (HOUSE NO.)

ENUMERATED WITH   Painter, David

RELATIONSHIP TO ABOVE   Son

REMARKS

This card is used because the son's surname is different from the father's.

1880 CENSUS-INDEX   *   underisplanable
DEPARTMENT OF COMMERCE
BUREAU OF THE CENSUS   A-1

FIGURE 4
INSTITUTION CARD (1880 SOUNDEX)

Use the same data as on Family and Individual Cards to access schedule

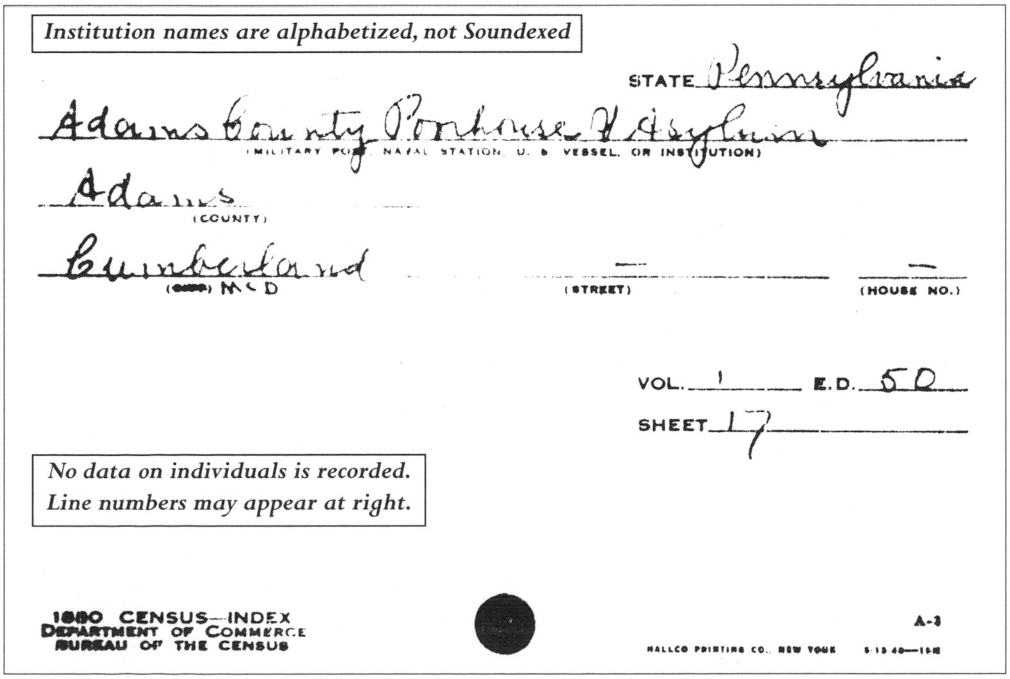

Institution names are alphabetized, not Soundexed

STATE Pennsylvania

Adams County Poorhouse & Asylum
(MILITARY POST, NAVAL STATION, U. S. VESSEL, OR INSTITUTION)

Adams
(COUNTY)

Cumberland   (STREET)   (HOUSE NO.)
(CITY) M C D

VOL. 1   E.D. 50
SHEET 17

No data on individuals is recorded.
Line numbers may appear at right.

1880 CENSUS—INDEX
DEPARTMENT OF COMMERCE
BUREAU OF THE CENSUS

HALLCO PRINTING CO. NEW YORK   A-3

Figure 5
Facsimile of Family Card (1880 Soundex)

Key data for accessing the schedule are bold

```
[SOUNDEX CODE]                          (NAME OF STATE OR OTHER JURISDICTION
                                         IS PRINTED, STAMPED, OR WRITTEN)

_____   VOL. _____  * E.D. _____

                                        ** SHEET _____ *** LINE _____

(COLOR)        (SEX)        (AGE)              (BIRTHPLACE)

        (County)                        (MCD)  (MINOR CIVIL DIVISION)

    (CITY)                  (STREET)                 (HOUSE NO.)

                OTHER MEMBERS OF FAMILY
```

NAME	RELATION-SHIP	AGE	BIRTHPLACE

1880 CENSUS — INDEX
DEPARTMENT OF COMMERCE
BUREAU OF THE CENSUS   [NAME OF PRIVATE PRINTING FIRM APPEARS HERE]   [FORM] A-1a

Figure 6
Facsimile of Other Members of Family – Continued Card (1880 Soundex)

Use bold key data on Family Card to access the schedule

```
[NO SOUNDEX CODE APPEARS HERE]          (NAME OF STATE OR OTHER JURISDICTION
                                         IS PRINTED, STAMPED, OR WRITTEN)


_____   [NO VOLUME, ED, SHEET,
    (HEAD OF FAMILY — Continued)          OR LINE NOS. APPEAR HERE]


                OTHER MEMBERS OF FAMILY — Continued
```

NAME	RELATION-SHIP	AGE	BIRTHPLACE

1880 CENSUS — INDEX
DEPARTMENT OF COMMERCE
BUREAU OF THE CENSUS   [NAME OF PRIVATE PRINTING FIRM APPEARS HERE]   [FORM] A-1b

FIGURE 7
FACSIMILE OF INDIVIDUAL CARD (1880 SOUNDEX)

Key data for accessing the schedule are bold

[SOUNDEX CODE]   **(NAME OF STATE OR OTHER JURISDICTION IS PRINTED, STAMPED, OR WRITTEN)**

(INDIVIDUAL)   **VOL.** _____ * **E.D.** _____

                                                    ** **SHEET** _____ *** **LINE** _____

(COLOR)   (SEX)   (AGE)   (BIRTHPLACE)

(County)   **(MCD)** **(MINOR CIVIL DIVISION)**

(CITY)   (STREET)   (HOUSE NO.)

ENUMERATED WITH _____

RELATIONSHIP TO ABOVE _____

REMARKS _____

1880 CENSUS — INDEX   [FORM] A-2
DEPARTMENT OF COMMERCE
BUREAU OF THE CENSUS   [NAME OF PRIVATE PRINTING FIRM APPEARS HERE]

FIGURE 8
FACSIMILE OF INSTITUTION CARD (1880 SOUNDEX)

Key data for accessing the schedule are bold

[NO SOUNDEX CODE APPEARS HERE]   **(NAME OF STATE OR OTHER JURISDICTION IS PRINTED, STAMPED, OR WRITTEN)**

(MILITARY POST, NAVAL STATION, U.S. VESSEL, OR INSTITUTION)

(COUNTY)

(CITY)   (STREET)   (HOUSE NO.)

                                                    VOL. _____ * **E.D.** _____

                                                    ** **SHEET** _____
                                                    [LINE NOS. MAY APPEAR BELOW]

[TOTAL NUMBER OF RESIDENTS WITHOUT NAMES MAY APPEAR HERE]

1880 CENSUS — INDEX   [FORM] A-3
DEPARTMENT OF COMMERCE
BUREAU OF THE CENSUS   [NAME OF PRIVATE PRINTING FIRM APPEARS HERE]

Card ordinarily is the only card referencing a particular child.

Institution Cards appear at the end of the last roll of Soundex microfilm for a state or territory.

The Institution Cards, unlike the three other Soundex cards, are alphabetically arranged, not Soundex coded, by the first name of the institution. The card shown in figure 4 was the first to appear in roll 168 because it names an institution whose name began with A—Adams County, PA, Poorhouse. The Institution Cards exclude personal data on individuals and, at most, may note only the number of inhabitants.

Institution Cards include jurisdictional data necessary to find the correct census schedules (e.g., State, county, city, and ED). Street and house numbers also often appear on the cards. The cards exclude a printed heading for MCDs, but as figure 4 suggests, some indexers inserted this information on the line for city. Also, the cards have no caption for line numbers pertinent to the schedules, but some indexers inserted this information near the line for sheet number.

Not-Reported Data

Occasionally, some people gave the enumerator only a surname, without any given or middle name, or the indexer may have found this information missing or illegible. Under these circumstances, Not Reported (NR) or a blank can appear on a card after a surname. Cards with this NR feature appear first within a code.

On census schedules, after the surname, some enumerators may have recorded only initials for a person or an initial before the middle name. Such cards are arranged alphabetically and may appear after those with the NR-first name. They ordinarily precede cards with full names bearing the same first letter.

The indexers may also have encountered an NR surname, with or without a given name and initials. Cards with an NR surname for the head of family are on the last Soundex roll for a state or territory, usually before the Institution Cards. Roll 34 of California's Soundex (T737) states "Not Reported thru Institutions," but most roll listings in this catalog do not reference this feature.

The NR-surname cards may include enough personal information such as color, sex, age, street, and house number to identify a person. Some cards also list members of the family or household by surname and may include an indexer's remarks about possible relationships.

Mixed Codes

"Mixed codes" means that codes on the cards may appear in non-consecutive order; e.g., M-200 is followed by M-190, M-205, and then by M-189. In these instances, which divider cards usually note, researchers should disregard the codes and focus on the alphabetized given names.

This catalog alphabetically lists the States, District of Columbia, and territories; references the microfilm rolls at the far left; and then describes their coverage. The arrangement first cites the names of counties, which usually are in alphabetical order. Names of cities often appear separately from counties. Roll 1188 in figure 9, for example, covers part of the city of Philadelphia. Within cities or large urban areas, MCDs such as wards may be numbered and then usually listed in consecutive order.

Within counties, cities, or MCDs, EDs are the next most important data that the catalog notes, often in numerical order. In figure 9, rolls 1190–1194 pertain to Schuylkill County, EDs 1–238. In many instances, the catalog notes that rolls include certain sheets for an ED or other jurisdiction.

Match the county, city, MCD, ED, and sheet number listed on the Soundex card with the information or range provided in the catalog.

FIGURE 9
SAMPLE ROLL LISTINGS FOR 1880 CENSUS (MICROFILM PUBLICATION T9)

State and territorial names are alphabetized in catalog

76	PENNSYLVANIA 1880 — SOUTH CAROLINA 1880

Counties

1157. Monroe (cont'd: E.D. 215, sheet 13—end) and Montgomery (part: E.D. 1—10, sheet 18) Counties

1158. Montgomery County (cont'd: E.D. 10, sheet 19—E.D. 30, sheet 22)

1159. Montgomery County (cont'd: E.D. 30, sheet 23—E.D. 52, sheet 14)

1160. Montgomery (cont'd: E.D. 52, sheet 15—end), Montour, and Northampton (part: E.D. 1—66, sheet 2) Counties

1161. Northampton County (cont'd: E.D. 66, sheet 3—E.D. 77, sheet 39)

1162. Northampton County (cont'd: E.D. 78, sheet 1—E.D. 91, sheet 26)

1163. Northampton (cont'd: E.D. 91, sheet 27—end) and Northumberland (part: E.D. 1—146, sheet 50) Counties

1188. City of Philadelphia, ward 29 (cont'd: E.D. 610, sheet 1—E.D. 642, sheet 38)

1189. City of Philadelphia, wards 30 and 31 (cont'd: E.D. 643, sheet 1—E.D. 670, sheet 4)

1190. City of Philadelphia, ward 31 (cont'd: E.D. 670, sheet 5—end), and Schuylkill County (part: E.D. 1—176, sheet 62)

1191. Schuylkill County (cont'd: E.D. 176, sheet 63—E.D. 192, sheet 64)

1192. Schuylkill County (cont'd: E.D. 192, sheet 65—E.D. 215, sheet 32)

1193. Schuylkill County (cont'd: E.D. 215, sheet 33—E.D. 238, sheet 6)

1194. Schuylkill (cont'd: E.D. 238, sheet 7—end), Snyder, and Somerset (part: E.D. 1, sheet 6) Counties

1195. Somerset (cont'd: E.D. 1, sheet 7—end) and Sullivan Counties

Roll numbers

Counties, MCDs, EDs and sheets noted on Soundex cards

The 1880 schedule consists of four sides. Enumerators usually recorded the names of the city, county, and state and the number or name of the ward or other MCD only on the front of the schedule. In figure 10, for example, these spaces were originally blank. Handwritten ED numbers are on the upper left side, on the third line.

Next match the sheet number recorded on the Soundex card with the page number on the first line of the upper left side of the schedule. On the card for Levi Cook, for example, the sheet number is 9, which corresponds to that on the schedule in figure 10. The handwritten numbers on the schedules ordinarily start at 1 in each ED and continue consecutively on each sheet, A–D. Disregard the stamped numbers usually at the right side of the schedules. The Soundex card for Levi Cook notes line 15. In figure 10, an arrow points to this line.

ENUMERATION DISTRICT DESCRIPTIONS AND MAPS

Researchers who cannot find a name in Soundex or a commercial index may want to consult enumeration district (ED) descriptions and maps.

An ED refers to the area assigned to a single census-taker. ED descriptions pertinent to the schedules covered by this catalog are in *Descriptions of Census Enumeration Districts, 1830–1890 and 1910–1950* (T1224). Table 2, ED Descriptions, 1830–90, in T1224, explains coverage of the 17 rolls pertinent to this catalog. An overview of these aids appears in Bruce Carpenter, "Using Soundex Alternatives: Enumeration Districts, 1880–1920," *Prologue: Quarterly of the National Archives* 25 (Spring 1993): 90–93. A case study on the approach appears in Keith R. Schlesinger, "An Urban Finding Aid for the Federal Census," in *Our Family, Our Town: Essays on Family and Local History Sources in the National Archives,*

FIGURE 10
TOP PART OF AN 1880 CENSUS SCHEDULE

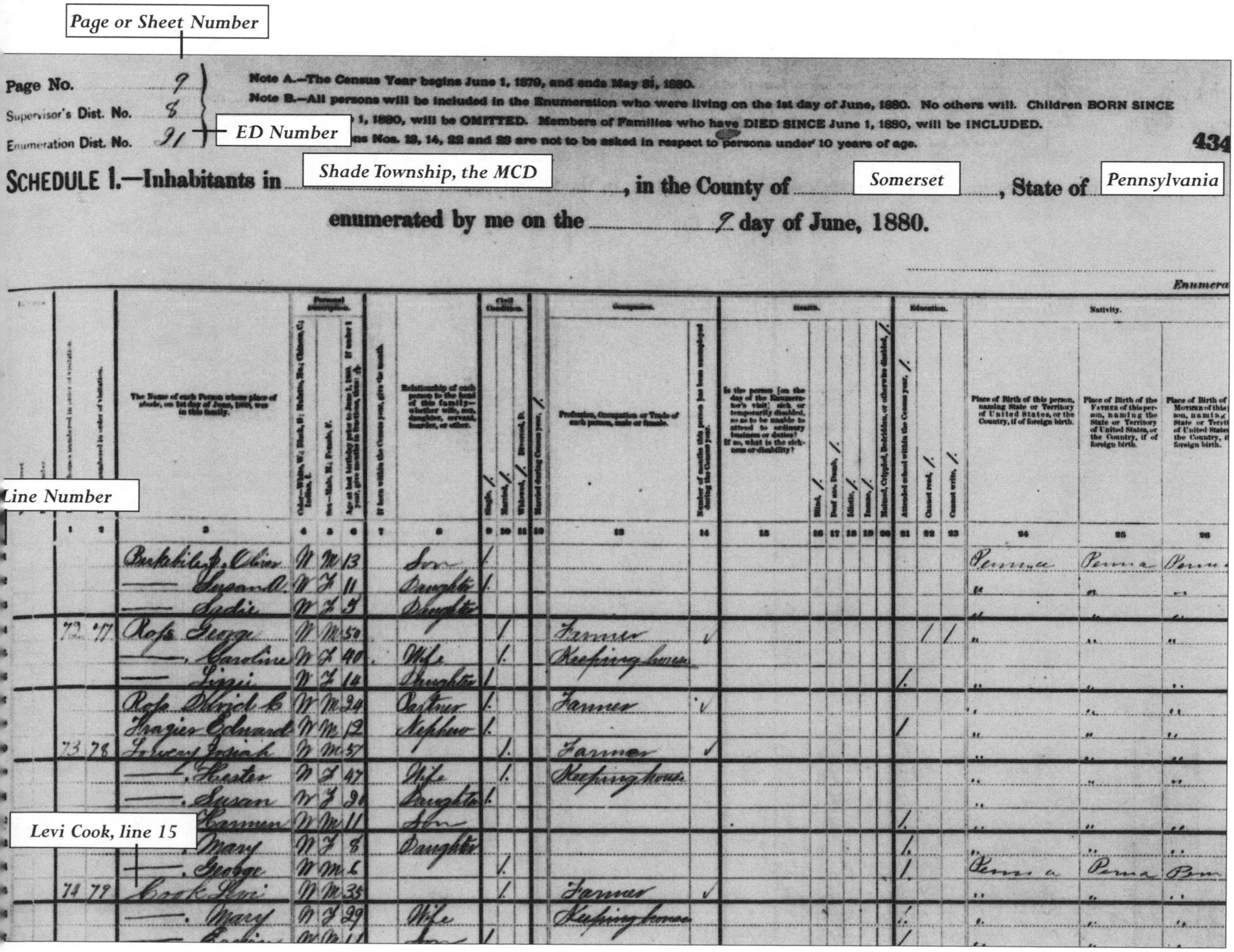

comp. Timothy Walch (Washington, DC: National Archives and Records Administration, 1987), pp. 126–140.

The title of T1224 contains a misnomer because EDs, strictly defined, were not used until the 1880 census. The early censuses used the term subdivision to refer to part of a supervisor's or marshal's division or district. Subdivisions in the early censuses comprised towns, townships, or other units comparable to MCDs.

Researchers must determine the state or territory and try to identify the county. Descriptions found in T1224 may help narrow the search by specifying what county certain localities (including MCDs, neighborhoods, or post offices) were in during certain census years.

The descriptions note street names or ranges and specify the corresponding EDs. An example using Cook County, IL, appears in figure 11, Enumeration District Description (1880). This example lists street ranges in the middle of the page and post office addresses at the right. An arrow points to the corresponding ED numbers at the far left. For example, the post office at 2924 Fifth Avenue in Chicago in the fifth ward, was in ED 31. The same research steps can help researchers find the 1890–1920 schedules, but most ED numbers changed for each census.

Maps can complement ED descriptions or provide substitutes for them. The National Archives does not have ED descriptions or ED maps for censuses from 1790 through 1820, therefore commercially or privately published maps are especially helpful and practical. Many commercial indexes for censuses include maps for a particular year and state. William Thorndale and William Dollarhide, *Map Guide to the U.S. Federal Census, 1790–1920* (Baltimore: Genealogical Publishing Company, 1992) is especially useful in identifying counties and many localities in existence in

---

TABLE 2
ED DESCRIPTIONS, 1830–90, IN T1224

An asterisk (*) notes alphabetized states and territories

Census Year	Roll Number	Remarks
1830-40	1	**Arranged by region**
1850-60 *	2	**No 1850 data for** Oregon Territory
1870	3	**No data for Montana** Territory but separate category for "Indians— All States"
1880 *	4–6	**No data for Alabama,** Arizona Territory, Arkansas, California, Colorado, Connecticut, Montana Territory, Ohio, Oregon, Pennsylvania, and Wisconsin. Roll 4, DK–KY; roll 5, LA–MO; and roll 6, NB–WY.
1890 *	7–17	**Roll 7, AL–DE; roll 8,** DC–IL; roll 9, IN–KS; roll 10, KY–MD; roll 11, MA–MN; roll 12, MS–NM; roll 13, NY; roll 14, NC–OR; roll 15, PA; roll 16, RI–TX; roll 17, UT–WY

FIGURE 11
ENUMERATION DISTRICT DESCRIPTION (1880)

After matching a person's address or location with a post office address or street name or range shown below, use the ED number at the far left to help find the microfilm roll that copies that ED's census schedules.

early census years.

While the National Archives research rooms have some maps that can help researchers, the agency's Cartographic and Architectural Branch has some specially marked ED ("office copy") maps. They show streets, locations, or neighborhoods within cities and specify the ED.

Cartographic Records of the Bureau of the Census, Preliminary Inventory (PI) 103 (Washington, DC: National Archives and Records Service, 1958) discusses ED maps available in the National Archives. The appendix to PI 103 lists the maps by alphabetizing the names of States, specifying counties or other localities, and noting availability for the years 1880–1940.

The National Archives has no pre-1880 ED maps, and maps for the 1880 census exist for only Washington, DC; Rockwall County, TX; and Atlanta in Fulton County, GA. Part of the last map appears in figure 12, Enumeration District Description Map (1880). The large handwritten numbers are ED numbers corresponding to those in this catalog.

Only 11 ED maps exist for the 1890 census, and only one pertains to the remaining schedules. The exception is the map of Washington, DC, which shows part of the area to which a few schedules pertain; but this map is far less helpful than M496, the alphabetical index, in locating these schedules.

To order copies of ED maps, write to the Cartographic Section, Special Media Archives Services Division (NWCS), National Archives at College Park, 8601 Adelphi Road, College Park, MD

FIGURE 12
ENUMERATION DISTRICT DESCRIPTION MAP (1880)

The large handwritten numbers indicate ED numbers

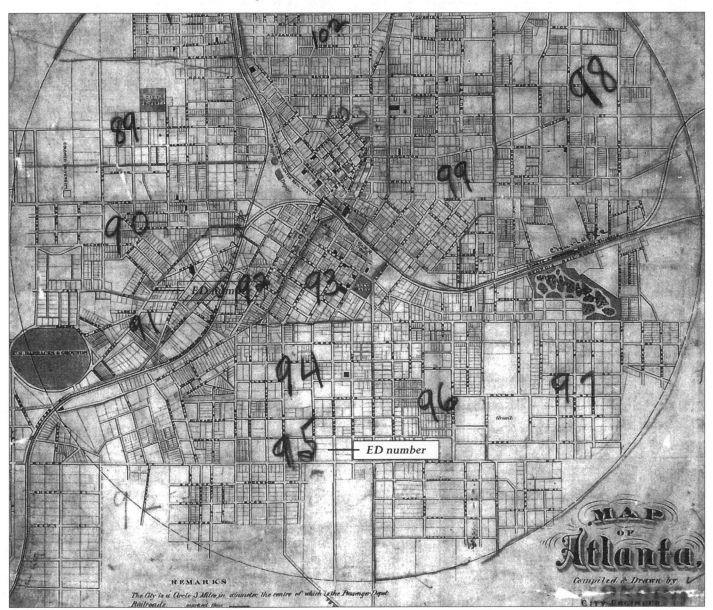

20740-6001. Prices vary with the map size. Even full-scale maps, though, may be difficult to read, especially because black-and-white copies may obscure colored ED boundaries.

OTHER SCHEDULES

While this catalog focuses on decennial population schedules, the National Archives has custody of numerous other Federal census records that can supplement and enrich genealogical projects and other research. Many of these records are microfilmed and can be purchased.

The Government occasionally conducted territorial and special censuses in interdecennial periods. The 1885 special census enumerated Colorado, Nebraska, New Mexico, South Dakota, and South Dakota. The Government also used many special or supplemental schedules to collect nonpopulation data, which mostly concern manufacturing, agriculture, social statistics, and mortality (causes of death) in the year before the decennial census. The 1880 census, for example, included 4 supplemental schedules as well as 12 special manufacturing schedules and 7 schedules involving the defective, dependent, and delinquent classes.

Indians

Census enumerators did not count Indians not taxed, that is, Indians who lived on reservations or who roamed as nomads over unsettled tracts of land. Whether or not they were of mixed blood, Indians who had severed their tribal affiliations and lived among the general population or on the outskirts of towns, were counted as part of the ordinary population. Before 1870, however, there is seldom a way to identify such Indians in the census. *Schedules of a Special Census of Indians, 1880* (M1791) reproduces a special 1880 enumeration of Indians living near military installations in Washington, Dakota Territories, and California. All other Indians should be enumerated in the state, county, or locality where they resided. Not until 1890 did the decennial census schedules enumerate the Indian population with any accuracy.

The records of the Bureau of Indian Affairs include many tribal census rolls, which are completely unrelated to the decennial census schedules. These are described in chapter 11 of *Genealogical Research in the National Archives.*

Blacks

The first listing of all blacks by name in a Federal census was made in 1870, the first Federal census taken after the Civil War and the abolition of slavery. In 1850 and 1860, slave statistics were gathered, but the census schedules did not list slaves by name; they were tallied unnamed in age and sex categories. These slave schedules are useful, however as circumstantial evidence that a slave of a certain age and sex was the property of a particular owner in 1850 or 1860.

Free blacks who were heads of households were enumerated by name in the censuses from 1790 to 1840, and the names of all free household members were included in the censuses of 1850 and 1860.

For more information see *Genealogical Research in the National Archives*, section 12.2, Census Records, page 173.

RESEARCH HINTS

The following tips may be useful:

✦ The 1810 census includes some schedules or fragments dealing with that year's census of manufactures. For coverage, see PI 161, appendix IX.

✦ Some transcribed data on the 1820 census of manufactures appears in T911, *Compilation of Tennessee Census Reports, 1820.*

✦ In some cities, the Government conducted second enumerations because of questions about the accuracy of the first. Researchers should determine whether or not two microfilm rolls copy schedules for the same area. For example, rolls 975 and 1014 of M593, *Ninth Census of the United States, 1870,* copy schedules for New York City, ward 1.

✦ A fire destroyed most of the 1870 Minnesota schedules. M593, rolls 716–719, copies the remaining Federal schedules, while T132 reproduces the State copy. T132 also is noteworthy because it includes some mortality schedules interfiled with the population schedules.

USEFUL PUBLICATIONS

Details on many of these records appear in *Guide to Genealogical Research in the National Archives*, chapter 1. *National Archives Microfilm Resources for Research: A Comprehensive Catalog* (pp. 6–11) notes other nonpopulation and territorial censuses as well as special aids and Bureau of the Census publications.

Numerous details on little-known census records, including unmicrofilmed records, also appear in *Records of the Bureau of the Census*, PI 161 (Washington, DC: National Archives and Records Service, 1964). This free work is available from National Archives and Records Administration, Research Support Branch (NWCC1), Room 403, 700 Pennsylvania Avenue, NW, Washington, DC 20408. Ordering information is on page xix. Researchers interested in unmicrofilmed records covered by PI 161 or in other census-related topics may write to the Textual Archives Services Division, Old military and Civil Records (NWCTB), National Archives and Records Administration, Washington, DC 20408.

Free literature includes *Aids for Genealogical Research* which describes microfilm catalogs, such as the *1900 Federal Population Census, The 1910 Federal Population Census*, and *The 1920 Federal Population Census.*

Other free literature includes *Using Records in the National Archives for Genealogical Research*, General Information Leaflet (GIL) No. 5; *Military Service Records in the National Archives of the United States*, GIL No. 7; *Information about the National Archives for Prospective Researchers*, GIL No. 30; *The Regional Archives System of the National*

Archives, GIL No. 22; *Fast Facts About the 1920 Census*, GIL No. 43, which explains the most current publicly released decennial census; and *Select List of Publications of the National Archives and Records Administration*, GIL 3, which covers many additional free works such as preliminary inventories and reference information papers. GIL No. 5 is also important because it includes guidance on how to formally cite microfilmed census records.

Genealogy Web Page

The National Archives and Records Administration's Web site is at *http://www.nara.gov*. The Genealogy Web site includes copies of the census catalogs and a "Soundex machine" that automatically converts a name to a Soundex code.

CENSUS AVAILABILITY AND ACCESS

Microfilmed copies of census records are available at the National Archives Building in Washington, DC, at NARA's 13 regional records services facilities, and at many large libraries and genealogical societies that have purchased all or some of the microfilm. The public can also request mail-order paper copies of census schedules, rent the microfilm, or purchase microfilm rolls.

Ordering Paper Copies by Mail

The National Archives in Washington, DC, can provide paper copies of specifically identified pages of Federal population census schedules through the mail. To receive this photocopying service, use *Order for Copies of Census Records*, NATF Form 82 (rev. 1992) and provide the following information: the name of the individual, the page number, census year, state, and county. Researchers may request copies of NATF Form 82 by writing to the Textual Reference Branch (NWCTB-C), National Archives and Records Administration, Washington, DC 20408. For the 1880 through 1920 censuses, the enumeration district is also necessary. Ordinarily, it is possible to use a Government or privately printed census index to locate this information.

National Archives Microfilm Rental Program

The National Archives Microfilm Rental Program offers microfilm of Federal population schedules from 1790 through 1920 and Soundexes from 1880 through 1920. The program also rents microfilm of American Revolutionary War military service records and indexes, pension files, and bounty-land warrant files. For a free brochure that describes the program, write or call National Archives Microfilm Rental Program, P.O. Box 30, Annapolis Junction, MD 20701-0030, 301-604-3699.

Buying the Microfilm

Microfilm copies of census records are also available for purchase. The schedules are on 35mm microfilm; the Soundex is on 16mm. Schedules for an entire county or enumeration district may be on one or more rolls of microfilm.

All microfilm publications of National Archives records are for sale. Individual rolls or a complete set (all rolls) are for sale. The current prices for silver-halide positive film copies are $34 a roll for domestic orders and $39 for foreign orders, shipping is included. These prices are subject to change without advance notice. Checks and money orders should be made payable to the "National Archives Trust Fund (NATF)." VISA, MasterCard, American Express, and Discover credit card orders must include the expiration date and the cardholder's signature. Do NOT send cash. Federal, state, and local government agencies only may purchase microfilm on an accounts-receivable basis, but they must submit a signed purchase order within 10 working days of placing an order. U.S. Treasury regulations require a minimum amount of $25 for foreign checks. To order microfilm, write to: **National Archives Trust Fund (NATF), P.O. Box 100793, Atlanta, GA 30384-0793.** When ordering microfilm, please state the microfilm publication number and specific roll numbers.

Check the order immediately upon receipt for errors, completeness, or damage in shipping. Notify the Product Sales Section of any problems within 60 days. Do not return microfilm orders without written permission from the Product Sales Section.

For more information on how to order or for help identifying which rolls of a publication you may wish to purchase, contact: **National Archives and Records Administration, Research Support Branch (NWCC2), Room 1000, 8601 Adelphi Road, College Park, MD 20740-6001, 1-800-234-8861, 301-713-6800, fax 301-713-6169.**

Include the census year, the state, and the county or enumeration district.

Copies of National Archives microfilm publications may also be purchased from Scholarly Resources, Inc., 104 Greenhill Avenue, Wilmington, DE 19805 (telephone 302-654-7713/fax 302-654-3871). Copies available for sale from other sources have not been authorized or duplicated by the National Archives and may be one or more generations removed from the master negative, and therefore are of poorer quality and legibility.

SELECT BIBLIOGRAPHY

In addition to the works mentioned in this introduction, most of which are described in *Aids for Genealogical Research*, the following literature includes chapters or information that may help with census research. Bibliographies in the commercial works refer to additional helpful sources. Also, the National Archives sells many commercial works not listed here that explain census research. An asterisk (*) below notes two National Archives works that are out of print, but researchers may examine copies in the National Archives library.

Delle Donne, Carmen R. *Federal Census Schedules, 1850–1880: Primary Sources for Historical Research*. Reference Information Paper 67. National Archives and Records Service, 1973. *

Eakle, Arlene and Johni Cerny, eds. *The Source: A Guidebook of American Genealogy*. Salt Lake City: Ancestry Inc., 1984.

Federal Population and Mortality Census Schedules, 1790–1910, in the National Archives and the States: Outline of a Lecture on Their Availability, Content and Use. Special List 24. National Archives and Records Service, rev. 1986.

Fishbein, Meyer H. *The Censuses of Manufactures, 1810–1890*. Reference Information Paper 50. National Archives and Records Service, 1973. *

Greene, Evarts B. and Virginia D. Harrington. *American Population Before the Federal Census of 1790*. Baltimore: Genealogical Publishing Co., Inc., reprint 1993.

Greenwood, Val D. *The Researcher's Guide to American Genealogy*. 2d ed. Baltimore: Genealogical Publishing Company, Inc., 1990.

Guide to the Federal Records in the National Archives of the United States. Washington, DC: National Archives and Records Administration, 3 vols., 1995.

Lainhart, Ann S. *State Census Records*. Baltimore: Genealogical Publishing Company, Inc., 1992.

Publications of the Bureau of the Census, 1790–1916. National Archives Microfilm Publication T825 (42 rolls).

Szucs, Loretto Dennis and Sandra Hargreaves Luebking. *The Archives: A Guide to the National Archives Field Branches*. Salt Lake City: Ancestry, Inc. 1988.

Wright, Carroll D. and William C. Hunt. *The History and Growth of the United States Census*. 56th Cong., 1st sess. S. Doc. 194. Serial 3856. (A commercial reprint is available.)

Regional Archives

NARA–Northeast Region (Boston)
380 Trapelo Road
Waltham, MA 02452-6399
781-647-8104
Email: waltham.archives@nara.gov
Areas Served: Connecticut, Maine, Massachusetts, New Hampshire,
Rhode Island, and Vermont

NARA–Northeast Region (Pittsfield)
10 Conte Drive
Pittsfield, MA 01201-8230
413-445-6885
Email: pittsfield.archives@nara.gov
(no accessioned records, only microfilm related to genealogy)

NARA–Northeast Region (New York City)
201 Varick Street, 12th Floor
New York, NY 10014-4811
212-337-1300
Email: newyork.archives@nara.gov
Area Served: New Jersey, New York, Puerto Rico, and the Virgin Islands

NARA–Mid Atlantic Region (Center City Philadelphia)
900 Market Street
Philadelphia, PA 19107-4292
215-597-3000
Email: philadelphia.archives@nara.gov
Area Served: Delaware, Pennsylvania, Maryland, Virginia, and West
Virginia

NARA–Southeast Region
1557 St. Joseph Avenue
East Point, GA 30344-2593
404-763-7477
Email: atlanta.archives@nara.gov
Area Served: Alabama, Florida, Georgia, Kentucky, Mississippi, North
Carolina, South Carolina, and Tennessee

NARA–Great Lakes Region (Chicago)
7358 South Pulaski Road
Chicago, IL 60629-5898
773-581-7816
Email: chicago.archives@nara.gov
Area Served: Illinois, Indiana, Michigan, Minnesota, Ohio, and Wisconsin

NARA–Central Plains Region (Kansas City)
2312 East Bannister Road
Kansas City, MO 64131-3011
816-926-6272
Email: kansascity.archives@nara.gov
Area Served: Iowa, Kansas, Missouri, and Nebraska

NARA–Southwest Region
501 West Felix Street, P.O. Box 6216
Fort Worth, TX 76115-0216
817-334-5525
Email: ftworth.archives@nara.gov
Area Served: Arkansas, Louisiana, Oklahoma, and Texas

NARA–Rocky Mountain Region
Building 48, Denver Federal Center
West 6th Avenue and Kipling Street
Denver, CO 80225
P.O. Box 25307
Denver, CO 80225-0307
303-236-0817
Email: denver.archives@nara.gov
Area Served: Colorado, Montana, New Mexico, North Dakota, South
Dakota, Utah, and Wyoming

NARA–Pacific Region (Laguna Niguel)
24000 Avila Road, First Floor, East Entrance
Laguna Niguel, CA 92677-3497
P.O. Box 6719
Laguna Niguel, CA 92607-6719
949-360-2641
Email: laguna.archives@nara.gov
Area Served: Arizona; southern California, and Clark County, Nevada

NARA–Pacific Region (San Francisco)
1000 Commodore Drive
San Bruno, CA 94066-2350
650-876-9009
Email: sanbruno.archives@nara.gov
Area Served: Northern California, Hawaii, Nevada (except Clark
County), American Samoa, and the Pacific Trust Territories.

NARA–Pacific Alaska Region (Seattle)
6125 Sand Point Way NE
Seattle, WA 98115-7999
206-526-6507
Email: seattle.archives@nara.gov
Area Served: Idaho, Oregon, and Washington

NARA–Pacific Alaska Region (Anchorage)
654 West Third Avenue
Anchorage, AK 99501-2145
907-271-2441
Email: alaska.archives@nara.gov
Area Served: Alaska

Abbreviations & Terms used in Soundex Cards

A	Aunt		GA	Great aunt
Ad	Adopted		Gcl	Grandchild
AdCl	Adopted child		GD	Granddaughter
AdD	Adopted daughter		GF	Grandfather
AdGcl	Adopted grandchild		GGF	Great-grandfather
AdM	Adopted mother		GGGF	Great-great-grandfather
AdS	Adopted son		GGGM	Great-great-grandmother
Al	Aunt-in-law		GGM	Great-grandmother
Ap	Apprentice		GM	Grandmother
Asst	Assistant		Gml	Grandmother-in-law
At	Attendant		GN	Grand or great nephew
B	Brother		GNi	Grand or great niece
Bar	Bartender		Go	Governess
BBoy	Bound boy		God Cl	God child
BGirl	Bound girl		GS	Grandson
Bl	Brother-in-law		Gsl	Grand son-in-law
Bo	Boarder		GU	Great uncle
Boy	Boy		Gua	Guardian
Bu	Butler		Guest	Guest
C	Cousin		Hb	Half brother
Cap	Captain		Hbl	Half brother-in-law
Cha	Chamber Maid		He	Herder
Cil	Cousin-in-law		Help	Help
Cl	Child		H.Gi	Hired girl
Coa	Coachman		Hh	Hired hand
Com	Companion		Hk	Housekeeper
Cook	Cook		Hlg	Hireling
D	Daughter		Hm	Hired man
Dl	Daughter-in-law		HMaid	Housemaid
Dla	Day laborer		HSi	Half sister
Dom	Domestic		HSil	Half sister-in-law
Dw	Dishwasher		Husband	Husband
Emp	Employee		Hw	Houseworker
En	Engineer		I	Inmate
F	Father		L	Lodger
FaH	Farm hand		La	Laborer
FaL	Farm laborer		Lau	Launderer
FaW	Farm worker		M	Mother
FB	Foster brother		Maid	Maid
FF	Foster father		Man	Manager
Fi	Fireman		Mat	Matron
First C	First cousin		ML	Mother-in-law
FL	Father-in-law		N	Nephew
FM	Foster mother		Ni	Niece
FoB	Foster brother		Nil	Niece-in-law
FoS	Foster son		Nl	Nephew-in-law
FoSi	Foster sister		Nu	Nurse

O	Officer
P	Patient
Pa	Partner
Ph	Physician
Por	Porter
Pr	Prisoner
Pri	Principal
Prv	Private
Pu	Pupil
R	Roomer
S	Son
Sa	Sailor
Sal	Saleslady
Sb	Stepbrother
Sbl	Step brother-in-law
Scl	Step child
Sd	Stepdaugther
Sdl	Step daughter-in-law
Se	Servant
Se.Cl	Servant's child
Sf	Stepfather
Sfl	Step father-in-law
Sgd	Step granddaughter
Sgs	Step grandson
Si	Sister
Sl	Son-in-law
Sm	Stepmother
Sml	Step mother-in-law
Ss	Stepson
Ssi	Stepsister
Ssil	Step sister-in-law
Ssl	Step son-in-law
Su	Superintendant
Ten	Tenant
U	Uncle
Ul	Uncle-in-law
Vi	Visitor
W	Wife
Wa	Warden
Wai	Waitress
Ward	Ward
Wkm	Workman
Wt	Waiter

FIRST CENSUS OF THE UNITED STATES, 1790. M637. 12 ROLLS.
These are the original census schedules for 1790. Schedules for some counties are missing. No schedules are known to exist for Delaware, Georgia, Kentucky, New Jersey, Tennessee, and Virginia; apparently they were destroyed during the British attack on Washington during the War of 1812. The 1790 schedules for Virginia that appear on microfilm publication T498 were reconstructed from State enumerations.

1. Connecticut
2. Maine
3. Maryland
4. Massachusetts
5. New Hampshire
6. New York
7. North Carolina
8. Pennsylvania: Berks, Chester, Delaware, Huntington, Mifflin (part), Luzerne, Dauphin, Northampton, Cumberland, Fayette, Westmoreland (part), Bucks, and Lancaster Counties
9. Pennsylvania: Montgomery, Westmoreland (part), Allegheny, Washington, Bedford, Franklin, York, Northumberland, Mifflin (part) and Philadelphia Counties
10. Rhode Island
11. South Carolina
12. Vermont

FIRST CENSUS OF THE UNITED STATES, 1790. T498. 3 ROLLS.
These are the printed schedules as published by the Bureau of the Census in 1907-8. At the end of roll 3, the 1840 Census of Pensioners for Revolutionary or Military Services has also been reproduced.

1. Connecticut, Maine, Maryland, Massachusetts, and New Hampshire
2. New York, North Carolina, and Pennsylvania
3. Rhode Island, South Carolina, Vermont, and Virginia

SECOND CENSUS OF THE UNITED STATES, 1800. M32. 52 ROLLS.

Connecticut.
1. Fairfield and Hartford Counties

2. Litchfield, New Haven, Tolland, and Windham Counties
3. Middlesex and New London Counties

Delaware.
4. Entire state

District of Columbia.
5. Entire district

Maine.
6. Cumberland and Lincoln Counties
7. Hancock and Kennebec Counties
8. Washington and York Counties

Maryland.
9. Allegany and Anne Arundel Counties, Baltimore City, and Calvert County
10. Caroline, Cecil, Charles, Frederick, and Kent Counties
11. Dorchester, Harford, Montgomery, Prince Georges, and Queen Annes Counties
12. St. Mary's, Somerset, Talbot, Washington, and Worcester Counties

Massachusetts.
13. Barnstable and Berkshire Counties
14. Essex County
15. Hampshire County
16. Plymouth, Suffolk, and Worcester Counties; and State recapitulation
17. Middlesex County
18. Nantucket and Norfolk Counties
19. Bristol and Dukes Counties

New Hampshire.
20. Entire state

New York.
21. Dutchess, Ulster, Orange, and Herkimer Counties
22. Albany, Clinton, Columbia, Delaware, Essex, and Greene Counties
23. Kings, New York, and Oneida Counties
24. Montgomery, Onondaga, Steuben, and Tioga Counties
25. Otsego, Queens, Richmond, and Rockland Counties

26. Rensselaer, Schoharie, and Washington Counties
27. Saratoga, Suffolk, and Westchester Counties
28. Ontario, Cayuga, and Chenango Counties

North Carolina.

29. Anson, Ashe, Brunswick, Buncombe, Burke, Cabarrus, Iredell, and Lincoln Counties
30. Beaufort, Bertie, Camden, Chowan, Currituck, Edgecombe, Gates, and Halifax Counties
31. Bladen, Carteret, Caswell, Chatham, Craven, Cumberland, Duplin, Franklin, Granville, Greene, Guilford, Hertford, Johnston, and Jones Counties
32. Lenoir, Moore, Nash, Onslow, Person, Pitt, Randolph, Robeson, Rockingham, Sampson, Stokes, Surry, Wake, Warren, and Wayne Counties
33. Mecklenburg, Montgomery, New Hanover, Richmond, Rowan, Rutherford, and Wilkes Counties
34. Hyde, Martin, Northampton, Orange, Pasquotank, Perquimans, Tyrrell, and Washington Counties

Pennsylvania.

35. Adams, Allegheny, Armstrong, and Berks Counties
36. Beaver, Bedford, Bucks, Butler, and Chester Counties
37. Centre, Mifflin, Northampton, and Northumberland Counties
38. Crawford, Cumberland, Delaware, Fayette, and Franklin Counties
39. Lancaster, Luzerne, and Mercer Counties
40. Dauphin, Erie, Greene, and Huntingdon Counties
41. Lycoming, Montgomery, and Westmoreland Counties
42. Philadelphia County (excluding the city of Philadelphia)
43. City of Philadelphia and Somerset and Venango Counties
44. Warren, Washington, Wayne, and York Counties

Rhode Island.

45. Bristol, Kent, and Providence Counties
46. Newport and Washington Counties

South Carolina.

47. Abbeville, Barnwell, Chester, Chesterfield, Darlington, Edgefield, Fairfield, and Greenville Counties and Districts
48. Beaufort, Charleston, and Colleton Districts
49. Georgetown, Winyaw, Waccamaw, Kingston, Kershaw, Marion, Liberty, Williamsburg, Orangeburg, Lexington, Orange, Lexington (additional schedules), Sumter, Claremont, Clarendon, Selem, and York Counties and Districts
50. Lancaster, Laurens, Marlboro, Newberry, Pendleton, Spartanburg, and Union Districts

Vermont.

51. Addison, Bennington, Caledonia, Chittenden, Essex, Franklin,

Orange, and Orleans Counties
52. Rutland, Windsor, and Windham Counties

THIRD CENSUS OF THE UNITED STATES, 1810. M252. 71 ROLLS.

Connecticut.

1. Fairfield and Hartford Counties
2. Litchfield, Middlesex, and New Haven Counties
3. New London, Tolland, and Windham Counties

Delaware.

4. Entire state

Kentucky.

5. Adair, Barren, Boone, Bourbon, Bracken, Breckinridge, Bullitt, and Butler Counties
6. Estill, Fayette, Fleming, Floyd, Franklin, Gallatin, Garrard, Grayson, Green, Greenup, Hardin, Harrison, Henderson, Henry, and Hopkins Counties
7. Jefferson, Jessamine, Knox, Lewis, Lincoln, Livingston, Logan, Madison, Mason, Mercer, Montgomery, and Muhlenberg Counties
8. Nelson, Nicholas, Ohio, Pendleton, Pulaski, Rockcastle, Scott, Shelby, Warren, Washington, Wayne, and Woodford Counties
9. Caldwell, Campbell, Casey, Christian, Clark, Clay, and Cumberland Counties

Louisiana.

10. Ascension, Assumption, Atacapas, Avoyelles, Baton Rouge, Catahoula, Concordia, Iberville, Lafourche, Natchitoches, Orleans, Opelousas, Ouachita, Plaquemines, Pointe Coupee, Rapides, St. Bernard, St. Charles, St. James, and St. John the Baptist Parishes

Maine.

11. Cumberland, Hancock, and Kennebec Counties
12. Lincoln, Oxford, Somerset, Washington, and York Counties; and State recapitulation

Maryland.

13. City of Baltimore and Baltimore County
14. Allegany, Anne Arundel, Harford, Kent, Montgomery, and Talbot Counties
15. Calvert, Caroline, Cecil, Charles, Dorchester, and Frederick Counties
16. Prince Georges, Queen Annes, St. Mary's, Somerset, Washington, and Worcester Counties

Massachusetts.

17. Barnstable, Berkshire, and Bristol Counties

18. Dukes, Essex, Nantucket, and Norfolk Counties
19. Hampshire County
20. Middlesex County
21. Plymouth and Suffolk Counties
22. Worcester County

New Hampshire.
23. Cheshire and Grafton (part) Counties
24. Grafton (part) and Hillsboro Counties
25. Coos, Rockingham, and Strafford Counties; and State recapitulation

New York.
26. Albany, Broome, Chenango, and Delaware Counties
27. Essex, Franklin, Genesee, Greene, and Herkimer Counties
28. Jefferson, Kings, Lewis, and Madison Counties
29. Montgomery, Niagara, and Orange Counties
30. Allegany, Clinton, Dutchess, Sullivan, and Washington Counties
31. Cayuga and Columbia Counties
32. New York County (including New York City)
33. Oneida and Ontario Counties
34. Onondaga, Otsego, Queens, and Richmond Counties
35. Rensselaer, Rockland, and Saratoga Counties
36. St. Lawrence, Schoharie, Seneca, and Suffolk Counties
37. Schenectady, Steuben, Tioga, Ulster, and Westchester Counties

North Carolina.
38. Anson, Brunswick, Caswell, Currituck, Halifax, Person, Randolph, Richmond, and Robeson Counties
39. Ashe, Beaufort, Bertie, Buncombe, Burke, Cabarrus, Camden, Carteret, Chatham, Chowan, and Cumberland Counties
40. Duplin, Edgecombe, Franklin, Gates, Granville, Guilford, Haywood, Hertford, Hyde, Iredell, Johnston, Jones, Lenoir, and Lincoln Counties
41. Martin, Montgomery, Moore, Nash, Onslow, Orange, Pasquotank, Perquimans, and Pitt Counties
42. Bladen, Columbus, Mecklenburg, Northampton, Rutherford, Sampson, and Warren Counties
43. Rockingham, Rowan, Stokes, Surry, Tyrrell, Washington, Wayne, and Wilkes Counties

Pennsylvania.
44. Adams, Allegheny, and Armstrong Counties.
45. Beaver, Bedford (part), and Berks Counties
46. Bedford (part), Bucks, Butler, Cambria, and Centre Counties
47. Chester, Clearfield, Crawford, and Delaware Counties
48. Cumberland and Erie Counties
49. Greene, Indiana, and Luzerne Counties
50. Lancaster County
51. Huntingdon, Jefferson, McKean, Mifflin, Northampton, Tioga, and Westmoreland Counties
52. Lycoming, Mercer, and Montgomery Counties
53. Northumberland, Potter, Somerset, Venango, and Warren Counties
54. Dauphin, Fayette, and Franklin Counties
55. City of Philadelphia
56. Philadelphia County (excluding the city of Philadelphia)
57. Washington, Wayne, and York Counties

Rhode Island.
58. Bristol and Providence Counties
59. Kent, Newport, and Washington Counties; and State recapitulation

South Carolina.
60. Abbeville, Barnwell, Beaufort, Charleston, Chester, Chesterfield, and Colleton Counties
61. Lancaster, Laurens, Lexington, Marion, Marlboro, Newberry, Orangeburg, Pendleton, Richland, Spartanburg, Sumter, Union, Williamsburg, and York Counties; and State recapitulation
62. Darlington, Edgefield, Greenville, Horry, Kershaw, Fairfield, and Georgetown Counties

Tennessee.
63. Rutherford County

Vermont.
64. Addison, Bennington, Caledonia, Chittenden, Essex, Franklin, Grand Isle, Orange, and Orleans Counties
65. Rutland, Windham, and Windsor Counties; and State recapitulation

Virginia (including present-day West Virginia).
66. Accomack, Albemarle, Amelia, Amherst, Augusta, Bath, Berkeley, Botetourt, Brooke, Brunswick, and Buckingham Counties
67. Bedford, Caroline, Chesterfield, and Dinwiddie Counties, the borough of Norfolk, the town of Petersburg, and Rockingham County
68. Campbell, Charles City, Charlotte, Culpeper, Cumberland, Elizabeth City, Essex, Fairfax, Fauquier, Fluvanna, Franklin, Frederick, Giles, Gloucester, Goochland, and Greensville Counties
69. Hampshire, Hanover, Harrison, Henrico (excluding the city of Richmond), Isle of Wight, Jefferson, Kanawha, King and Queen, King George, Lancaster, Lee (recapitulation only), Loudoun, Lunenburg, Madison, Mason, Mathews, Middlesex, and Monongalia Counties
70. Monroe, Montgomery, Nelson, New Kent, Norfolk (excluding the borough of Norfolk), Northumberland, Nottoway,

Ohio, Pendleton, Powhatan, Prince Edward, Prince George, Prince William, Princess Anne, Randolph, and Richmond Counties, the city of Richmond, and Rockbridge County

71. Shenandoah, Southampton, Spotsylvania, Stafford, Surry, Sussex, Warwick, Washington, Westmoreland, Wood, Wythe, and York Counties

FOURTH CENSUS OF THE UNITED STATES, 1820. M33. 142 ROLLS.

Connecticut.

1. Fairfield and Litchfield Counties
2. Hartford, Middlesex, New London, and Tolland Counties
3. New Haven and Windham Counties

Delaware.

4. Entire state

District of Columbia.

5. Entire district

Georgia.

6. Appling, Baldwin, Emanuel, Habersham, Hall, Irwin, and Jasper Counties
7. Bryan, Bulloch, Columbia, Early, Glynn, Effingham, Hancock, Jones, Lincoln, Oglethorpe, Richmond, Screven, and Warren Counties
8. Burke, Camden, Chatham, Clarke, Elbert, Greene, Gwinnett, Jackson, and Liberty Counties
9. Laurens, McIntosh, Madison, Montgomery, Pulaski, Putnam, Tattnall, Washington, Wayne, Wilkes, and Wilkerson Counties
10. Jefferson, Morgan, Telfair, and Walton Counties

Illinois.

11. Alexander, Edwards, Franklin, Gallatin, Jackson, Jefferson, Johnson, Madison, Union, Wayne, and White Counties
12. Bond, Clark, Crawford, Monroe, Pope, Randolph, St. Clair, and Washington Counties

Indiana.

13. Clark, Dearborn, Floyd, Franklin, Gibson, Jackson, Jefferson, Pike, Posey, and Randolph Counties
14. Crawford, Delaware, Dubois, Harrison, Jennings, Knox, Lawrence, Martin, Monroe, Orange, Owen, Perry, Scott, Switzerland, Vanderburgh, Vigo, Wabash, and Washington Counties
15. Fayette, Ripley, Spencer, Sullivan, Warrick, and Wayne Counties

Kentucky.

16. Adair, Allen, Bath, Breckinridge, and Butler Counties
17. Barren, Estill, Fayette, Gallatin, Grant, and Hart Counties
18. Boone, Bourbon, Bullitt, and Casey Counties
19. Bracken, Caldwell, Clark, Clay, Cumberland, and Nelson Counties
20. Campbell, Christian, Green, Lewis, Nicholas, Muhlenberg, and Union Counties
21. Daviess, Fleming, Garrard, Grayson, and Greenup Counties
22. Floyd, Franklin, and Henry Counties
23. Hardin, Harlan, Harrison, Hopkins, and Knox Counties
24. Henderson, Jefferson, Jessamine, Owen, and Shelby Counties
25. Lincoln, Madison, Monroe, and Montgomery Counties
26. Livingston, Logan, Mason, Mercer, and Todd Counties
27. Ohio, Pendleton, Pulaski, Rockcastle, and Scott Counties
28. Simpson, Warren, Wayne, and Whitley Counties
29. Trigg, Washington, and Woodford Counties

Louisiana.

30. Ascension, Assumption, Lafourche, St. Bernard, St. Charles, St. Helena, St. Jacques, St. John the Baptist, and St. Landry Parishes
31. Avoyelles, Catahoula, Concordia, Feliciana, Iberville, West Baton Rouge, Natchitoches, Ouachita, Pointe Coupee, Rapides, St. Mary, St. Martin, St. Tammany, and Washington Parishes
32. East Baton Rouge Parish, New Orleans City, and Orleans and Plaquemines Parishes

Maine.

33. Cumberland County (part)
34. Cumberland (part) and Hancock Counties
35. Kennebec County
36. Lincoln County
37. Oxford and Washington Counties
38. Penobscot and Somerset Counties
39. York County

Maryland.

40. Allegany, Calvert, Caroline, Cecil, and Charles Counties
41. Baltimore and Anne Arundel Counties
42. City of Baltimore
43. Dorchester and Frederick Counties
44. Harford, Kent, Montgomery, and Prince Georges Counties
45. Queen Annes, St. Mary's, and Somerset Counties
46. Talbot, Washington, and Worcester Counties

Massachusetts.

47. Barnstable, Bristol, and Dukes Counties
48. Berkshire and Hampden Counties
49. Essex County
50. Franklin, Hampshire and Plymouth Counties
51. Middlesex County

52. Nantucket and Norfolk Counties
53. Suffolk County
54. Worcester County (part)
55. Worcester County (part)

Michigan.
56. Oakland, Wayne, Michilimackinac, Brown, Crawford, Monroe, and Macomb Counties

Mississippi.
57. Adams, Amite, Franklin, Greene, Lawrence, Marion, Perry, and Wayne Counties
58. Claiborne, Covington, Hancock, Jackson, Jefferson, Monroe, Pike, Warren, and Wilkinson Counties

New Hampshire.
59. Cheshire and Coos Counties
60. Rockingham County
61. Hillsboro and Strafford Counties and State recapitulation

New York.
62. Ontario County
63. Albany and Montgomery Counties
64. Allegany, Greene, Kings, and Orange Counties
65. Broome, Delaware, Richmond, Schenectady, and Schoharie Counties
66. Cattaraugus, Chautauqua, Chenango, Clinton, Cortland, and Franklin Counties
67. Herkimer and Onondago Counties
68. Cayuga and Rensselaer Counties
69. Essex and Niagara Counties
70. Columbia County
71. Dutchess and Sullivan Counties
72. Genesee, Hamilton, and Jefferson Counties
73. Madison and Oneida Counties
74. Otsego, Steuben, and Suffolk Counties
75. Lewis, Seneca, and Westchester Counties
76. Tompkins, Ulster, Warren, and Washington Counties
77. New York County (New York City, wards 1-7)
78. New York (New York City, wards 8-10), Queens, and Rockland Counties
79. Oswego, Putnam, St. Lawrence, Saratoga, and Tioga Counties

North Carolina.
80. Anson, Buncombe, Cabarrus, Duplin, Haywood, Iredell, Johnston, Lenoir, Moore, Onslow, Rutherford, and Washington Counties
81. Ashe, Caswell, Chowan, Perquimans, Richmond, Rowan, and Tyrrell Counties
82. Beaufort, Bertie, Bladen, Chatham, Greene, Orange, Person, Pitt, Rockingham, Surry, and Warren Counties

83. Burke, Carteret, Cumberland, Hyde, Jones, Lincoln, Nash, Wayne, and Wilkes Counties
84. Brunswick, Camden, Columbus, Craven, Edgecombe, Gates, Mecklenburg, New Hanover, Pasquotank, Robeson, and Stokes Counties
85. Granville, Guilford, Halifax, Hertford, Northampton, and Sampson Counties

Ohio.
86. Adams, Athens, Belmont, Brown, and Champaign Counties
87. Ashtabula, Butler, Fairfield, Hamilton, and Warren Counties
88. Clark, Coshocton, Gallia, Hocking, Huron, Knox, Lawrence, Meigs, and Monroe Counties
89. Clermont, Darke, Mercer, Delaware, Jackson, Pickaway, Pike, and Trumbull Counties
90. Clinton, Cuyahoga, Logan, Hardin, and Medina Counties
91. Columbiana, Geauga, Green, Guernsey, and Jefferson Counties
92. Fayette, Highland, Morgan, Muskingum, Richland, and Ross Counties
93. Harrison and Wayne Counties
94. Licking, Madison, Miami, Montgomery, Sandusky, Stark, and Union Counties
95. Perry, Portage, Preble, Scioto, Shelby, Tuscarawas, and Washington Counties; and State recapitulation

Pennsylvania.
96. Adams, Beaver, and Chester Counties
97. Allegheny and Armstrong Counties 98. Bedford, Bradford, Butler, Cambria, Centre, Clearfield, and Greene Counties
99. Berks and Bucks (part) Counties
100. Bucks (part) and Montgomery Counties
101. Columbia, Crawford, and Franklin Counties
102. Cumberland, Dauphin, Erie, and Mifflin Counties
103. Delaware and Fayette Counties
104. Huntington, Lehigh, Northampton, and Perry Counties
105. Indiana, Jefferson, Lebanon, and Luzerne Counties
106. Lancaster County
107. Northumberland, Lycoming, Mercer, McKean, and Potter Counties
108. City of Philadelphia
109. Philadelphia County (part)
110. Philadelphia County (part)
111. Pike, Schuylkill, and Somerset Counties
112. Susquehanna, Wayne, and Westmoreland Counties
113. Tioga, Union, Warren, and Washington Counties
114. Venango and York Counties and State recapitulation

Rhode Island.
115. Bristol and Washington Counties
116. Kent and Newport Counties

117. Providence County

South Carolina.

118. Abbeville, Colleton, Darlington, Edgefield, Fairfield, Lancaster, and Orangeburg Counties

119. Barnwell, Charleston, Chesterfield, Horry, and Kershaw Counties

120. Beaufort, Chester, Georgetown, Greenville, Pendleton, Spartanburg, and Williamsburg Counties

121. Laurens, Lexington, Marion, Marlboro, Richland, Sumter, Union, and York Counties

Tennessee.

122. Bedford, Davidson, Hardin, Hickman, Humphreys, Montgomery, Overton, Perry, Warren, Wayne, White, and Wilson Counties

123. Dickson, Franklin, Jackson, Lawrence, and Lincoln Counties

124. Giles, Maury, Rutherford, Shelby, Stewart, and Sumner Counties

125. Robertson, Smith, and Williamson Counties

Vermont.

126. Addison, Bennington, Grand Isle, and Rutland Counties

127. Caledonia, Chittenden, Essex, Franklin, Orange, and Orleans Counties

128. Washington, Windham, and Windsor Counties

Virginia (including present-day West Virginia).

129. Accomack, Bath, Berkeley, Campbell, Caroline, and Chesterfield Counties

130. Albemarle, Botetourt, Cabell, Cumberland, Giles, Lee, Mecklenburg, Montgomery, Nelson, Nicholas, Northampton, Preston, Prince William, Randolph, and Rockbridge Counties

131. Amelia, Amherst, Grayson, Halifax, Madison, Norfolk (excluding the borough of Norfolk), and Prince Edward Counties, and the city of Richmond

132. Augusta, Brooke, Buckingham, Greenbrier, Henrico (excluding the city of Richmond), and Isle of Wight Counties

133. Bedford, Culpeper, Elizabeth City, Lancaster, Lewis, Monroe, New Kent, Richmond, and Tazewell Counties

134. Brunswick, Fluvanna, Jefferson, King George, and Princess Anne Counties

135. Charles City, Powhatan, Prince George, Spotsylvania, Sussex, and Westmoreland Counties, city of Williamsburg, and York County

136. Charlotte, Fauquier, Franklin, Gloucester, Hampshire, and King William Counties

137. Dinwiddie (excluding the town of Petersburg), Essex, Fairfax, Hardy, James City (excluding the city of Williamsburg), Loudoun, and Lunenburg Counties

138. Frederick, Hanover, Harrison, Mason, Shenandoah, Warwick, and Wood Counties

139. Goochland, Henry, Louisa, and Nansemond Counties, the town of Petersburg, and Rockingham, Scott, and Wythe Counties

140. Greensville, Ohio, Pendleton, Pittsylvania, and Tyler Counties

141. Morgan, Northumberland, Nottoway, Orange, Patrick, Russell, Stafford, and Washington Counties

142. Kanawha, King and Queen, Mathews, Middlesex, and Monongalia Counties, the borough of Norfolk, and Southampton and Surry Counties

FIFTH CENSUS OF THE UNITED STATES, 1830. M19. 201 ROLLS.

Alabama.

1. Blount, Franklin, Jackson, Jefferson, Lauderdale, and Lawrence Counties

2. Mobile (excluding the city of Mobile), Baldwin, Monroe, Dallas, Pickens, Bibb, Montgomery, Clarke, Shelby, Butler, Henry, Marengo, and Greene Counties

3. Pike, Perry, Connecuh, Autauga, Wilcox, Fayette, Dale, Covington, Washington, Lowndes, and Tuscaloosa Counties and Mobile City

4. Limestone, Madison, Marion, Morgan, St. Clair, and Walker Counties

Arkansas.

5. Entire state

Connecticut.

6. Fairfield County

7. Hartford County

8. Middlesex and Tolland Counties

9. New Haven County

10. New London County

11. Windham and Litchfield Counties

Delaware.

12. Newcastle and Kent Counties

13. Sussex County

District of Columbia.

14. Entire district

Florida.

15. Entire state

Georgia.

16. Appling, Baker, Baldwin, Bibb, Bryan, Bulloch, Burke, Butts, Camden, Campbell, Carroll, Chatham, Clarke, Columbia,

Coweta, and Crawford Counties

17. Decatur, DeKalb, Dooly, Early, Effingham, Elbert, Emanuel, Fayette, Franklin, Glynn, Greene, and Gwinnett Counties

18. Habersham, Hall, Hancock, Harris, Henry, Houston, Irwin, Jackson, Jasper, Jefferson, and Jones Counties

19. Laurens, Lee, Liberty, Lincoln, Lowndes, Madison, McIntosh, Marion, Meriwether, Monroe, Montgomery, Morgan, and Muscogee Counties

20. Newton, Oglethorpe, Pike, Pulaski, Putnam, Rabun, Randolph, Richmond, Screven, Talbot, Taliaferro, and Tattnall Counties

21. Telfair, Thomas, Troup, Twiggs, Upson, Walton, Ware, Warren, Washington, Wayne, Wilkes, and Wilkinson Counties

Illinois.

22. Alexander, Pope, Union, Johnson, Jackson, Franklin, Perry, Randolph, Monroe, Washington, Marion, Jefferson, Hamilton, and Gallatin Counties

23. Crawford, Edgar, Clark, Schuyler, McDonough, Vermilion, Macon, Shelby, Tazewell, Montgomery, and Macoupin Counties

24. Greene, Morgan, Sangamon, Calhoun, Pike, Fulton, Knox, Henry, Adams, Hancock, Warren, Mercer, Peoria, Putnam, and Jo Daviess Counties

25. White, Edwards, Wabash, Wayne, Clay, Clinton, St. Clair, Madison, Bond, Fayette, and Lawrence Counties

Indiana.

26. Fayette, Lawrence, Gibson, Sullivan, Boone, Vermillion, Hamilton, Rush, Martin, Madison, Allen, Pike, Decatur, St. Joseph, and Elkhart Counties

27. Cass, Johnson, Dubois, Harrison, Jennings, Dearborn, and Franklin Counties

28. Clark, Jefferson, Spencer, Marion, Crawford, Warrick, Delaware, Perry, Floyd, and Shelby Counties

29. Hancock, Randolph, Wayne, Posey, Jackson, and Owen Counties

30. Montgomery, Clinton, Vigo, Hendricks, Monroe, Putnam, Morgan, and Scott Counties

31. Orange, Henry, Tippecanoe, Greene, Bartholomew, Carroll, Knox, Washington, and Daviess Counties

32. Ripley, Switzerland, Parke, Fountain, Warren, Vanderburgh, Union, and Clay Counties

Kentucky.

33. Adair, Allen, Anderson, Barren, Bath, Boone, and Bourbon Counties

34. Bracken, Breckinridge, Butler, Bullitt, Caldwell, Calloway, Campbell, and Casey Counties

35. Christian, Clark, Cumberland, Clay, Daviess, Edmonson, Estill, and Fayette Counties

36. Fleming, Floyd, Franklin, Gallatin, Garrard, Grant, Graves, and Grayson Counties

37. Green, Greenup, Hancock, Harlan, Harrison, Hart, Henderson, Henry, and Hardin Counties

38. Hickman, Hopkins, Jefferson, Jessamine, Knox, Laurel, Lawrence, Lewis, and Lincoln Counties

39. Livingston, Logan, Madison, Mason, McCracken, Meade, Mercer, and Monroe Counties

40. Montgomery, Morgan, Muhlenberg, Nelson, Nicholas, Ohio, Oldham, Owen, Perry, and Pike Counties

41. Pulaski, Pendleton, Rockcastle, Russell, Scott, Shelby, Simpson, Spencer, and Todd Counties

42. Trigg, Union, Warren, Washington, Wayne, Whitley, and Woodford Counties

Louisiana.

43. Lafourche, Ascension, St. Helena, St. Tammany, Washington, Assumption, Terrebonne, Iberville, Concordia, Jefferson, Plaquemines, East Feliciana, West Feliciana, East Baton Rouge, West Baton Rouge, St. James, Pointe Coupee, St. John the Baptist, St. Bernard, and St. Charles Parishes

44. St. Landry, Natchitoches, Rapides, St. Martin, St. Mary, Lafayette, Ouachita, Avoyelles, Catahoula, and Claiborne Parishes

45. Orleans Parish

Maine.

46. Cumberland County

47. Hancock and Washington Counties and a few entries for Penobscot and Lincoln Counties

48. Kennebec County

49. Lincoln County

50. Oxford and Waldo Counties

51. Somerset and Penobscot Counties

52. York County

Maryland.

53. Allegany and Anne Arundel Counties

54. City of Baltimore

55. Baltimore (excluding the city of Baltimore), Calvert, and Caroline Counties

56. Cecil, Charles, and Dorchester Counties

57. Frederick, Harford, and Kent Counties

58. Talbot, Washington, and Worcester Counties

Massachusetts.

59. Bristol County

60. Norfolk and Barnstable Counties

61. Essex County

62. Franklin, Dukes, and Berkshire Counties

63. Hampden County and a few entries for the town of Paxton in

Worcester County

64. Suffolk (excluding the city of Boston), Nantucket, Plymouth, and Hampshire Counties

65. City of Boston

66. Middlesex County (part)

67. Middlesex County (part)

68. Worcester County

Michigan.

69. Wayne, Monroe, Oakland, Lenawee, Macomb, St. Clair, Washtenaw, St. Joseph, Berrien, Cass, Van Buren, Michilimackinack, Brown, Crawford, Chippewa, and Iowa Counties

Mississippi.

70. Adams, Amite, Claiborne, Copiah, Covington, Franklin, Greene, Hancock, and Hinds Counties

71. Jackson, Jones, Jefferson, Lawrence, Lowndes, Madison, Marion, Monroe, Perry, Rankin, Simpson, Warren, Washington, Wayne, Wilkinson, and Yazoo Counties

Missouri.

72. Lincoln, Marion, Chariton, Washington, Jefferson, Franklin, Gasconade, Crawford, Cole, Montgomery, Pike, St. Charles, St. Louis, Ste. Genevieve, Perry, St. Francois, and Cape Girardeau Counties

73. Scott, New Madrid, Wayne, Callaway, Boone, Howard, Cooper, Saline, Lafayette, Clay, Jackson, Randolph, Madison, Ralls, and Ray Counties

New Hampshire.

74. Cheshire and Sullivan Counties

75. Grafton and Coos Counties

76. Merrimack and Hillsboro Counties

77. Rockingham County

78. Strafford County

New Jersey.

79. Bergan and Essex Counties

80. Burlington and Monmouth Counties

81. Gloucester, Cape May, Salem, and Cumberland Counties

82. Morris, Sussex, and Warren Counties

83. Somerset, Middlesex, and Hunterdon Counties

New York.

84. Allegany and Albany Counties

85. Broome, Cattaraugus, and Clinton Counties

86. Chenango and Chautauqua Counties

87. Columbia County

88. Cortland and Cayuga Counties

89. Delaware County

90. Franklin and Genesee Counties

91. Herkimer and Hamilton Counties

92. Jefferson and Lewis Counties

93. Livingston and Madison Counties

94. Monroe County

95. Montgomery and Niagara Counties

96. New York City, wards 1-6

97. New York City, wards 7-9

98. New York City, wards 10-14

99. Oneida County

100. Onondaga County

101. Ontario County

102. Otsego County

103. Putnam, Rockland, and Suffolk Counties

104. Queens and Dutchess Counties

105. Rensselaer County

106. Richmond and Ulster Counties

107. St. Lawrence and Steuben Counties

108. Saratoga County

109. Seneca, Tioga, and Tompkins Counties

110. Sullivan and Greene Counties

111. Warren and Washington Counties

112. Westchester and Kings Counties

113. Orange County

114. Erie and Essex Counties

115. Orleans and Oswego Counties

116. Schoharie and Schenectady Counties

117. Wayne and Yates Counties

North Carolina.

118. Ashe, Anson, Burke, Buncombe, Brunswick, and Bertie Counties

119. Beaufort, Bladen, Craven, Cabarrus, Currituck, Caswell, Chowan, Camden, and Chatham Counties

120. Columbus, Cumberland, Carteret, Duplin, Davidson, Edgecombe, and Franklin Counties

121. Granville, Gates, Guilford, Greene, Hyde, Halifax, Haywood, and Hertford Counties

122. Iredell, Johnston, Jones, Lincoln, Lenoir, Mecklenburg, Martin, and Moore Counties

123. Macon, Montgomery, Northampton, New Hanover, Nash, Onslow, and Orange Counties

124. Person, Pitt, Perquimans, Pasquotank, Richmond, Robeson, Rockingham, Rowan, and Rutherford Counties

125. Randolph, Surry, Sampson, Stokes, Tyrrell, Wilkes, Wake, Wayne, Washington, and Warren Counties

Ohio.

126. Adams, Ashtabula, Athens, Mercer, Van Wert, and Allen Counties

127. Butler, Belmont, and Brown Counties

128. Champaign, Clark, Clermont, and Columbiana Counties
129. Coshocton, Cuyahoga, Crawford, and Clinton Counties
130. Darke, Delaware, Fairfield, and Fayette Counties
131. Franklin, Gallia, Geauga, Greene, and Guernsey Counties
132. Hamilton and Hocking Counties
133. Highland, Harrison, Hancock, Holmes, and Huron Counties
134. Jefferson, Jackson, Knox, Lawrence, and Licking Counties
135. Lorain, Logan, Hardin, Madison, Marion, Medina, and Meigs Counties
136. Miami, Monroe, and Montgomery Counties
137. Morgan, Muskingum, and Perry Counties
138. Pickaway, Pike, Portage, and Preble Counties
139. Richland and Ross Counties
140. Sandusky, Shelby, Scioto, Seneca, and Stark Counties
141. Tuscarawas, Trumbull, Union, and Washington Counties
142. Wayne, Williams, Paulding, Henry, Putnam, Warren, and Wood Counties

Pennsylvania.
143. Adams and Berks Counties
144. Allegheny County
145. Bradford, Armstrong, and Luzerne Counties
146. Bucks County
147. Butler, Northumberland, Erie, and Mifflin Counties
148. Chester County
149. Crawford, Mercer, and Union Counties
150. Cumberland and Delaware Counties
151. Dauphin and Franklin Counties
152. Bedford and Indiana Counties
153. Lancaster County
154. Lebanon and Montgomery Counties
155. Lehigh County
156. Northampton and Perry Counties
157. Philadelphia County (part)
158. Philadelphia County (part)
159. City of Philadelphia
160. Pike, Schuylkill, Wayne, and York Counties
161. Somerset, McKean, Potter, Jefferson, Cambria, and Clearfield Counties
162. Susquehanna, Fayette, and Greene Counties
163. Tioga and Washington Counties
164. Venango and Westmoreland Counties
165. Warren, Columbia, Beaver, and Centre Counties
166. Huntington and Lycoming Counties

Rhode Island.
167. Newport, Washington, Kent, and Bristol Counties
168. Providence County

South Carolina.
169. Abbeville, Barnwell, Laurens, Chester, and Fairfield Counties

170. Charleston, Georgetown, Williamsburg, Horry, and Beaufort Counties
171. Kershaw, Marlboro, Newberry, Union, Spartanburg, Lexington, Richland, and Colleton Counties
172. Marion, Sumter, Edgefield, Chesterfield, and Greenville Counties
173. Orangeburg, Lancaster, Anderson, Darlington, Pickens, and York Counties

Tennessee.
174. Bedford, Carroll, Davidson, Dickson, and Dyer Counties
175. Carter, Marion, Monroe, Anderson, Washington, Bledsoe, Sullivan, and Rhea Counties
176. Fentress, Fayette, Franklin, Giles, Gibson, Hickman, Humphreys, Hardeman, Hardin, and Haywood Counties
177. Henry, Henderson, Jackson, Lincoln, Lawrence, and Maury Counties
178. Hawkins, Sevier, McMinn, Campbell, Blount, and Knox Counties
179. Montgomery, Madison, McNairy, Obion, Overton, Perry, Rutherford, and Robertson Counties
180. Roane, Hamilton, Morgan, Claiborne, Greene, Cocke, Jefferson, and Grainger Counties
181. Shelby, Smith, Sumner, Stewart, Tipton, and Warren Counties
182. White, Wilson, Williamson, Wayne, and Weakley Counties

Vermont.
183. Franklin, Orleans, and Washington Counties
184. Grand Isle, Bennington, and Addison Counties
185. Essex and Orange Counties
186. Windham and Chittenden Counties
187. Windsor and Caledonia Counties
188. Rutland County

Virginia (including present-day West Virginia).
189. Augusta, Alleghany, Brooke, Bath, Berkeley, and Botetourt Counties
190. Cabell, Frederick, Greenbrier, Giles, Grayson, and Harrison Counties
191. Hampshire, Hardy, Jefferson, Kanawha, Lewis, Logan, Lee, and Monongalia Counties
192. James City, New Kent, Franklin, Westmoreland, Goochland, Cumberland, Isle of Wight, Accomack, and Halifax Counties
193. Loudoun, Essex, Gloucester, Nansemond, Powhatan, and Buckingham Counties
194. Louisa, King George, Richmond, Charles City, Bedford, Hanover, Princess Anne, Campbell, Fauquier, Amherst, and Lancaster Counties
195. Lunenburg, Stafford, Spotsylvania, Northampton, Patrick, Henry, Nottoway, Brunswick, Henrico, and Fluvanna Counties and the city of Richmond

196. Madison, Greensville, Prince William, Nelson, Mathews, Middlesex, Elizabeth City, Charlotte, Southampton, Orange, Dinwiddie, and Chesterfield Counties

197. Mecklenburg, Culpeper, Warwick, Caroline, Albemarle, and Norfolk Counties

198. Monroe, Montgomery, Morgan, Mason, Nicholas, and Ohio Counties

199. Preston, Pendleton, Pocahontas, Randolph, Russell, Rockingham, and Rockbridge Counties

200. Scott, Shenandoah, Tyler, Tazewell, Washington, Wythe, and Wood Counties

201. Sussex, Prince Georges, King William, Prince Edward, Amelia, Surry, Northumberland, Fairfax, King and Queen, Pittsylvania, and York Counties

SIXTH CENSUS OF THE UNITED STATES, 1840. M704. 580 ROLLS.

Alabama.

1. Autauga, Barbour, Baldwin, Bibb, and Butler Counties
2. Chambers, Clarke, Conecuh, Coosa, and Covington Counties
3. Blount, Benton, and Cherokee Counties
4. De Kalb, Fayette, and Franklin Counties
5. Dale, Dallas, and Greene Counties
6. Henry, Jefferson, and Lowndes Counties
7. Jackson and Lauderdale Counties
8. Limestone and Lawrence Counties
9. Macon, Marengo, and Mobile Counties
10. City of Mobile and Montgomery County
11. City of Montgomery and Monroe and Perry Counties
12. Pickens and Pike Counties
13. Morgan, Marion, Marshall, and Madison Counties
14. Randolph, St. Clair, and Talladega Counties
15. Russell, Shelby, Sumter, and Tallapoosa Counties
16. Tuscaloosa, Washington, Walker, and Wilcox Counties

Arkansas.

17. Arkansas, Benton, Carroll, Chicot, Clark, Conway, Crawford, Crittenden, Desha, Franklin, and Greene Counties
18. Hempstead, Hot Springs, Independence, Izard, Jackson, Jefferson, and Johnson Counties
19. Lafayette, Lawrence, Madison, Marion, Mississippi, Monroe, Phillips, Pike, Poinsett, Pope, and Pulaski Counties
20. Randolph, St. Francis, Saline, Scott, Searcy, Sevier, Union, Van Buren, Washington, and White Counties

Connecticut.

21. Fairfield County (part)
22. Fairfield County (part)
23. Hartford County (part)
24. Hartford County (part)
25. Litchfield County
26. Middlesex County
27. New Haven County (part)
28. New Haven County (part)
29. New London County (part)
30. New London County (part)
31. Tolland County
32. Windham County

Delaware.

33. Kent and New Castle Counties
34. Sussex County

District of Columbia.

35. Washington City, Washington County, Georgetown, and Alexandria County

Florida.

36. Walton, Escambia, Madison, Jefferson, Leon, Hamilton, Gadsden, St. Johns, Nassau, Mosquito, Hillsborough, Duval, Columbia, Alachua, Monroe, Dade, Washington, Jackson, Franklin, and Calhoun Counties

Georgia.

37. Appling, Baker, Baldwin, Bibb, Bryan, Bullock, Burke, and Butts Counties
38. Camden, Campbell, Carroll, Cass, Chatham, Chattooga, and Cherokee Counties
39. Clarke, Cobb, Columbia, Coweta, and Crawford Counties
40. Decatur, De Kalb, Dade, Dooly, Early, Effingham, and Elbert Counties
41. Emanuel, Fayette, Floyd, Forsyth, and Franklin Counties
42. Gilmer, Glynn, Greene, Gwinnett, Hall, and Habersham Counties
43. Hancock, Harris, Heard, Henry, and Houston Counties
44. Irwin, Jackson, Jasper, Jefferson, and Jones Counties
45. Laurens, Lee, Liberty, Lincoln, Lowndes, and Lumpkin Counties
46. Macon, Madison, Marion, McIntosh, and Meriwether Counties
47. Monroe, Montgomery, Morgan, Murray, and Muscogee Counties
48. Newton, Oglethorpe, Paulding, and Pike Counties
49. Pulaski, Putnam, Rabun, Randolph, and Richmond Counties
50. Screven, Stewart, and Sumter Counties
51. Talbot, Taliaferro, Tattnall, Telfair, Thomas, Troup, and Twiggs Counties
52. Union, Upson, Walker, Walton, and Ware Counties
53. Warren, Washington, Wayne, Wilkes, and Wilkinson Counties

Illinois.

54. Adams and Alexander Counties

55. Bond, Boone, Brown, and Bureau Counties
56. Calhoun, Carroll, Cass, Champaign, Christian, Clark, Clay, and Clinton Counties
57. Coles, Cook, and Crawford Counties
58. De Kalb, De Witt, Du Page, Edgar, Edwards, and Effingham Counties
59. Fayette, Franklin, and Fulton Counties
60. Gallatin, Greene, Hamilton, Hancock, and Hardin Counties
61. Henry, Iroquois, Jackson, Jasper, Jefferson, Jersey, Jo Daviess, and Johnson Counties
62. Kane, Knox, and Lake Counties
63. La Salle, Lawrence, Lee, Livingston, and Logan Counties
64. Macon, Macoupin, Madison, and Marion Counties
65. Marshall, McDonough, McHenry, McLean, and Menard Counties
66. Mercer, Monroe, Montgomery, and Morgan Counties
67. Ogle, Peoria, Perry, and Pike Counties
68. Pope, Putnam, Randolph, and Rock Island Counties
69. Sangamon, Schuyler, and Scott Counties
70. Shelby, Stark, Stephenson, and St. Clair Counties
71. Tazewell, Union, Vermilion, and Wabash Counties
72. Warren, Washington, and Wayne Counties
73. White, Will, Whiteside, Williamson, and Winnebago Counties

Indiana.
74. Adams, Allen, Blackford, Bartholomew, Benton, and Boone Counties
75. Brown, Cass, and Clark Counties
76. Clay, Clinton, Carroll, and Crawford Counties
77. Daviess and Dearborn Counties
78. Decatur, De Kalb, Delaware, and Dubois Counties
79. Elkhart, Fayette, and Floyd Counties
80. Fountain, Franklin, and Fulton Counties
81. Gibson, Grant, and Greene Counties
82. Hamilton, Hancock, and Harrison Counties
83. Jackson, Jasper, Jay, and Jefferson Counties
84. Jennings and Johnson Counties
85. Kosciusko, Knox, Lake, and La Porte Counties
86. Lagrange and Lawrence Counties
87. Hendricks and Henry Counties
88. Huntington, Madison, and Marion Counties
89. Orange, Owen, and Parke Counties
90. Perry, Pike, Porter, and Posey Counties
91. Pulaski and Putnam Counties
92. Randolph and Ripley Counties
93. Rush, Scott, Shelby, and Spencer Counties
94. St. Joseph, Starke, Sullivan, and Steuben Counties
95. Switzerland, Tippecanoe, and Union Counties
96. Vanderburgh, Vermillion , and Vigo Counties
97. Wabash, Warren, Warrick, and Washington Counties

98. Wells, White, Whitley, and Wayne Counties
99. Marshall, Martin, Miami, and Monroe Counties
100. Montgomery, Morgan, and Noble Counties

Iowa.
101. Clayton, Clinton, Cedar, Dubuque, Des Moines, Delaware, Henry, Johnson, and Jefferson Counties
102. Jackson, Jones, Linn, Lee, Louisa, Muscantine, Scott, Van Buren, and Washington Counties

Kentucky.
103. Adair, Allen, Anderson, and Barren Counties
104. Bath, Boone, and Bourbon Counties
105. Bracken, Butler, Breathitt, Breckinridge, and Bullitt Counties
106. Caldwell, Calloway, and Campbell Counties
107. Carroll, Casey, Christian, and Carter Counties
108. Clark, Clay, Clinton, and Cumberland Counties
109. Daviess, Estill, Edmonson, and Fayette Counties
110. Fleming, Floyd, and Franklin Counties
111. Gallatin, Garrard, Grant, and Graves Counties
112. Grayson, Green, and Greenup Counties
113. Hancock, Hardin, Harlan, Harrison, and Hart Counties
114. Henderson, Henry, Hickman, and Hopkins Counties
115. Jefferson County
116. Jessamine, Kenton, and Knox Counties
117. Laurel, Lawrence, Lewis, Lincoln, and Livingston Counties
118. Logan, Madison, and Marion Counties
119. Mason, McCracken, Meade, and Mercer Counties
120. Monroe, Morgan, Montgomery, and Muhlenberg Counties
121. Nelson, Nicholas, Ohio, and Oldham Counties
122. Owen, Pendleton, Perry, Pike, and Pulaski Counties
123. Rockcastle, Russell, Scott, and Shelby Counties
124. Simpson, Spencer, Todd, Trigg, and Trimble Counties
125. Union, Warren, and Washington Counties
126. Wayne, Whitley, and Woodford Counties

Louisiana.
127. Lafayette, Caddo, Catahoula, Calcasieu, Caldwell, Claiborne, Ouachita, and Natchitoches Parishes
128. Rapides, St. Landry, Avoyelles, St. Martin, St. Mary, and Union Parishes
129. Lafourche, Terrebonne, Iberville, West Baton Rouge, East Baton Rouge, Washington, Madison, Carroll, and St. Tammany Parishes
130. Concordia, Pointe Coupee, West Feliciana, Jefferson, East Feliciana, St. Helena, and Livingston Parishes
131. Orleans Parish (excluding the city of New Orleans)
132. City of New Orleans, municipality no. 1

133. City of New Orleans, municipality no. 2
134. City of New Orleans, municipality no. 3
135. Plaquemines, St. Bernard, St. Charles, St. John the Baptist, St. James, Ascension, and Assumption Parishes

Maine.
136. Aroostook County
137. Cumberland County (part), city of Portland
138. Cumberland County (part) (excluding the city of Portland)
139. Cumberland County (part) (excluding the city of Portland)
140. Franklin County
141. Hancock County
142. Kennebec County (part)
143. Kennebec County (part)
144. Lincoln County (part)
145. Lincoln County (part)
146. Oxford County (part)
147. Oxford County (part)
148. Penobscot County (part)
149. Penobscot County (part)
150. Piscataquis County
151. Somerset County
152. Washington County
153. Waldo County
154. York County (part)
155. York County (part)

Maryland.
156. Allegany County
157. Anne Arundel County
158. Baltimore County, city of Baltimore, wards 1-3
159. City of Baltimore, wards 4-6
160. City of Baltimore, wards 7-10
161. City of Baltimore, wards 11 and 12
162. Baltimore County (part) (excluding the city of Baltimore), collection districts 1-5
163. Carroll, Calvert, and Charles Counties
164. Cecil and Caroline Counties
165. Dorchester and Frederick (part) Counties
166. Frederick County (part)
167. Harford and Kent Counties
168. Montgomery County
169. Prince Gèorge and Queen Annes Counties
170. St. Mary's and Somerset Counties
171. Talbot and Washington Counties
172. Worcester County

Massachusetts.
173. Barnstable County
174. Dukes County
175. Berkshire County (part)

176. Berkshire County (part)
177. Bristol County (part)
178. Bristol County (part)
179. Essex County (part)
180. Essex County (part)
181. Essex County (part)
182. Essex County (part)
183. Franklin County
184. Hampshire County
185. Hampden County (part)
186. Hampden County (part)
187. Middlesex County (part)
188. Middlesex County (part)
189. Middlesex County (part)
190. Middlesex County (part)
191. Norfolk County (part)
192. Norfolk County (part)
193. Nantucket County
194. Plymouth County (part)
195. Plymouth County (part)
196. Suffolk County, city of Chelsea and city of Boston, wards 9-12
197. Suffolk County, city of Boston, wards 5-8
198. Suffolk County, city of Boston, wards 1-4
199. Worcester County (part)
200. Worcester County (part)
201. Worcester County (part)
202. Worcester County (part)

Michigan.
203. Allegan, Berrien, Barry, Branch, and Calhoun Counties
204. Cass, Chippewa, Clinton, and Eaton Counties
205. Genesee, Hillsdale, Ingham, and Ionia Counties
206. Jackson, Kalamazoo, and Kent Counties
207. Lapeer and Lenawee Counties
208. Livingston, Mackinac, Macomb, and Monroe Counties
209. Oakland, Ottawa, and Oceana Counties
210. Saginaw, Shiawassee, St. Clair, and St. Joseph Counties
211. Van Buren and Washtenaw Counties
212. Wayne County

Mississippi.
213. Adams, Amite, Claiborne, Copiah, Clarke, Covington, Greene, and Franklin Counties
214. Jasper, Hinds, Hancock, Holmes, Jackson, Jefferson, and Jones Counties
215. Attala, Bolivar, Carroll, Chickasaw, Choctaw, Coahoma, De Soto, Itawamba, Lafayette, and Lowndes Counties
216. Kemper, Leake, Lauderdale, Lawrence, Madison, Marion, Nesoba, Newton, and Pike Counties
217. Perry, Rankin, Scott, Simpson, Smith, Wayne, Washington, Warren, Wilkinson, and Yazoo Counties

218. Marshall, Monroe, Noxubee, Oktibbeha, Panola, and Pontotoc Counties
219. Tallahatchie, Tippah, Tishomingo, Tunica, Winston, and Yalobush Counties

Missouri.

220. Audrain, Barry, Benton, Boone, and Buchanan Counties
221. Caldwell, Callaway, Carroll, Cape Girardeau, Chariton, and Clark Counties
222. Clay, Clinton, Cole, and Cooper Counties
223. Crawford, Daviess, Franklin, Gasconade, and Greene Counties
224. Howard, Jackson, Jefferson, Johnson, and Lafayette Counties
225. Lewis, Lincoln, Linn, and Livingston Counties
226. Macon, Madison, Marion, Miller, and Monroe Counties
227. Morgan, Montgomery, New Madrid, and Newton Counties
228. Perry, Pettis, Pike, Platte, and Polk Counties
229. Pulaski, Ralls, Randolph, Ray, Ripley, and Rives Counties
230. St. Charles, St. Francois, and Ste. Genevieve Counties
231. St. Louis County
232. Stoddard, Shelby, Scott, Saline, Taney, and Van Buren Counties
233. Warren, Washington, and Wayne Counties

New Hampshire.

234. Cheshire County
235. Coos County
236. Grafton County (part)
237. Grafton County (part)
238. Hillsboro County (part)
239. Hillsboro County (part)
240. Merrimack County (part)
241. Merrimack County (part)
242. Rockingham County (part)
243. Rockingham County (part)
244. Sullivan County
245. Strafford County (part)
246. Strafford County (part)

New Jersey.

247. Atlantic and Bergen Counties
248. Burlington County
249. Cape May and Cumberland Counties
250. Essex County (part), city of Newark
251. Essex County (part) (excluding the city of Newark)
252. Gloucester County
253. Hudson and Hunterdon Counties
254. Mercer County
255. Monmouth County
256. Middlesex County
257. Morris County
258. Passaic County

259. Somerset County
260. Sussex County
261. Salem County
262. Warren County

New York.

263. Albany County (part) (excluding the city of Albany)
264. Albany County (part), city of Albany, wards 1-5
265. Allegany County
266. Broome County
267. Cattaragus County
268. Chemung County
269. Cayuga County (part)
270. Cayuga County (part)
271. Chautauqua County (part)
272. Chautauqua County (part)
273. Chenango County
274. Delaware County
275. Cortland County
276. Clinton County
277. Columbia County
278. Dutchess County (part)
279. Dutchess County (part)
280. Erie County (part)
281. Erie County (part) (including the city of Buffalo)
282. Essex County
283. Franklin County
284. Fulton County
285. Genesee County (part)
286. Genesee County (part)
287. Genesee County (part)
288. Greene County
289. Kings County
290. Herkimer and Hamilton Counties
291. Jefferson County (part)
292. Jefferson County (part)
293. Lewis County
294. Livingston County
295. Madison County
296. Montgomery County
297. Monroe County (part)
298. Monroe County (part)
299. New York County, city of New York, wards 1-3
300. City of New York, wards 4 and 5
301. City of New York, wards 6 and 7
302. City of New York, ward 8
303. City of New York, ward 9
304. City of New York, ward 10
305. City of New York, wards 11 and 12
306. City of New York, ward 13
307. City of New York, ward 14

308. City of New York, ward 15
309. City of New York, ward 16
310. City of New York, ward 17
311. Niagara County
312. Oneida County (part)
313. Oneida County (part)
314. Oneida County (part)
315. Oneida County (part)
316. Onondaga County (part)
317. Onondaga County (part)
318. Onondaga County (part)
319. Ontario County (part)
320. Ontario County (part)
321. Orleans County
322. Orange County (part)
323. Orange County (part)
324. Putnam County
325. Oswego County (part)
326. Oswego County (part)
327. Otsego County (part)
328. Otsego County (part)
329. Otsego County (part)
330. Queens County
331. Rockland and Richmond Counties
332. Rensselaer County (part)
333. Rensselaer County (part)
334. St. Lawrence County (part)
335. St. Lawrence County (part)
336. Saratoga County
337. Schenectady County
338. Schoharie County
339. Seneca County
340. Steuben County (part)
341. Steuben County (part)
342. Sullivan County
343. Suffolk County
344. Tioga County
345. Tompkins County
346. Ulster County (part)
347. Ulster County (part)
348. Washington County
349. Warren County
350. Wayne County
351. Yates County
352. Westchester County (part)
353. Westchester County (part)

North Carolina.

354. Ashe, Anson, Bertie, and Buncombe Counties
355. Bladen, Brunswick, Beaufort, and Burke Counties
356. Cabarrus, Columbus, Carteret, and Currituck Counties

357. Chatham, Chowan, Cherokee, and Cumberland Counties
358. Camden, Caswell, and Craven Counties
359. Duplin, Davie, and Davidson Counties
360. Edgecombe, Franklin, and Granville Counties
361. Gates, Greene, and Guilford Counties
362. Halifax, Hertford, Hyde, Haywood, and Henderson Counties
363. Iredell, Johnston, and Jones Counties
364. Lenoir, Lincoln, Macon, and Moore Counties
365. Montgomery, Mecklenburg, and Martin Counties
366. New Hanover, Nash, and Northampton Counties
367. Onslow and Orange Counties
368. Person. Pasquotank, Perquimans, and Pitt Counties
369. Rowan, Randolph, and Rockingham Counties
370. Robeson, Richmond, and Rutherford Counties
371. Sampson and Surry Counties
372. Stokes, Tyrell, and Warren Counties
373. Washington and Wilkes Counties
374. Wayne, Wake, and Yancey Counties

Ohio.

375. Adams and Allen Counties
376. Ashtabula County
377. Athens County
378. Belmont County
379. Brown County
380. Butler County
381. Carroll County
382. Champaign County
383. Clark County
384. Clermont County
385. Clinton County
386. Columbiana County
387. Coshocton County
388. Crawford County
389. Cuyahoga County
390. Darke County
391. Delaware County
392. Erie County
393. Fayette and Franklin Counties
394. Fairfield County
395. Gallia and Geauga Counties
396. Greene County
397. Guernsey County
398. Hamilton County, city of Cincinnati, wards 1-4
399. City of Cincinnati, wards 5-7
400. Hamilton County (part) (excluding the city of Cincinnati)
401. Hancock and Hardin Counties
402. Harrison and Henry Counties
403. Highland and Hocking Counties
404. Holmes and Huron Counties
405. Jackson and Jefferson Counties

406. Knox County
407. Lawrence and Lake Counties
408. Licking County
409. Logan and Lorain Counties
410. Lucas County
411. Madison and Marion Counties
412. Medina County
413. Meigs and Mercer Counties
414. Montgomery County
415. Miami County
416. Monroe County
417. Morgan County
418. Muskingum County
419. Ottawa, Paulding, and Perry Counties
420. Pickaway County
421. Pike and Preble Counties
422. Portage and Putnam Counties
423. Richland County
424. Ross County
425. Sandusky and Scioto Counties
426. Seneca and Shelby Counties
427. Stark County
428. Summit County
429. Trumbull County
430. Tuscarawas County
431. Union, Van Wert, and Warren Counties
432. Wayne County
433. Williams and Washington Counties
434. Wood County

Pennsylvania.
435. Adams County
436. Berks County (part)
437. Berks County (part)
438. Berks County (part)
439. Allegheny County (part)
440. Allegheny County (part)
441. Allegheny County (part)
442. Armstrong County
443. Bradford County
444. Beaver County
445. Bedford County
446. Bucks County (part)
447. Bucks County (part)
448. Butler County
449. Columbia County
450. Clinton County
451. Cambria and Centre Counties
452. Crawford County
453. Chester County (part)
454. Chester County (part)

455. Cumberland County
456. Dauphin County
457. Delaware County
458. Franklin County
459. Erie County
460. Fayette County
461. Greene County
462. Huntingdon County
463. Indiana County
464. Jefferson and Juniata Counties
465. Lancaster County (part)
466. Lancaster County (part)
467. Lancaster County (part)
468. Lebanon County
469. Lehigh County
470. Monroe County
471. Luzerne County (part)
472. Luzerne County (part)
473. Lycoming County
474. Mercer County
475. Mifflin, McKean, and Northumberland Counties
476. Potter and Susquehanna Counties
477. Montgomery County (part)
478. Montgomery County (part)
479. Northampton County
480. Perry County
481. Philadelphia County, city of Philadelphia, North Mulberry, South Mulberry, and Upper Delaware Wards
482. City of Philadelphia, North, High Street, Chestnut, and Middle Wards
483. City of Philadelphia, South, Walnut, Dock, and Locust Wards
484. City of Philadelphia, New Market, Cedar, and Pine Wards
485. Philadelphia County, city of Northern Liberties, wards 1-7
486. Philadelphia County, Southwark, wards 1-5
487. Philadelphia County, Spring Garden, wards 1-4
488. Philadelphia County, Kensington, wards 1-5
489. Philadelphia County (part)
490. Philadelphia County (part)
491. Philadelphia County (part)
492. Pike and Schuylkill Counties
493. Wayne County
494. Somerset County
495. Tioga County
496. Union County
497. Venango County
498. Westmoreland County
499. Washington County
500. Clearfield and Warren Counties
501. York County (part)
502. York County (part)
503. York County (part)

Rhode Island.
504. Bristol, Kent, and Newport Counties
505. Providence County
506. Washington County

South Carolina.
507. Abbeville and Anderson Districts
508. Barnwell and Beaufort Districts
509. Charleston District
510. Colleton, Chester, and Chesterfield Districts
511. Darlington, Edgefield, and Fairfield Districts
512. Greenville, Georgetown, Horry, Kershaw, and Lancaster Districts
513. Laurens, Lexington, Marion, and Marlboro Districts
514. Newberry, Orangeburg, Pickens, and Richland Districts
515. Sumter and Spartanburg Districts
516. Union, Williamsburg, and York Districts

Tennessee.
517. Anderson, Bradley, Blount, and Bledsoe Counties
518. Carter, Claiborne, Cocke, and Campbell Counties
519. Bedford, Cannon, and Coffee Counties
520. Dickson, De Kalb, and Davidson Counties
521. Benton, Carroll, Dyer, Fayette, and Gibson Counties
522. Hardin, Hardeman, Haywood, Henderson, and Henry Counties
523. Fentress, Franklin, and Giles Counties
524. Hickman, Humphreys, and Jackson Counties
525. Greene, Grainger, and Hamilton Counties
526. Hawkins, Johnson, and Jefferson Counties
527. Knox and McMinn Counties
528. Monroe, Morgan, Meigs, and Marion Counties
529. Lauderdale, McNairy, Madison, and Obion Counties
530. Perry, Shelby, Tipton, and Weakley Counties
531. Lincoln, Lawrence, and Marshall Counties
532. Montgomery and Maury Counties
533. Overton, Rutherford, and Robertson Counties
534. Smith, Stewart, and Sumner Counties
535. Polk, Rhea, Roane, Sullivan, Sevier, and Washington Counties
536. White and Wayne Counties
537. Williamson, Wilson, and Warren Counties

Vermont.
538. Addison County
539. Bennington County
540. Caledonia County
541. Chittenden and Essex Counties
542. Franklin and Grand Isle Counties
543. Lamoille and Orange Counties
544. Orleans County

545. Rutland County
546. Washington County
547. Windham County
548. Windsor County

Virginia.
549. Accomack, Albermarle, and Amelia Counties
550. Amherst, Bedford, Brunswick, and Buckingham Counties
551. Augusta, Alleghany, Bath, and Berkeley Counties
552. Brooke, Braxton, and Botetourt Counties
553. Campbell, Caroline, and Charles City Counties
554. Charlotte, Chesterfield, Culpeper, and Cumberland Counties
555. Clarke, Cabell, Frederick, and Fayette Counties
556. Floyd, Giles, Greenbrier, and Grayson Counties
557. Dinwiddie, Elizabeth City, and Essex Counties
558. Fairfax, Fauquier, and Fluvanna Counties
559. Franklin, Gloucester, Goochland, Greensville, and Greene Counties
560. Halifax and Hanover Counties
561. Henrico and Henry Counties
562. Harrison and Hardy Counties
563. Hampshire, Jackson, and Jefferson Counties
564. Isle of Wight, James City, King George, King William, King and Queen, Lancaster, and Loudoun Counties
565. Louisa, Lunenburg, Madison, Mathews, Mecklenburg, and Middlesex Counties
566. Kanawha, Logan, Lee, and Lewis Counties
567. Montgomery, Monongalia, and Monroe Counties
568. Morgan, Mason, Mercer, and Marshall Counties
569. Nansemond, Nelson, and New Kent Counties
570. Norfolk, Northampton, Northumberland, and Nottoway Counties
571. Nicholas, Ohio, and Pocahontas Counties
572. Pendleton, Page, Pulaski, and Preston Counties
573. Orange, Patrick, and Pittsylvania Counties
574. Powhatan, Princess Anne, Prince Edward, Prince George, and Prince William Counties
575. Rappahannock, Richmond, Southampton, and Spotsylvania Counties
576. Stafford, Surry, Sussex, Warwick, Westmoreland, and York Counties
577. Russell, Rockingham, and Rockbridge Counties
578. Roanoke, Randolph, Scott, Shenandoah, and Smyth Counties
579. Tyler, Tazewell, Wythe, Wood, Warren, and Washington Counties

Wisconsin.
580. Calumet, Fond du Lac, Crawford, St. Croix, Grant, Iowa, Racine, Rock, Brown, Washington, Sheboygan, Manitowoc, Winnebago, Marquette, Dodge, Portage, Dane, Sauk, Green, Jefferson, Milwaukee, and Walworth Counties

**SEVENTH CENSUS OF THE UNITED STATES, 1850. M432.
1,009 ROLLS.**

Alabama.

FREE SCHEDULES.

1. Autauga, Baldwin, Barbour, and Benton Counties
2. Bibb, Blount, Butler, and Chambers Counties
3. Cherokee, Choctaw, Clarke, Coffee, and Conecuh Counties
4. Coosa, Covington, Dale, and Dallas Counties
5. De Kalb, Fayette, and Franklin Counties
6. Greene, Hancock, and Henry Counties
7. Jackson, Jefferson, and Lauderdale Counties
8. Lawrence, Limestone, and Lowndes Counties
9. Macon and Madison Counties
10. Marengo, Marion, and Marshall Counties
11. Mobile and Monroe Counties
12. Montgomery, Morgan, and Perry Counties
13. Pickens and Pike Counties
14. Randolph, Russell, St. Clair, and Shelby Counties
15. Sumter, Talladega, and Tallapoosa Counties
16. Tuscaloosa, Walker, Washington, and Wilcox Counties

SLAVE SCHEDULES.

17. Autauga, Baldwin, Barbour, Benton, Bibb, Blount, Butler, and Chambers Counties
18. Cherokee, Choctaw, Clarke, Coffee, Conecuh, Coosa, Covington, Dale, and Dallas Counties
19. De Kalb, Fayette, Franklin, Greene, Hancock, Henry, Jackson, Jefferson, and Lauderdale Counties
20. Lawrence, Limestone, Lowndes, and Macon Counties
21. Madison, Marengo, Marion, and Marshall Counties
22. Mobile, Monroe, Montgomery, and Morgan Counties
23. Perry, Pickens, Pike, Randolph, and Russell Counties
24. St. Clair, Shelby, Sumter, Talladega, Tallapoosa, Tuscaloosa, Walker, Washington, and Wilcox Counties

Arkansas.

FREE SCHEDULES.

25. Arkansas, Ashley, Benton, Bradley, Carroll, Chicot, Clark, Conway, Crawford, and Crittenden Counties
26. Dallas, Desha, Drew, Franklin, Fulton, Greene, Hempstead, Hot Spring, and Independence Counties
27. Izard, Jackson, Jefferson, Johnson, Lafayette, Lawrence, and Madison Counties
28. Marion, Mississippi, Izard, Monroe, Montgomery, Newton, Ouachita, and Perry Counties
29. Phillips, Pike, Poinsett, Polk, Pope, Prairie, and Pulaski Counties
30. Randolph, St. Francis, Saline, Scott, Searcy, Sevier, and Union Counties
31. Van Buren, Washington, White, and Yell Counties

SLAVE SCHEDULES.

32. Entire state

California.

33. Butte and Calaveras Counties
34. El Dorado County
35. Los Angeles, Marin, Mariposa, Mendocino, Monterey, Napa, Sacramento, Santa Barbara, Santa Cruz, San Diego, San Joaquin, and San Luis Obispo Counties
36. Solano, Sonoma, Sutter, Colusa, Shasta, Trinity, Tuolumme, Yolo, and Yuba Counties

Connecticut.

37. Fairfield County (part)
38. Fairfield County (part)
39. Hartford County (part)
40. Hartford County (part)
41. Hartford County (part)
42. Litchfield County (part)
43. Litchfield County (part)
44. Middlesex County
45. New Haven County (part)
46. New Haven County (part)
47. New Haven County (part)
48. New London County (part)
49. New London County (part)
50. Tolland County
51. Windham County

Delaware.

52. Kent County
53. New Castle County (part)
54. New Castle County (part)
55. Sussex County and slave schedules

District of Columbia.

56. Washington City
57. Georgetown, Washington County, and slave schedules

Florida.

FREE SCHEDULES.

58. Alachua, Benton, Calhoun, Columbia, Dade, Duval, Escambia, Franklin, Gadsden, Hamilton, Hillsborough, Holmes, and Jackson Counties
59. Jefferson, Leon, Levy, Madison, Marion, Monroe, Nassau, Orange, Putnam, St. Johns, St. Lucie, Santa Rosa, Wakulla, Walton, and Washington Counties

SLAVE SCHEDULES.

60. Entire state

Georgia.

FREE SCHEDULES.

61. Appling, Baker, Baldwin, and Bibb Counties
62. Bryan, Bulloch, Burke, Butts, Camden, and Campbell Counties
63. Carroll and Cass Counties
64. Chatham and Chattooga Counties
65. Cherokee, Clarke, and Clinch Counties
66. Cobb, Columbia, and Coweta Counties
67. Crawford, Dade, Decatur, and De Kalb Counties
68. Dooly, Early, Effingham, Elbert, and Emanuel Counties
69. Fayette, Floyd, and Forsyth Counties
70. Franklin and Gilmer Counties
71. Glynn, Gordon, Greene, and Gwinnett Counties
72. Habersham, Hall, and Hancock Counties
73. Harris, Heard, and Henry Counties
74. Houston, Irwin, Jackson, and Jasper Counties
75. Jefferson, Jones, Laurens, Lee, Liberty, Lincoln, and Lowndes Counties
76. Lumpkin, Macon, and Madison Counties
77. McIntosh, Marion, and Meriwether Counties
78. Monroe, Montgomery, Morgan, and Murray Counties
79. Muscogee and Newton Counties
80. Oglethorpe, Paulding, Pike, and Pulaski Counties
81. Putnam, Rabun, Randolph, and Richmond Counties
82. Screven, Stewart, and Sumter Counties
83. Talbot, Taliaferro, Tattnall, Telfair, and Thomas Counties
84. Troup, Twiggs, and Union Counties
85. Upson and Walker Counties
86. Walton, Ware, and Warren Counties
87. Washington, Wayne, Wilkes, and Wilkinson Counties

SLAVE SCHEDULES.

88. Appling, Baker, Baldwin, Bibb, Bryan, Bullock, Burke, Butts, Camden, Campbell, Carroll, and Cass Counties
89. Chatham, Chattooga, Cherokee, Clarke, Clinch, Cobb, Columbia, Coweta, and Crawford Counties
90. Dade, Decatur, De Kalb, Dooly, Early, Effingham, Elbert, Emanuel, Fayette, Floyd, Forsyth, Franklin, Gilmer, Glynn, Gordon, Greene, and Gwinnett Counties
91. Habersham, Hall, Hancock, Harris, Heard, Henry, Houston, Irwin, Jackson, and Jasper Counties
92. Jefferson, Jones, Laurens, Lee, Liberty, Lincoln, Lowndes, Lumpkin, Macon, Madison, and McIntosh Counties
93. Marion, Meriwether, Monroe, Montgomery, Morgan, Murray, and Muscogee Counties
94. Newton, Oglethorpe, Paulding, Pike, Pulaski, Putnam, Rabun, Randolph, and Richmond Counties
95. Screven, Stewart, Sumter, Talbot, Taliaferro, Tattnall, Telfair, Thomas, and Troup Counties
96. Twiggs, Union, Upson, Walker, Walton, Ware, Warren, Washington, Wayne, Wilkes, and Wilkinson Counties

Illinois.

97. Adams County.
98. Alexander, Bond, Boone, and Brown Counties
99. Bureau, Calhoun, Carroll, Cass, and Champaign Counties
100. Christian, Clark, Clay, and Clinton Counties
101. Coles County
102. City of Chicago
103. Cook County (excluding the city of Chicago)
104. Crawford, Cumberland, De Kalb, and De Witt Counties
105. Du Page, Edgar, Edwards, and Effingham Counties
106. Fayette and Franklin Counties
107. Fulton and Gallatin Counties
108. Greene, Grundy, and Hamilton Counties
109. Hancock, Hardin, Henderson, and Henry Counties
110. Iroquois, Jackson, Jasper, and Jefferson Counties
111. Jersey and Jo Daviess Counties
112. Johnson and Kane Counties
113. Kendall and Knox Counties
114. Lake County
115. La Salle and Lawrence Counties
116. Lee, Livingston, Logan, and McDonough Counties
117. McHenry and McLean Counties
118. Macon and Macoupin Counties
119. Madison and Marion Counties
120. Marshall, Mason, Massac, Menard, and Mercer Counties
121. Monroe and Montgomery Counties
122. Morgan and Moultrie Counties
123. Ogle and Peoria Counties
124. Perry, Piatt, and Pike Counties
125. Pope, Pulaski, Putnam, Randolph, and Richland Counties
126. Rock Island and St. Clair Counties
127. Saline and Sangamon Counties
128. Schuyler, Scott, and Shelby Counties
129. Stark, Stephenson, and Tazewell Counties
130. Union, Vermilion, and Wabash Counties
131. Warren, Washington, and Wayne Counties
132. White and Whiteside Counties
133. Will and Williamson Counties
134. Winnebago and Woodford Counties

Indiana.

135. Adams and Allen Counties
136. Bartholomew, Benton, Blackford, and Boone Counties
137. Brown, Carroll, and Cass Counties
138. Clark and Clay Counties
139. Clinton and Crawford Counties
140. Daviess County
141. Dearborn County
142. Decatur and De Kalb Counties
143. Delaware and Dubois Counties
144. Elkhart and Fayette Counties

145. Floyd and Fountain Counties
146. Franklin and Fulton Counties
147. Gibson and Grant Counties
148. Greene and Hamilton Counties
149. Hancock and Harrison Counties
150. Hendricks County
151. Henry and Howard Counties
152. Huntington, Jackson, and Jasper Counties
153. Jay County
154. Jefferson County
155. Jennings and Johnson Counties
156. Knox and Kosciusko Counties
157. Lagrange, Lake, and La Porte Counties
158. Lawrence and Madison Counties
159. Marion County
160. Marshall, Martin, and Miami Counties
161. Monroe and Montgomery Counties
162. Morgan and Noble Counties
163. Ohio and Orange Counties
164. Owen and Parke Counties
165. Perry, Pike, and Porter Counties
166. Posey and Pulaski Counties
167. Putnam County
168. Randolph County
169. Ripley County
170. Rush County
171. St. Joseph and Scott Counties
172. Shelby, Spencer, and Starke Counties
173. Steuben and Sullivan Counties
174. Switzerland County
175. Tippecanoe County
176. Tipton, Union, and Vanderburgh Counties
177. Vermillion and Vigo Counties
178. Wabash and Warren Counties
179. Warrick and Washington Counties
180. Wayne County
181. Wells, White, and Whitley Counties

Iowa.

182. Allamakee, Appanoose, Benton, Black Hawk, Boone, Buchanan, Cedar, Clarke, Clayton, Clinton, Dallas, and Davis Counties
183. Decatur, Delaware, Des Moines, and Dubuque Counties
184. Fayette, Fremont, Henry, Iowa, Jackson, and Jasper Counties
185. Jefferson, Johnson, Jones, and Keokuk Counties
186. Lee and Linn Counties
187. Louisa, Lucas, Madison, Mahaska, Marion, Marshall, Monroe, and Muscatine Counties
188. Page, Polk, Pottawattamie, Poweshiek, Scott, Tama, and Taylor Counties
189. Van Buren, Wapello, Warren, Washington, Wayne, and Winneshiek Counties

Kentucky.

FREE SCHEDULES.

190. Adair, Allen, Anderson, and Ballard Counties
191. Barren and Bath Counties
192. Boone, Bourbon, and Boyle Counties
193. Bracken, Breathitt, Breckinridge, and Bullitt Counties
194. Butler, Caldwell, and Calloway Counties
195. Campbell, Carroll, and Carter Counties
196. Casey, Christian, and Clark Counties
197. Clay, Clinton, Crittenden, and Cumberland Counties
198. Daviess, Edmonson, and Estill Counties
199. Fayette and Fleming Counties
200. Floyd, Franklin, Fulton, and Gallatin Counties
201. Garrard, Grant, and Graves Counties
202. Grayson, Green, Greenup, and Hancock Counties
203. Hardin, Harlan, and Harrison Counties
204. Hart, Henderson, and Henry Counties
205. Hickman and Hopkins Counties and Jefferson County (excluding the city of Louisville)
206. City of Louisville, districts 1 and 2
207. City of Louisville, districts 3 and 4
208. Jessamine, Johnson, and Kenton Counties
209. Knox, Larue, Laurel, Lawrence, and Letcher Counties
210. Lewis, Lincoln, and Livingston Counties
211. Logan, McCracken, and Madison Counties
212. Marion, Marshall, and Mason Counties
213. Meade, Mercer, and Monroe Counties
214. Montgomery, Morgan, and Muhlenberg Counties
215. Nelson, Nicholas, and Ohio Counties
216. Oldham, Owen, Owsley, Pendleton, and Perry Counties
217. Pike, Pulaski, Rockcastle, and Russell Counties
218. Shelby, Scott, and Simpson Counties
219. Spencer, Taylor, Todd, and Trigg Counties
220. Trimble, Union, and Warren Counties
221. Washington and Wayne Counties
222. Whitley and Woodford Counties

SLAVE SCHEDULES.

223. Adair, Allen, Anderson, Ballard, Barren, Bath, Boone, Bourbon, Boyle, Bracken, Breathitt, Breckinridge, Bullitt, Butler, Caldwell, Calloway, Campbell, Carroll, Carter, and Casey Counties
224. Christian, Clark, Clay, Clinton, Crittenden, Cumberland, Daviess, Edmonson, Estill, Fayette, Fleming, Floyd, Franklin, and Fulton Counties
225. Gallatin, Garrard, Grant, Graves, Grayson, Green, Greenup, Hancock, Hardin, Harlan, Harrison, Hart, Henderson, Henry, Hickman, Hopkins, and Jefferson Counties
226. Jessamine, Johnson, Kenton, Knox, Larue, Laurel, Lawrence,

Letcher, Lewis, Lincoln, Livingston, Logan, McCracken, Madison, Marion, Marshall, Mason, Meade, and Mercer Counties

227. Monroe, Montgomery, Morgan, Muhlenberg, Nelson, Nicholas, Ohio, Oldham, Owen, Owsley, Pendleton, Perry, Pike, Pulaski, Rockcastle, Russell, Scott, Shelby, and Simpson Counties

228. Spencer, Taylor, Todd, Trigg, Trimble, Union, Warren, Washington, Wayne, Whitley, and Woodford Counties

Louisiana.

FREE SCHEDULES.

229. Ascension, Assumption, Avoyelles, East Baton Rouge, and West Baton Rouge Parishes

230. Bienville, Bossier, Caddo, Calcasieu, Caldwell, Carroll, Catahoula, Claiborne, and Concordia Parishes

231. De Soto, East Feliciana, West Feliciana, Franklin, Iberville, and Jackson Parishes

232. Jefferson, Lafayette, and Lafourche Parishes

233. Livingston, Madison, Morehouse, and Natchitoches Parishes

234. Orleans Parish (excluding the city of New Orleans)

235. City of New Orleans, wards 1-4 (1st municipality)

236. City of New Orleans, wards 5-7 (1st municipality)

237. City of New Orleans, 2nd municipality

238. City of New Orleans, 3d municipality, and Ouachita and Plaquemines Parishes

239. Pointe Coupee, Rapides, Sabine, St. Bernard, St. Charles, St. Helena, St. James, and St. John the Baptist Parishes

240. St. Landry, St. Martin, and St. Mary Parishes

241. St. Tammany, Tensas, Terrebonne, Union, Vermilion, and Washington Parishes

SLAVE SCHEDULES.

242. Ascension, Assumption, East Baton Rouge, West Baton Rouge, Avoyelles, Bienville, Bossier, Caddo, Calcasieu, and Caldwell Parishes

243. Carroll, Catahoula, Claiborne, Concordia, De Soto, East Feliciana, and West Feliciana Parishes

244. Franklin, Iberville, Jackson, Jefferson, Lafayette, Lafourche, Livingston, Madison, Morehouse, and Natchitoches Parishes

245. Orleans (including the city of New Orleans), Ouachita, Plaquemines, Pointe Coupee, and Rapides Parishes

246. Sabine, St. Bernard, St. Charles, St. Helena, St. James, St. John the Baptist, and St. Landry Parishes

247. St. Martin, St. Mary, St. Tammany, Tensas, Terrebonne, Union, Vermilion, and Washington Parishes

Maine.

248. Aroostook County

249. Cumberland County (part)

250. Cumberland County (part)

251. Cumberland County (part)

252. City of Portland

253. Franklin County

254. Hancock County (part)

255. Hancock County (part)

256. Kennebec County (part)

257. Kennebec County (part)

258. Kennebec County (part)

259. Lincoln County (part)

260. Lincoln County (part)

261. Lincoln County (part)

262. Oxford County (part)

263. Oxford County (part)

264. Penobscot County (part)

265. Penobscot County (part)

266. Penobscot County (part)

267. Piscataquis County

268. Somerset County (part)

269. Somerset County (part)

270. Waldo County (part)

271. Waldo County (part)

272. Washington County (part)

273. Washington County (part)

274. York County (part)

275. York County (part)

276. York County (part)

Maryland.

FREE SCHEDULES.

277. Allegany County

278. Anne Arundel County

279. Baltimore County (part) (eastern, 2d, and 6th districts)

280. Baltimore County (part) (6th and 1st districts)

281. City of Baltimore (part), wards 1-2

282. City of Baltimore (part), wards 3-4

283. City of Baltimore (part), wards 5-7

284. City of Baltimore (part), wards 8-11

285. City of Baltimore (part), wards 12-14

286. City of Baltimore (part), wards 15-17

287. City of Baltimore (part), wards 18-20

288. Calvert and Caroline Counties

289. Carroll County

290. Cecil and Charles Counties

291. Dorchester County

292. Frederick County (part)

293. Frederick County (part)

294. Harford and Kent Counties

295. Montgomery and Prince Georges Counties

296. Queen Annes and St. Mary's Counties

297. Somerset and Talbot Counties

298. Washington County
299. Worcester County

SLAVE SCHEDULES.
300. Allegany, Anne Arundel, and Baltimore Counties, city of Baltimore and Calvert, Caroline, Carroll, Cecil, and Charles Counties
301. Dorchester, Frederick, Harford, Kent, Montgomery, and Prince Georges Counties
302. Queen Annes, St. Mary's, Somerset, Talbot, Washington, and Worcester Counties

Massachusetts.
303. Barnstable County (part)
304. Barnstable County (part)
305. Berkshire County (part)
306. Berkshire County (part)
307. Bristol County (part)
308. Bristol County (part)
309. Bristol (part) and Dukes Counties
310. Essex County (part)
311. Essex County (part) and city of Lynn
312. Essex County (part) and city of Salem
313. Essex County (part)
314. Essex County (part)
315. Essex County (part)
316. Franklin County (part)
317. Franklin County (part)
318. Hampden County (part)
319. Hampden County (part)
320. Hampshire County (part)
321. Hampshire County (part)
322. Middlesex County (part)
323. Middlesex County (part)
324. Middlesex County (part)
325. Middlesex County (part)
326. Middlesex County (part) and city of Lowell, ward 5
327. City of Lowell (excluding ward 5)
328. Nantucket County
329. Norfolk County (part)
330. Norfolk County (part)
331. Norfolk County (part)
332. Plymouth County (part)
333. Plymouth County (part)
334. City of Boston, wards 1-3
335. City of Boston, wards 4-5
336. City of Boston, wards 6-8
337. City of Boston, wards 9-10
338. City of Boston, ward 11
339. City of Boston, ward 12, and Suffolk County (part)
340. Worcester County (part)
341. Worcester County (part)
342. Worcester County (part)
343. Worcester County (part)
344. Worcester County (part)
345. Worcester County (part)

Michigan.
346. Allegan, Barry, and Berrien Counties
347. Branch County
348. Calhoun County
349. Cass, Chippewa, Clinton, and Eaton Counties
350. Genesee County
351. Hillsdale, Houghton, Huron, and Ingham Counties
352. Ionia and Jackson Counties
353. Kalamazoo and Kent Counties
354. Lapeer County
355. Lenawee County
356. Livingston County
357. Macomb, Marquette, Mason, Mackinac, and Midland Counties
358. Monroe and Montcalm Counties
359. Newaygo and Oakland (part) Counties
360. Oakland County (part)
361. Oceana, Ontonagon, Ottawa, and Saginaw Counties
362. St. Clair and St. Joseph Counties
363. Sanilac, Schoolcraft, Shiawassee, Tuscola, and Van Buren Counties
364. Washtenaw County
365. Wayne County (part) and city of Detroit
366. Wayne County (part)

Minnesota.
367. Entire territory

Mississippi.
FREE SCHEDULES.
368. Adams, Amite, Attala, and Bolivar Counties
369. Carroll and Chickasaw Counties
370. Choctaw, Claiborne, Clarke, and Coahoma Counties
371. Copiah, Covington, and De Soto Counties
372. Franklin, Greene, Hancock, Harrison, and Hinds Counties
373. Holmes, Issaquena, and Itawamba Counties
374. Jackson, Jasper, Jefferson, Jones, and Kemper Counties
375. Lafayette, Lauderdale, and Lawrence Counties
376. Leake, Lowndes, Madison, and Marion Counties
377. Marshall County
378. Monroe, Neshoba, and Newton Counties
379. Noxubee, Oktibbeha, Panola, and Perry Counties
380. Pike, Pontotoc, and Rankin Counties
381. Scott, Simpson, Smith, Sunflower, Tallahatchie, and Tippah Counties

382. Tishomingo, Tunica, Warren, Washington, Wayne, Wilkinson, Winston, Yalobusha, and Yazoo Counties

SLAVE SCHEDULES.

383. Adams, Amite, Attala, Bolivar, Carroll, Chickasaw, and Choctaw Counties

384. Claiborne, Clarke, Coahoma, Copiah, Covington, De Soto, Franklin, Greene, Hancock, and Harrison Counties

385. Hinds, Holmes, Issaquena, Itawamba, Jackson, Jasper, and Jefferson Counties

386. Jones, Kemper, Lafayette, Lauderdale, Lawrence, Leake, Lowndes, and Madison Counties

387. Marion, Marshall, Monroe, Neshoba, Newton, and Noxubee Counties

388. Oktibbeha, Panola, Perry, Pike, Pontotoc, Rankin, Scott, Simpson, Smith, Sunflower, Tallahatchie, and Tippah Counties

389. Tishomingo, Tunica, Warren, Washington, Wayne, and Wilkinson Counties

390. Winston, Yalobusha, and Yazoo Counties

Missouri.
FREE SCHEDULES.

391. Adair, Andrew, Atchison, Audrain, and Barry Counties
392. Bates, Benton, and Boone Counties
393. Buchanan, Butler, Caldwell, and Callaway Counties
394. Camden and Cape Girardeau Counties
395. Carroll, Cass, Cedar, and Chariton Counties
396. Clark, Clay, and Clinton Counties
397. Cole, Cooper, and Crawford Counties
398. Dade, Dallas, Daviess, and De Kalb Counties
399. Dodge, Dunklin, Franklin, Gasconade, and Gentry Counties
400. Greene, Grundy, and Harrison Counties
401. Henry, Hickory, Holt, and Howard Counties
402. Jackson, Jasper, and Jefferson Counties
403. Johnson, Knox, Laclede, and Lafayette Counties
404. Lawrence, Lewis, and Lincoln Counties
405. Linn, Livingston, McDonald, Macon, and Madison Counties
406. Marion, Mercer, Miller, and Mississippi Counties
407. Moniteau, Monroe, and Montgomery Counties
408. Morgan, New Madrid, Newton, Nodaway, Oregon, and Osage Counties
409. Ozark, Perry, Pettis, and Pike Counties
410. Platee County
411. Polk, Pulaski, Putnam, Ralls, and Randolph Counties
412. Ray, Reynolds, and Ripley Counties
413. St. Charles, St. Clair, St. Francois, and Ste. Genevieve Counties
414. St. Louis County (part)(excluding the city of St. Louis)
415. St. Louis County (part) and city of St. Louis, wards 1-2
416. St. Louis County (part) and city of St. Louis, ward 3

417. St. Louis County (part) and city of St. Louis, wards 4-5
418. St. Louis County (part) and city of St. Louis, ward 6
419. Saline, Schuyler, Scotland, and Scott Counties
420. Shannon, Shelby, Stoddard, Sullivan, and Taney Counties
421. Texas, Warren, Washington, Wayne, and Wright Counties

SLAVE SCHEDULES.

422. Adair, Andrew, Atchison, Audrain, Barry, Bates, Benton, Boone, Buchanan, Butler, Caldwell, Callaway, Camden, Cape Girardeau, Carroll, Cass, Cedar, Chariton, Clark, Clay, Clinton, Cole, Cooper, Crawford, Dade, Dallas, Daviess, De Kalb, Dodge, Dunklin, and Franklin Counties

423. Gasconade, Gentry, Greene, Grundy, Harrison, Henry, Hickory, Holt, Howard, Jackson, Jasper, Jefferson, Johnson, Knox, Laclede, Lafayette, Lawrence, Lewis, Lincoln, Linn, Livingston, McDonald, Macon, Madison, Marion, Mercer, Miller, Mississippi, Moniteau, Monroe, and Montgomery Counties

424. Morgan, New Madrid, Newton, Nodaway, Oregon, Osage, Ozark, Perry, Pettis, Pike, Platte, Polk, Pulaski, Putnam, Ralls, Randolph, Ray, Reynolds, Ripley, St. Charles, St. Clair, St. Francois, Ste. Genevieve, Saint Louis, Saline, Schuyler, Scotland, Scott, Shannon, Shelby, Stoddard, Sullivan, Taney, Texas, Warren, Washington, Wayne, and Wright Counties

New Hampshire.

425. Belknap County
426. Carroll County
427. Cheshire County (part)
428. Cheshire County (part)
429. Coos County
430. Grafton County (part)
431. Grafton County (part)
432. Hillsboro County (part)
433. Hillsboro County (part)
434. Hillsboro County (part)
435. Merrimack County (part)
436. Merrimack County (part)
437. Rockingham County (part)
438. Rockingham County (part)
439. Strafford County (part)
440. Strafford County (part)
441. Sullivan County

New Jersey.
FREE SCHEDULES.

442. Atlantic and Bergen Counties
443. Burlington County (part)
444. Burlington County (part)
445. Camden County

446. Cape May and Cumberland Counties
447. City of Newark, north, east, and south wards
448. City of Newark, west and 5th wards
449. Essex County (part) (excluding the city of Newark)
450. Essex County (part) (excluding the city of Newark)
451. Gloucester County
452. Hudson County
453. Hunterdon County
454. Mercer County
455. Middlesex County
456. Monmouth County (part)
457. Monmouth County (part)
458. Morris County (part)
459. Morris County (part)
460. Ocean County
461. Passaic County
462. Salem County
463. Somerset County
464. Sussex County
465. Warren County

SLAVE SCHEDULES.
466. Entire state

New Mexico.
467. Bernalillo and Rio Arriba Counties
468. Santa Ana and Santa Fe Counties
469. San Miguel and Taos Counties
470. Valencia County

New York.
471. Albany County (part) and city of Albany, wards 1-5
472. Albany County (part) and city of Albany, wards 6-10
473. Albany County (part)
474. Albany County (part)
475. Allegany County (part)
476. Allegany County (part)
477. Broome County (part)
478. Broome County (part)
479. Cattaraugus County (part)
480. Cattaraugus County (part)
481. Cayuga County (part)
482. Cayuga County (part)
483. Cayuga County (part)
484. Chautauqua County (part)
485. Chautauqua County (part)
486. Chemung County
487. Chenango County (part)
488. Chenango County (part)
489. Clinton County (part)
490. Clinton County (part)

491. Columbia County (part)
492. Columbia County (part)
493. Cortland County
494. Delaware County (part)
495. Delaware County (part)
496. Dutchess County (part)
497. Dutchess County (part)
498. Erie County (part)
499. Erie County (part)
500. Erie County (part)
501. Erie County (part) and city of Buffalo, wards 1-3
502. Erie County (part) and city of Buffalo, wards 4-5
503. Essex County (part)
504. Essex County (part)
505. Franklin County (part)
506. Fulton County
507. Genesee County (part)
508. Genesee County (part)
509. Greene County (part)
510. Greene County (part)
511. Hamilton County
512. Herkimer County (part)
513. Herkimer County (part)
514. Jefferson County (part)
515. Jefferson County (part)
516. Jefferson County (part)
517. Kings County (part) and city of Brooklyn, wards 1 -3
518. Kings County (part) and city of Brooklyn, wards 4-5
519. Kings County (part) and city of Brooklyn, wards 6-8
520. Kings County (part) and city of Brooklyn, wards 9-11
521. Kings County (part)
522. Kings County (part)
523. Lewis County
524. Livingston County (part)
525. Livingston County (part)
526. Madison County (part)
527. Madison County (part)
528. Monroe County (part)
529. Monroe County (part)
530. Monroe County (part) and city of Rochester, wards 1-5
531. Monroe County (part) and city of Rochester, wards 6-9
532. Montgomery County (part)
533. Montgomery County (part)
534. New York County (part) and New York City, ward 1
535. New York County (part) and New York City, wards 2-3
536. New York County (part) and New York City, ward 4
537. New York County (part) and New York City, ward 5
538. New York County (part) and New York City, ward 6
539. New York County (part) and New York City, ward 7 (part)
540. New York County (part) and New York City, ward 7 (part)
541. New York County (part) and New York City, ward 8 (part)

542. New York County (part) and New York City, ward 8 (part)
543. New York County (part) and New York City, ward 9 (part)
544. New York County (part) and New York City, ward 9 (part)
545. New York County (part) and New York City, ward 10
546. New York County (part) and New York City, ward 11 (part)
547. New York County (part) and New York City, ward 11 (part)
548. New York County (part) and New York City, ward 12 (part)
549. New York County (part) and New York City, ward 12 (part)
550. New York County (part) and New York City, ward 1-3
551. New York County (part) and New York City, ward 14
552. New York County (part) and New York City, ward 15
553. New York County (part) and New York City, ward 16 (part)
554. New York County (part) and New York City, ward 16 (part)
555. New York County (part) and New York City, ward 17 (part)
556. New York County (part) and New York City, ward 17 (part)
557. New York County (part) and New York City, ward 18 (part)
558. New York County (part) and New York City, ward 18 (part)
559. New York County (part) and New York City, ward 19
560. Niagara County (part)
561. Niagara County (part)
562. Oneida County (part)
563. Oneida County (part) and city of Utica
564. Oneida County (part)
565. Oneida County (part)
566. Oneida County (part)
567. Onondaga County (part)
568. Onondaga County (part)
569. Onondaga County (part) and city of Syracuse
570. Onondaga County (part)
571. Ontario County (part)
572. Ontario County (part)
573. Orange County (part)
574. Orange County (part)
575. Orleans County
576. Oswego County (part)
577. Oswego County (part)
578. Oswego County (part)
579. Otsego County (part)
580. Otsego County (part)
581. Putnam County
582. Queens County (part)
583. Queens County (part)
584. Rensselaer County (part)
585. Rensselaer County (part)
586. Rensselaer County (part)
587. Richmond County
588. Rockland County
589. St. Lawrence County (part)
590. St. Lawrence County (part)
591. St. Lawrence County (part)
592. Saratoga County (part)

593. Saratoga County (part)
594. Schenectady County
595. Schoharie County (part)
596. Schoharie County (part)
597. Seneca County
598. Steuben County (part)
599. Steuben County (part)
600. Steuben County (part)
601. Suffolk County (part)
602. Suffolk County (part)
603. Sullivan County
604. Tioga County
605. Tompkins County (part)
606. Tompkins County (part)
607. Ulster County (part)
608. Ulster County (part)
609. Warren County
610. Washington County (part)
611. Washington County (part)
612. Wayne County (part)
613. Wayne County (part)
614. Westchester County (part)
615. Westchester County (part)
616. Wyoming County (part)
617. Wyoming County (part)
618. Yates County

North Carolina.
FREE SCHEDULES.
619. Alamance, Alexander, and Anson Counties
620. Ashe and Beaufort Counties
621. Bertie, Bladen, and Brunswick Counties
622. Buncombe, Burke, and Cabarrus Counties
623. Caldwell, Camden, Carteret, and Caswell Counties
624. Catawba and Chatham Counties
625. Cherokee, Chowan, and Cleveland Counties
626. Columbus and Craven Counties
627. Cumberland and Currituck Counties
628. Davidson and Davie Counties
629. Duplin and Edgecomb Counties
630. Forsyth, Franklin, and Gaston Counties
631. Gates and Granville Counties
632. Greene and Guilford Counties
633. Halifax and Haywood Counties
634. Henderson, Hertford, Hyde, and Iredell Counties
635. Johnston, Jones, and Lenoir Counties
636. Lincoln, McDowell, Martin, and Macon Counties
637. Mecklenburg and Montgomery Counties
638. Moore, Nash, and New Hanover Counties
639. Northampton, Onslow, and Orange Counties
640. Pasquotank, Perquimans, and Person Counties

641. Pitt and Randolph Counties

642. Richmond and Robeson Counties

643. Rockingham and Rowan Counties

644. Rutherford and Sampson Counties

645. Stanly and Stokes Counties

646. Surry and Tyrell Counties

647. Union and Wake Counties

648. Warren, Washington, Watauga, and Wayne Counties

649. Wilkes and Yancey Counties

SLAVE SCHEDULES.

650. Alamance, Alexander, Anson, Ashe, Beaufort, Bertie, Bladen, Brunswick, Buncombe, Burke, Cabarrus, Caldwell, and Camden Counties

651. Carteret, Caswell, Catawba, Chatham, Cherokee, Chowan, Cleveland, Columbus, Craven, Cumberland, and Currituck Counties

652. Davidson, Davie, Duplin, Edgecomb, Forsyth, Franklin, Gaston, Gates, Granville, and Greene Counties

653. Guilford, Halifax, Haywood, Henderson, Hertford, Hyde, Iredell, Johnston, Jones, Lenoir, and Lincoln Counties

654. McDowell, Martin, Macon, Mecklenburg, Montgomery, Moore, New Hanover, Northampton, and Onslow Counties

655. Orange, Pasquotank, Perquimans, Person, Pitt, Randolph, Richmond, Robeson, Rockingham, and Rowan Counties

656. Rutherford, Sampson, Stanly, Stokes, Surry, Tyrell, Union, Wake, Warren, Washington, Watauga, Wayne, Wilkes, and Yancey Counties

Ohio.

657. Adams and Allen Counties

658. Ashland County

659. Ashtabula County

660. Athens and Auglaize Counties

661. Belmont County

662. Brown County

663. Butler County

664. Carroll County

665. Champaign County

666. Clark County

667. Clermont County

668. Clinton County

669. Columbiana County

670. Coshocton County

671. Crawford County

672. Cuyahoga County (part)

673. Cuyahoga County (part)

674. Darke and Defiance Counties

675. Delaware County

676. Erie County

677. Fairfield County

678. Fayette County

679. Franklin County (part)

680. Franklin County (part)

681. Fulton and Gallia Counties

682. Geauga County

683. Greene County

684. Guernsey County

685. Hamilton County (part)

686. Hamilton County (part)

687. Hamilton County (part) and city of Cincinnati, wards 1-3

688. Hamilton County (part) and city of Cincinnati, wards 4-5

689. Hamilton County (part) and city of Cincinnati, wards 6-7

690. Hamilton County (part) and city of Cincinnati, wards 8-9

691. Hamilton County (part) and city of Cincinnati, wards 10-11

692. Hancock and Hardin Counties

693. Harrison and Henry Counties

694. Highland County

695. Hocking County

696. Holmes County

697. Huron County

698. Jackson County

699. Jefferson County

700. Knox County

701. Lake and Lawrence Counties

702. Licking County (part)

703. Licking County (part)

704. Logan County

705. Lorain County

706. Lucas and Madison Counties

707. Mahoning County

708. Marion County

709. Medina County

710. Meigs and Mercer Counties

711. Miami County

712. Monroe County

713. Montgomery County (part)

714. Montgomery County (part)

715. Morgan County

716. Morrow County

717. Muskingum County (part)

718. Muskingum County (part)

719. Ottawa, Paulding, and Perry Counties

720. Pickaway County

721. Pike County

722. Portage County

723. Preble and Putnam Counties

724. Richland County

725. Ross County

726. Sandusky County

727. Scioto County

728. Seneca County
729. Shelby County
730. Stark County (part)
731. Stark County (part)
732. Summit County
733. Trumbull County
734. Tuscarawas County (part)
735. Tuscarawas County (part)
736. Union, Van Wert, and Vinton Counties
737. Warren County
738. Washington County
739. Wayne County (part)
740. Wayne County (part)
741. Williams, Wood, and Wyandot Counties

Oregon.
742. Entire territory

Pennsylvania.
743. Adams County
744. Allegheny County (part)
745. Allegheny County (part) and city of Pittsburgh, wards 1-4
746. Allegheny County (part) and city of Pittsburgh, wards 5-9
747. Allegheny County (part)
748. Allegheny County (part)
749. Armstrong County
750. Beaver County
751. Bedford County
752. Berks County (part)
753. Berks County (part)
754. Berks County (part)
755. Blair County
756. Bradford County (part)
757. Bradford County (part)
758. Bucks County (part)
759. Bucks County (part)
760. Butler County
761. Cambria County
762. Carbon County
763. Centre County
764. Chester County (part)
765. Chester County (part)
766. Chester County (part)
767. Clarion County
768. Clearfield and Clinton Counties
769. Columbia County
770. Crawford County (part)
771. Crawford County (part)
772. Cumberland County (part)
773. Cumberland County (part)
774. Dauphin County (part)

775. Dauphin County (part)
776. Delaware and Elk Counties
777. Erie County (part)
778. Erie County (part)
779. Fayette County (part)
780. Fayette County (part)
781. Franklin County (part)
782. Franklin County (part)
783. Fulton and Greene Counties
784. Huntingdon County
785. Indiana County
786. Jefferson and Juniata Counties
787. Lancaster County (part)
788. Lancaster County (part)
789. Lancaster County (part)
790. Lawrence County
791. Lebanon County
792. Lehigh County
793. Luzerne County (part)
794. Luzerne County (part)
795. Lycoming and McKean Counties
796. Mercer County
797. Mifflin County
798. Monroe County
799. Montgomery County (part)
800. Montgomery County (part)
801. Montour County
802. Northampton County (part)
803. Northampton County (part)
804. Northumberland County
805. Perry County
806. Philadelphia County (excluding the city of Philadelphia) (part): Kensington, wards 1-4
807. Philadelphia County (excluding the city of Philadelphia) (part): Kensington, wards 5-8
808. Philadelphia County (excluding the city of Philadelphia) (part)
809. Philadelphia County (excluding the city of Philadelphia) (part)
810. Philadelphia County (excluding the city of Philadelphia) (part): Northern Liberties, wards 1-4
811. Philadelphia County (excluding the city of Philadelphia) (part): Northern Liberties, wards 5-7
812. City of Philadelphia (part), wards: Cedar, South, and Lombard
813. City of Philadelphia (part), wards: Pine, Spruce, Walnut, and Chestnut
814. City of Philadelphia (part), wards: Middle and Locust
815. City of Philadelphia (part), wards: North Mulberry and South Mulberry
816. City of Philadelphia (part), wards: Lower Delaware, Upper

Delaware, and High Street
817. City of Philadelphia (part), wards: North, New Market, and Dock
818. Philadelphia County (excluding the city of Philadelphia) (part): Spring Garden District, wards 1-3
819. Philadelphia County (excluding the city of Philadelphia) (part): Spring Garden District, wards 4-7
820. Philadelphia County (excluding the city of Philadelphia) (part)
821. Philadelphia County (excluding the city of Philadelphia) (part): Southwark, wards 1-3
822. Philadelphia County (excluding the city of Philadelphia) (part): Southwark, wards 4-6
823. Philadelphia County (excluding the city of Philadelphia) (part)
824. Philadelphia County (excluding the city of Philadelphia) (part)
825. Pike and Potter Counties
826. Schuylkill County (part)
827. Schuylkill County (part)
828. Somerset and Sullivan Counties
829. Susquehanna County
830. Tioga County
831. Union County
832. Venango and Warren Counties
833. Washington County (part)
834. Washington County (part)
835. Wayne County
836. Westmoreland County (part)
837. Westmoreland County (part)
838. Wyoming County
839. York County (part)
840. York County (part)

Rhode Island.
841. Bristol and Kent Counties
842. Newport County
843. Providence County (part)
844. Providence County (part) and city of Providence, wards 1-3
845. Providence County (part) and city of Providence, wards 1-6
846. Providence County (part)
847. Washington County

South Carolina.
FREE SCHEDULES.
848. Abbeville and Anderson Counties
849. Barnwell and Beaufort Counties
850. Charleston County
851. Chester, Chesterfield, Colleton, and Darlington Counties
852. Edgefield and Fairfield Counties
853. Georgetown and Greenville Counties

854. Horry, Kershaw, and Lancaster Counties
855. Laurens and Lexington Counties
856. Marion, Marlboro, and Newberry Counties
857. Orangeburg and Pickens Counties
858. Richland and Spartanburg Counties
859. Sumter and Union Counties
860. Williamsburg and York Counties

SLAVE SCHEDULES.
861. Abbeville, Anderson, Barnwell, and Beaufort Counties
862. Charleston County
863. Chesterfield, Colleton, and Darlington Counties
864. Edgefield, Georgetown, and Fairfield Counties
865. Greenville, Horry, Kershaw, Lancaster, and Laurens Counties
866. Lexington, Marion, Marlboro, Newberry, and Orangeburg Counties
867. Pickens, Richland, Spartanburg and Sumter Counties
868. Union, Williamsburg, and York Counties

Tennessee.
FREE SCHEDULES.
869. Anderson and Bedford Counties
870. Benton and Bledsoe Counties
871. Blount and Bradley Counties
872. Campbell and Cannon Counties
873. Carroll and Carter Counties
874. Claiborne and Cocke Counties
875. Coffee and Davidson Counties
876. Decatur, De Kalb, and Dickson Counties
877. Dyer, Fayette, and Fentress Counties
878. Franklin and Gibson Counties
879. Giles County
880. Grainger and Greene Counties
881. Grundy, Hamilton, Hancock, and Hardeman Counties
882. Hardin and Hawkins Counties
883. Haywood and Henderson Counties
884. Henry, Hickman, and Humphreys Counties
885. Jackson and Jefferson Counties
886. Johnson, Knox, Lauderdale, and Lawrence Counties
887. Lewis, Lincoln, and McMinn Counties
888. McNairy and Macon Counties
889. Madison and Marion Counties
890. Marshall, Maury, and Meigs Counties
891. Monroe, Montgomery, Morgan, and Obion Counties
892. Overton, Perry, and Polk Counties
893. Rhea and Roane Counties
894. Robertson and Rutherford Counties
895. Scott, Sevier, and Shelby Counties
896. Smith and Stewart Counties
897. Sullivan, Sumner, Tipton, and Van Buren Counties
898. Warren and Washington Counties

899. Wayne and Weakley Counties
900. White and Williamson Counties
901. Wilson County

SLAVE SCHEDULES.
902. Anderson, Bedford, Benton, Bledsoe, Blount, Bradley,
    Campbell, Cannon, Carroll, Carter, Claiborne, Cocke,
    Coffee, Davidson, Decatur, De Kalb, Dickson, and Dyer
    Counties
903. Fayette, Fentress, Franklin, Gibson, Giles, Grainger, Greene,
    Grundy, Hamilton, Hancock, and Hardeman Counties
904. Hardin, Hawkins, Haywood, Henderson, Henry, Hickman,
    Humphreys, Jackson, Jefferson, Johnson, Knox,
    Lauderdale, Lawrence, Lewis, and Lincoln Counties
905. McMinn, McNairy, Macon, Madison, Marion, Marshall,
    Maury, Meigs, Monroe, Montgomery, and Morgan
    Counties
906. Obion, Overton, Perry, Polk, Rhea, Roane, Robertson,
    Rutherford, Scott, Sevier, and Shelby Counties
907. Smith, Stewart, Sullivan, Sumner, Tipton, Van Buren,
    Warren, Washington, and Wilson Counties

Texas.
FREE SCHEDULES.
908. Anderson, Angelina, Austin, Bastrop, Bexar, Bowie, Brazoria,
    Brazos, and Burleson Counties
909. Caldwell, Calhoun, Cameron, Starr, Webb, Cass, and
    Cherokee Counties
910. Collin, Colorado, Comal, Cooke, Dallas, Denton, De Witt,
    Ellis, Tarrant, Fannin, Fayette, Fort Bend, Galveston,
    Guadalupe, Gillespie, Goliad, Gonzales, Grayson, and
    Grimes Counties
911. Harris, Harrison, Hays, Henderson, Hopkins, Houston, and
    Hunt Counties
912. Jackson, Jasper, Jefferson, Kaufman, Lamar, Lavaca, Leon,
    Liberty, Limestone, Matagorda, and Medina Counties
913. Milam, Montgomery, Nacogdoches, Navarro, Newton,
    Nueces, and Panola Counties
914. Polk, Red River, Refugio, Robertson, Rusk, Sabine, San
    Augustine, and San Patricio Counties
915. Shelby, Smith, Titus, Travis, and Tyler Counties
916. Upshur, Van Zandt, Victoria, Walker, Washington, Wharton,
    and Williamson Counties

SLAVE SCHEDULES.
917. Anderson, Angelina, Austin, Bastrop, Bexar, Bowie, Brazoria,
    Brazos, Burleson, Caldwell, Calhoun, Cameron, Webb,
    Cass, Cherokee, Collin, Colorado, Comal, Cooke, Dallas,
    Denton, De Witt, Fannin, Fayette, Fort Bend, Galveston,
    Guadalupe, Gillespie, Goliad, Gonzales, Grayson, Grimes,
    Harris, Harrison, Hays, Henderson, Hopkins, Houston,

Hunt, Jackson, Jasper, Jefferson, and Kaufman Counties
918. Lamar, Lavaca, Leon, Liberty, Limestone, Matagorda,
    Medina, Milam, Montgomery, Nacogdoches, Navarro,
    Newton, Nueces, Panola, Polk, Red River, Refugio,
    Robertson, Rusk, Sabine, San Augustine, Shelby, Smith,
    Ellis, Tarrant, Titus, Travis, Tyler, Upshur, Van Zandt,
    Victoria, Walker, Washington, Wharton, and Williamson
    Counties

Utah.
919. Entire territory

Vermont.
920. Addison County
921. Bennington County
922. Caledonia County
923. Chittenden and Essex Counties
924. Franklin and Grande Isle Counties
925. Lamoille and Orleans Counties
926. Orange County
927. Rutland County
928. Washington County
929. Windham County
930. Windsor County (part)
931. Windsor County (part)

Virginia.
FREE SCHEDULES.
932. Accomack, Albemarle, and Alexandria Counties
933. Alleghany, Amelia, Amherst, and Appomattox Counties
934. Augusta County
935. Barbour, Bath, and Bedford Counties
936. Berkeley, Boone, and Botetourt Counties
937. Braxton, Brooke, Brunswick, and Buckingham Counties
938. Cabell and Campbell Counties
939. Caroline, Carroll, and Charles City Counties
940. Charlotte, Chesterfield, and Clarke Counties
941. Culpeper, Cumberland, and Dinwiddie Counties
942. Doddridge, Elizabeth City, Essex, and Fairfax Counties
943. Fauquier, Fayette, and Floyd Counties
944. Fluvanna and Franklin Counties
945. Frederick and Giles Counties
946. Gilmer, Gloucester, and Goochland Counties
947. Grayson, Greenbrier, Greene and Greenesville Counties
948. Halifax and Hampshire Counties
949. Hancock and Hanover Counties
950. Hardy and Harrison Counties
951. Henrico County
952. Henry, Highland, and Isle of Wight Counties
953. Jackson, James City, and Jefferson Counties
954. Kanawah, King and Queen, and King George Counties

955. King William, Lancaster, and Lee Counties

956. Lewis and Logan Counties

957. Loudoun and Louisa Counties

958. Lunenburg, Madison, and Marion Counties

959. Marshall and Mason Counties

960. Mathews, Mecklenburg, and Mercer Counties

961. Middlesex, Monongalia, and Monroe Counties

962. Montgomery, Morgan, and Nansemond Counties

963. Nelson, New Kent, and Nicholas Counties

964. Norfolk County

965. Northampton, Northumberland, and Nottoway Counties

966. Ohio County

967. Orange, Page, and Patrick Counties

968. Pendleton and Pittsylvania Counties

969. Pocahontas, Powhatan, and Preston Counties

970. Prince Edward, Prince George, and Prince William Counties

971. Princess Anne, Pulaski, and Putnam Counties

972. Raleigh, Randolph, Rappahannock, and Richmond Counties

973. Ritchie, Roanoke, and Rockbridge Counties

974. Rockingham County

975. Russell and Scott Counties

976. Shenandoah and Smyth Counties

977. Southampton and Spotsylvania Counties

978. Stafford, Surry, Sussex, and Taylor Counties

979. Tazewell and Tyler Counties

980. Warren, Warwick, Washington, Wayne, and Westmoreland Counties

981. Wetzel, Wirt, and Wood Counties

982. Wyoming, Wythe, and York Counties

SLAVE SCHEDULES.

983. Accomack, Albemarle, Alleghany, Amelia, Amherst, Appomattox, and Augusta Counties

984. Barbour, Bath, Bedford, Berkeley, Boone, Botetourt, Braxton, Brooke, Brunswick, Buckingham, Cabell, and Campbell Counties

985. Caroline, Carroll, Charles City, Charlotte, Chesterfield, Clarke, and Culpeper Counties

986. Cumberland, Dinwiddie, Doddridge, Elizabeth City, Essex, Fairfax, Fauquier, Fayette, Floyd, and Fluvanna Counties

987. Franklin, Frederick, Giles, Gilmer, Gloucester, Goochland, Grayson, Greenbrier, Greene, Greenesville, and Halifax Counties

988. Hampshire, Hancock, Hanover, Hardy, Harrison, Henrico, Henry, Highland, Isle of Wight, Jackson, James City, and Jefferson Counties

989. Kanawha, King and Queen, King George, King William, Lancaster, Lee, Lewis, Logan, Loudoun, and Louisa

Counties

990. Lunenburg, Madison, Marion, Marshall, Mason, Mathews, Mecklenburg, Mercer, Middlesex, Monongalia, Monroe, Montgomery, Morgan, Nansemond, and Nelson Counties

991. New Kent, Nicholas, Norfolk, Northampton, Northumberland, Nottoway, Ohio, Orange, Page, and Patrick Counties

992. Pendleton, Pittsylvania, Pocahontas, Powhatan, Preston, Prince Edward, Prince George, Prince William, Princess Anne, Pulaski, Putnam, Raleigh, Randolph, and Rappahannock Counties

993. Richmond, Ritchie, Roanoke, Rockbridge, Rockingham, Russell, Scott, Shenandoah, Smyth, Southampton, Spotsylvania, Stafford, Surry, Sussex, Taylor, Tazewell, Tyler, Warren, Warwick, Washington, Wayne, Westmoreland, Wetzel, Wirt, Wood, Wyoming, Wythe, and York Counties

Wisconsin.

994. Adams, Brown, Calumet, Chippewa, and Columbia Counties

995. Crawford and Dane Counties

996. Dodge County

997. Fond du Lac County

998. Grant County

999. Green and Iowa Counties

1000. Jefferson and Kenosha Counties

1001. Lafayette County

1002. La Pointe, Manitowoc, Marathon, and Marquette Counties

1003. Milwaukee County

1004. Portage, Racine, and Richland Counties

1005. Rock County

1006. St. Croix, Sauk, and Sheboygan Counties

1007. Walworth County

1008. Washington County

1009. Waukesha and Winnebago Counties

EIGHTH CENSUS OF THE UNITED STATES, 1860. M653. 1,438 ROLLS.

Alabama.

FREE SCHEDULES.

1. Autauga, Baldwin, and Barbour Counties

2. Bibb and Blount Counties

3. Butler County

4. Calhoun and Chambers Counties

5. Cherokee and Choctaw Counties

6. Clarke, Coffee, and Conecuh Counties

7. Coosa and Covington Counties

8. Dale and Dallas Counties

9. De Kalb and Fayette Counties
10. Franklin and Greene Counties
11. Henry and Jackson Counties
12. Jefferson and Lawrence Counties
13. Lauderdale and Limestone Counties
14. Lowndes and Macon Counties
15. Madison and Marengo Counties
16. Marion and Marshall Counties
17. Mobile County
18. Monroe County
19. Montgomery and Morgan Counties
20. Perry and Pickens Counties
21. Pike County
22. Randolph and Russell Counties
23. St. Clair and Shelby Counties
24. Sumter and Talladego Counties
25. Tallapoosa and Tuscaloosa Counties
26. Walker, Winston, Wilcox, and Washington Counties

SLAVE SCHEDULES.
27. Autauga, Baldwin, Barbour, Bibb, Blount, Butler, and Calhoun Counties
28. Chambers, Cherokee, Choctaw, Clarke, Coffee, Conecuh, Coosa, and Covington Counties
29. Dale, Dallas, De Kalb, Fayette, and Franklin Counties
30. Greene, Henry, Jackson, Jefferson, and Madison Counties
31. Marengo, Lawrence, Lauderdale. and Limestone Counties
32. Lowndes, Marion, Marshall, and Macon Counties
33. Mobile, Monroe, and Montgomery Counties
34. Morgan, Pickens, Perry, and Pike Counties
35. Randolph, Russell, Shelby, St. Clair, Sumter, and Tallapoosa Counties
36. Talladega, Tuscaloosa, Walker, Washington, Wilcox, and Winston Counties

Arkansas.
FREE SCHEDULES.
37. Arkansas, Ashley, and Benton Counties
38. Bradley, Calhoun, Carroll, and Chicot Counties
39. Clark, Columbia, and Conway Counties
40. Crawford, Crittenden, Craighead, and Dallas Counties
41. Desha, Drew, Franklin, and Fulton Counties
42. Greene, Hempstead, and Hot Spring Counties
43. Independence and Izard Counties
44. Jackson, Jefferson, and Johnson Counties
45. Lafayette, Lawrence, and Madison Counties
46. Marion, Mississippi, Monroe, Montgomery, and Newton Counties
47. Ouachita, Perry, Phillips, and Pike Counties
48. Poinsett, Polk, Pope, and Prairie Counties
49. Pulaski, Randolph, and St. Francis Counties

50. Saline, Scott, Searcy, and Sebastian Counties
51. Sevier, Union, and Van Buren Counties
52. Washington, White, and Yell Counties; and Indian Lands

SLAVE SCHEDULES.
53. Arkansas, Ashley, Benton, Bradley, Calhoun, Carroll, Chicot, Clark, Columbia, Conway, Craighead, Crawford, Crittenden, Dallas, Desha, Drew, Franklin, Fulton, Greene, Hempstead, Hot Spring, Independence, Izard, Jackson, and Jefferson Counties
54. Johnson, Lafayette, Lawrence, Madison, Marion, Mississippi, Monroe, Montgomery, Newton, Ouachita, Perry, Phillips, Pike, Poinsett, Polk, Pope, Prairie, Pulaski, Randolph, St. Francis, Saline, Scott, Searcy, Sebastian, Sevier, Union, Van Buren, Washington, White, and Yell Counties; and Indian Lands

California.
55. Alameda and Amador Counties
56. Butte County
57. Calaveras, Colusa, and Contra Costa Counties
58. Del Norte and El Dorado Counties
59. Fresno, Humboldt, Klamath, and Los Angeles Counties
60. Mariposa, Marin, Mendocino, Merced, and Monterey Counties
61. Napa and Nevada Counties
62. Placer and Plumas Counties
63. Sacramento County
64. San Bernardino, San Diego, and San Joaquin Counties
65. San Luis Obispo, San Mateo, Santa Barbara, and Santa Clara Counties
66. Santa Cruz, Shasta, and Sierra Counties
67. City of San Francisco, districts 3, 11, 10, 12, 6, 5, 2
68. City of San Francisco, districts 1, 9, 4, 8, 7
69. Siskiyou, Solano, and Sonoma Counties
70. Stanislaus, Sutter, Tehama, and Trinity Counties
71. Tulare and Tuolumne Counties
72. Yolo and Yuba Counties

Connecticut.
73. Fairfield County (part)
74. Fairfield County (part)
75. Fairfield County (part)
76. Fairfield County (part)
77. Hartford County (part)
78. Hartford County (part), city of Hartford, districts 3, 1, and 2
79. Hartford County (part)
80. Tolland County
81. Litchfield County (part)
82. Litchfield County (part)
83. Middlesex County

84. New Haven County (part)
85. New Haven County (part)
86. City of New Haven, wards 1-3
87. City of New Haven, wards 4-8
88. New Haven County (part)
89. New London County (part)
90. New London County (part)
91. New London County (part)
92. Windham County (part)
93. Windham County (part)

Dakota.
94. Entire territory

Delaware.
FREE SCHEDULES.
95. Kent County
96. New Castle County (part)
97. New Castle County (part)
98. City of Wilmington
99. Sussex County

SLAVE SCHEDULES.
100. Entire state

District of Columbia.
FREE SCHEDULES.
101. Georgetown
102. City of Washington, wards 1-3
103. City of Washington, wards 4-5
104. City of Washington, wards 6-7

SLAVE SCHEDULES.
105. Georgetown and city of Washington

Florida.
FREE SCHEDULES.
106. Alachua, Brevard, Calhoun, Clay, Columbia, Dade, Duval, Escambia, Franklin, and Gadsden Counties
107. Hamilton, Hillsborough, Holmes, Jackson, Jefferson, and Lafayette Counties
108. Leon, Levy, Liberty, Madison, Manatee, Marion, Monroe, Nassau, and New River Counties
109. Orange, Putnam, St. Johns, Santa Rosa, Sumter, Suwannee, Taylor, Volusia, Wakulla, Walton, and Washington Counties

SLAVE SCHEDULES.
110. Entire state

Georgia.
FREE SCHEDULES

111. Appling, Baker, Baldwin, Banks, Berrien, and Bibb Counties
112. Brooks, Bryan, Bulloch, and Burke Counties
113. Butts, Calhoun, Camden, Campbell, and Carroll Counties
114. Cass and Catoosa Counties
115. Chatham, Charlton, and Chattahoochee Counties
116. Chattooga, Cherokee, and Clarke Counties
117. Clay, Clayton, Clinch, Cobb, and Coffee Counties
118. Colquitt, Columbia, Coweta, Crawford, and Dade Counties
119. Dawson, Decatur, De Kalb, and Dooly Counties .
120. Dougherty, Early, Echols, Effingham, Elbert, Emanuel, and Fannin Counties
121. Fayette, Floyd, Forsyth, and Franklin Counties
122. Fulton County (part), city of Atlanta
123. Fulton County (part) (excluding the city of Atlanta)
124. Gilmer, Glascock, Glynn, and Gordon Counties
125. Greene, Gwinnett, and Habersham Counties
126. Hall, Hancock, Haralson, Hart, and Harris Counties
127. Heard, Henry, and Houston Counties
128. Irwin, Jackson, Jasper, Jefferson, and Johnson Counties
129. Jones, Laurens, Lee, Liberty, Lincoln, Lowndes, and Lumpkin Counties
130. McIntosh, Macon, Madison, Marion, Meriwether, and Miller Counties
131. Milton, Mitchell, Monroe, Montgomery, and Morgan Counties
132. Murray and Muscogee Counties
133. Newton, Oglethorpe, Paulding, Pickens, and Pierce Counties
134. Pike, Polk, Pulaski, Putnam, Quitman, and Rabun Counties
135. Randolph and Richmond Counties
136. Schley, Screven, Spalding, Stewart, and Sumter Counties
137. Talbot, Taliaferro, Tattnall, Taylor, Telfair, and Terrell Counties
138. Thomas, Towns, Troup, Twiggs, and Union Counties
139. Upson, Walker, and Walton Counties
140. Warren, Ware, Washington, Wayne, Webster, and White Counties
141. Whitefield, Wilcox, Wilkes, Wilkinson, and Worth Counties

SLAVE SCHEDULES.
142. Appling, Baker, Baldwin, Banks, Berrien, Bibb, Brooks, Bryan, Bulloch, Burke, and Butts Counties
143. Calhoun, Camden, Campbell, Carroll, Cass, Catoosa, Chattahoochee, Charlton, Chattooga, and Chatham Counties
144. Cherokee, Clarke, Clay, Clayton, Clinch, Cobb, Colquitt, Columbia, Coffee, Coweta, Crawford, Dade, Dawson, and Decatur Counties
145. De Kalb, Dooly, Dougherty, Early, Echols, Effingham, Elbert, Emanuel, Fannin, Fayette, Floyd, Forsyth, Franklin, Fulton, Gilmer, and Glascock Counties
146. Glynn, Gordon, Greene, Gwinnett, Habersham, Hall, Hancock, Haralson, Hart, Harris, and Heard Counties

147. Henry, Houston, Irwin, Jackson, Jasper, Jefferson, Johnson, and Jones Counties

148. Laurens, Lee, Liberty, Lincoln, Lowndes, Lumpkin, Macon, Madison, Marion, McIntosh, and Meriwether Counties

149. Miller, Milton, Mitchell, Monroe, Montgomery, Morgan, Murray, and Muscogee Counties

150. Newton, Oglethorpe, Paulding, Pickens, Pierce, Pike, Polk, Pulaski, and Putnam Counties

151. Quitman, Rabun, Randolph, Richmond, Schley, Screven, Spalding, Stewart, and Sumter Counties

152. Talbot, Taliaferro, Tattnall, Taylor, Telfair, Terrell, Thomas, Towns, Troup, and Twiggs Counties

153. Union, Upson, Walker, Walton, Warren, Ware, Washington, Wayne, Webster, White, Whitfield, Wilcox, Wilkens, Wilkenson, and Worth Counties

Illinois.

154. Adams County (part), city of Quincy
155. Adams County (part) (excluding the city of Quincy)
156. Alexander and Bond Counties
157. Boone and Brown Counties
158. Bureau County
159. Calhoun and Carroll Counties
160. Cass and Champaign Counties
161. Christian County
162. Clark and Clay Counties
163. Clinton County
164. Cook County (part), city of Chicago, wards 1-2
165. Cook County (part), city of Chicago, wards 3-4
166. Cook County (part), city of Chicago, wards 5-6
167. Cook County (part), city of Chicago, ward 7
168. Cook County (part), city of Chicago, wards 8-10
169. Cook County (part) (excluding the city of Chicago)
170. Cook County (part) (excluding the city of Chicago)
171. Coles and Crawford Counties
172. Cumberland County
173. De Kalb County
174. De Witt and Douglas Counties
175. Du Page County
176. Edgar, Edwards, and Effingham Counties
177. Fayette, Ford, and Franklin Counties
178. Greene County
179. Fulton County
180. Gallatin County
181. Grundy and Henderson Counties
182. Henry County
183. Hamilton County
184. Hancock County
185. Hardin County
186. Iroquois and Jackson Counties
187. Jasper and Jefferson Counties

188. Jersey County
189. Jo Daviess County
190. Johnson County
191. Kane County
192. Kankakee County
193. Lake County
194. Kendall County
195. Knox County
196. La Salle County (part)
197. La Salle County (part)
198. Lawrence and Lee Counties
199. Livingston County
200. Logan County
201. McDonough County
202. McHenry County
203. Macon County
204. McLean County
205. Menard County
206. Macoupin County
207. Marion County
208. Madison County
209. Massac County
210. Marshall and Mason Counties
211. Mercer County
212. Monroe County
213. Morgan and Moultrie Counties
214. Montgomery County
215. Ogle County
216. Peoria County (part), city of Peoria
217. Peoria County (part) (excluding the city of Peoria)
218. Perry County
219. Pike County
220. Piatt, Pope, and Pulaski Counties
221. Putnam and Randolph Counties
222. Richland and Rock Island Counties
223. Saline County
224. St. Clair County (part)
225. St. Clair County (part)
226. Sangamon County
227. Scott County
228. Schuyler and Shelby Counties
229. Stark County
230. Stephenson County
231. Union County
232. Tazewell County
233. Vermilion County
234. Wabash and Warren Counties
235. Washington County
236. Wayne and White Counties
237. Whiteside County
238. Will County

239. Williamson County
240. Winnebago County
241. Woodford County

Indiana.
242. Adams County
243. Allen County
244. Bartholomew and Benton Counties
245. Blackford and Boone Counties
246. Brown and Carroll Counties
247. Cass County
248. Clark County
249. Clay County
250. Clinton and Crawford Counties
251. Daviess County
252. Dearborn County
253. Decatur County
254. De Kalb and Delaware Counties
255. Dubois County
256. Elkhart and Fayette Counties
257. Floyd County
258. Fountain County
259. Franklin County
260. Fulton and Gibson Counties
261. Grant County
262. Greene County
263. Hamilton and Hancock Counties
264. Harrison County
265. Hendricks County
266. Henry and Howard Counties
267. Huntington County
268. Jackson and Jasper Counties
269. Jay County
270. Jefferson County
271. Jennings and Johnson Counties
272. Knox County
273. Kosciusko County
274. Lagrange and Lake Counties
275. La Porte County
276. Lawrence County
277. Madison County
278. Marshall and Martin Counties
279. Marion County (part), city of Indianapolis
280. Marion County (part) (excluding the city of Indianapolis)
281. Miami County
282. Monroe and Newton Counties
283. Montgomery County
284. Morgan County
285. Noble and Ohio Counties
286. Orange County
287. Owen and Parke Counties

288. Perry County
289. Pike and Porter Counties
290. Posey and Pulaski Counties
291. Putnam County
292. Randolph County
293. Ripley County
294. Rush and Scott Counties
295. St. Joseph County
296. Shelby County
297. Spencer and Starke Counties
298. Steuben and Sullivan Counties
299. Switzerland County
300. Tippecanoe County
301. Tipton and Union Counties
302. Vanderburgh County
303. Vermillion and Vigo Counties
304. Wabash County
305. Warren and Warrick Counties
306. Washington County
307. White and Whitley Counties
308. Wayne County
309. Wells County

Iowa.
310. Adair, Adams, and Allamakee Counties
311. Appanoose, Audubon, and Benton Counties
312. Black Hawk, Boone, and Bremer Counties
313. Buchanan, Buena Vista, Butler, Calhoun, Carroll, Cass, Cerro, Gordo, Cherokee, and Chickasaw Counties
314. Cedar, Clarke, and Clay Counties
315. Clayton County
316. Clinton and Crawford Counties
317. Dallas and Davis Counties
318. Decatur and Delaware Counties
319. Des Moines and Dickinson Counties
320. Dubuque County
321. Emmet, Franklin, and Fremont Counties
322. Fayette, Floyd, Grundy, and Greene Counties
323. Guthrie, Hamilton, Hancock, Hardin, Harrison, Howard, Humboldt, and Ida Counties
324. Henry County
325. Iowa and Jasper Counties
326. Jackson County
327. Johnson County
328. Jefferson and Jones Counties
329. Keokuk County
330. Kossuth and Lee Counties
331. Louisa County
332. Linn County
333. Lucas and Madison Counties
334. Mahaska and Monona Counties

335. Marion and Marshall Counties

336. Plymouth, Pocahontas, Palo Alto, Mills, Mitchell, Monroe, and Montgomery Counties

337. Muscatine, O'Brien, and Page Counties

338. Polk, and Pottawattamie Counties

339. Poweshiek, Ringgold, Sac, Shelby, Sioux, Story, and Tama Counties

340. Scott County

341. Warren County

342. Taylor, Union, and Van Buren Counties

343. Wapello County

344. Washington and Wayne Counties

345. Webster, Winnebago, Winneshiek, Woodbury, Worth, and Wright Counties

Kansas.

346. Allen, Anderson, Atchison, Bourbon, and Breckenridge Counties

347. Brown, Chase, Butler, Otoe, Hunter, Clay, Coffey, Davis, Dickinson, Donipan, and Marion Counties

348. Arapahoe County

349. Dorn, Douglas, Franklin, and Jefferson Counties

350. Johnson and Leavenworth Counties

351. Linn, Lykins, McGhee, Madison, Marshall, Morris, Nemaha, and Osage Counties

352. Pottawatomie (535-564), Wabaunsee (565-582), Pottawatomie (583-602), Riley, Shawnee, Jackson, Wabaunsee (781-793), Washington, Woodson, Greenwood, Wilson, and Wyandott Counties

Kentucky.
FREE SCHEDULES.

353. Adair, Allen, and Anderson Counties

354. Ballard and Barren Counties

355. Bath and Boone Counties

356. Bourbon, Boyd, and Boyle Counties

357. Bracken and Breathitt Counties

358. Breckinridge, Bullitt, and Butler Counties

359. Caldwell and Calloway Counties

360. Campbell County

361. Carroll, Carter, and Casey Counties

362. Christian and Clark Counties

363. Clay, Clinton, and Crittenden Counties

364. Cumberland and Daviess Counties

365. Edmonson, Estill, and Fayette Counties

366. Fleming County

367. Floyd, Franklin, and Fulton Counties

368. Gallatin, Garrard, and Grant Counties

369. Graves and Grayson Counties

370. Green, Greenup, and Hancock Counties

371. Hardin and Harlan Counties

372. Harrison and Hart Counties

373. Henderson and Henry Counties

374. Hickman, Hopkins, and Jackson Counties

375. City of Louisville, wards 1-3

376. City of Louisville, wards 4-8

377. Jefferson County (part) (excluding the city of Louisville)

378. Jessamine and Johnson Counties

379. Kenton County

380. Knox, Larue, and Laurel Counties

381. Lawrence, Letcher, and Lewis Counties

382. Lincoln and Livingston Counties

383. Logan, Lyon, and McCracken Counties

384. McLean and Madison Counties

385. Magoffin, Marion, and Marshall Counties

386. Mason and Meade Counties

387. Mercer and Metcalfe Counties

388. Monroe, Montgomery, Morgan, and Muhlenberg Counties

389. Nelson and Nicholas Counties

390. Ohio and Oldham Counties

391. Owen and Owsley Counties

392. Pendleton, Perry, and Pike Counties

393. Powell, Pulaski, and Rockcastle Counties

394. Rowan, Russell, and Scott Counties

395. Shelby, Simpson, and Spencer Counties

396. Taylor and Todd Counties

397. Trigg and Trimble Counties

398. Union and Warren Counties

399. Washington, Wayne, and Webster Counties

400. Whitley and Woodford Counties

SLAVE SCHEDULES.

401. Adair, Allen, Anderson, Ballard, Barren, Bath, Boone, Bourbon, Boyd, Boyle, Bracken, Breathitt, Breckinridge, Bullitt, Butler, Caldwell, Calloway, Campbell, Carroll, Carter, and Casey Counties

402. Christian, Clark, Clay, Clinton, Crittenden, Cumberland, Daviess, Edmonson, Estill, Fayette, Fleming, Floyd, and Franklin Counties

403. Fulton, Gallatin, Garrard, Grant, Graves, Grayson, Green, Greenup, Hancock, Hardin, Harrison, Hart, Henderson, Henry, Hickman, Hopkins, Jackson, and Jefferson Counties

404. Jessamine, Johnson, Kenton, Knox, Larue, Laurel, Lawrence, Letcher, Lewis, Lincoln, Livingston, Logan, Lyon, McCracken, McLean, Madison, Magoffin, and Marion Counties

405. Marshall, Mason, Meade, Mercer, Metcalfe, Monroe, Montgomery, Morgan, Muhlenberg, Nelson, Nicholas, Ohio, Oldham, Owen, Owsley, Pendleton, Perry, Pike, Powell, Pulaski, Rockcastle, Rowan, Russell, Scott, and Shelby Counties

406. Simpson, Spencer, Taylor, Todd, Trigg, Trimble, Union,

Warren, Washington, Wayne, Webster, Whitley, and Woodford Counties

Louisiana.

FREE SCHEDULES.

407. Ascension, Assumption, and Avoyelles Parishes

408. East Baton Rouge, West Baton Rouge, and Bossier Parishes

409. Caddo, Calcasieu, Caldwell, and Carroll Parishes

410. Catahoula, Claiborne, Concordia, and De Soto Parishes

411. East Feliciana, West Feliciana, Franklin, Iberville, and Jackson Parishes

412. Jefferson and Lafayette Parishes

413. Lafourche, Livingston, Madison, and Morehouse Parishes

414. Natchitoches, Ouachita, Plaquemines, and Pointe Coupee Parishes

415. Orleans Parish, city of New Orleans, ward 1

416. City of New Orleans, wards 2 and 10

417. City of New Orleans, ward 3

418. City of New Orleans, ward 5

419. City of New Orleans, wards 6 and 7

420. City of New Orleans, ward 11

421. City of New Orleans, wards 4 and 8

422. City of New Orleans, ward 9

423. Rapides, Sabine, St. Bernard, St. Charles, St. Helena, and St. James Parishes

424. St. John the Baptist and St. Landry Parishes

425. St. Martin, St. Mary, St. Tammany, and Terrebonne Parishes

426. Tensas, Union, Vermilion, Washington, and Winn Parishes

SLAVE SCHEDULES.

427. Ascension, Assumption, Avoyelles, East Baton Rouge, West Baton Rouge, Bossier, Caddo, Calcasieu, Caldwell, Carroll, and Catahoula Parishes

428. Claiborne, Concordia, De Soto, East Feliciana, West Feliciana, Franklin, Iberville, Jackson, Jefferson, and Lafayette Parishes

429. Lafourche, Livingston, Madison, Morehouse, Natchitoches, and Orleans Parishes

430. Ouachita, Plaquemines, Pointe Coupee, Rapides, and Sabine Parishes

431. St. Bernard, St. Charles, St. Helena, St. James, St. John the Baptist, St. Landry, St. Martin, St. Mary, St. Tammany, Tensas, Terrebonne, Union, Vermilion, Washington, and Winn Parishes

Maine.

432. Androscoggin County

433. Piscataquis County

434. Aroostook County

435. Franklin County

436. Cumberland County (part)

437. Cumberland County (part)

438. Hancock County

439. Kennebec County (part)

440. Kennebec County (part)

441. Kennebec County (part)

442. Lincoln County

443. Knox County

444. Oxford County

445. Penobscot County (part)

446. Penobscot County (part)

447. Penobscot County (part)

448. Sagadahoc County

449. York County (part)

450. York County (part)

451. York County (part)

452. Somerset County

453. Waldo County

454. Washington County (part)

455. Washington County (part)

Maryland.

FREE SCHEDULES.

456. Allegany County

457. Anne Arundel County

458. Baltimore County (part), city of Baltimore, wards 1-2

459. Baltimore County (part), city of Baltimore, ward 3

460. Baltimore County (part), city of Baltimore, wards 4-6

461. Baltimore County (part), city of Baltimore, wards 7 and 10

462. Baltimore County (part), city of Baltimore, wards 8-9

463. Baltimore County (part), city of Baltimore, wards 11-12

464. Baltimore County (part), city of Baltimore, wards 13-16

465. Baltimore County (part), city of Baltimore, wards 17-18

466. Baltimore County (part), city of Baltimore, wards 19-20

467. Baltimore County (part) (excluding the city of Baltimore), districts 1-2

468. Baltimore County (part) (excluding the city of Baltimore), districts 3-9

469. Baltimore County (part) (excluding the city of Baltimore), districts 10-13

470. Calvert and Caroline Counties

471. Carroll County

472. Cecil County

473. Charles and Dorchester Counties

474. Frederick County (part)

475. Frederick County (part)

476. Harford County

477. Howard and Kent Counties

478. Montgomery and Prince Georges Counties

479. Queen Annes and St. Mary's Counties

480. Somerset County

481. Worcester County
482. Talbot County
483. Washington County

SLAVE SCHEDULES.
484. Allegany, Anne Arundel, Baltimore, Calvert, Caroline,
      Carroll, Cecil, Charles, Dorchester, Frederick, Harford,
      and Howard Counties
485. Kent, Montgomery, Prince Georges, Queen Annes, St.
      Marys, Somerset, Washington, and Worcester Counties

Massachusetts.
486. Barnstable County
487. Berkshire County (part)
488. Berkshire County (part)
489. Bristol County (part)
490. Bristol County (part), city of New Bedford
491. Bristol County (part)
492. Bristol County (part)
493. Dukes County
494. Essex County (part)
495. Essex County (part)
496. Essex County (part)
497. Essex County (part), city of Salem
498. Essex County (part)
499. Essex County (part)
500. Essex County (part)
501. Franklin County
502. Hampden County (part)
503. Hampden County (part)
504. Hampden County (part)
505. Hampshire County
506. Middlesex County (part)
507. Middlesex County (part), city of Lowell
508. Middlesex County (part), city of Cambridge
509. Middlesex County (part)
510. Middlesex County (part)
511. Middlesex County (part)
512. Middlesex County (part), city of Charlestown
513. Nantucket County
514. Norfolk County (part)
515. Norfolk County (part)
516. Norfolk County (part)
517. Norfolk County (part), city of Roxbury
518. Plymouth County (part)
519. Plymouth County (part)
520. Suffolk County (part), city of Boston, wards 1-2
521. Suffolk County (part), city of Boston, wards 3, 5, 6
522. Suffolk County (part), city of Boston, wards 7-9
523. Suffolk County (part), city of Boston, wards 4 and 10
524. Suffolk County (part), city of Boston, ward 11

525. Suffolk County (part), city of Boston, ward 12
526. Suffolk County (part) (excluding the city of Boston)
527. Worcester County (part), city of Worcester, wards 1, 2, 7, 8
528. Worcester County (part)
529. Worcester County (part)
530. Worcester County (part)
531. Worcester County (part)
532. Worcester County (part), city of Worcester, wards 3-6
533. Worcester County (part)
534. Worcester County (part)

Michigan.
535. Alpena, Alcona, Allegan, and Antrim Counties
536. Barry and Bay Counties
537. Berrien County
538. Branch County
539. Calhoun County
540. Clinton County
541. Cass and Chippewa Counties
542. Eaton, Emmet, Cheboygan, Presque Isle, Mackinac, and
Delta Counties
543. Midland, Gladwin, Manistee, Grand Traverse, Gratiot, and
      Hillsdale Counties
544. Genesee and Houghton Counties
545. Huron and Ingham Counties
546. Ionia County
547. Iosco, Isabella, and Jackson Counties
548. Kalamazoo County
549. Lapeer County
550. Kent, Leelanau, and Manitou Counties
551. Lenawee County
552. Livingston County
553. Macomb County
554. Marquette, Schoolcraft, Mason, Osceola, Mecosta, and
      Monroe Counties
555. Montcalm, Muskegon, and Newaygo Counties
556. Oakland County
557. Oceana, Ontonagon, and Ottawa Counties
558. Saginaw and Sanilac Counties
559. St. Clair County
560. Shiawassee County
561. St. Joseph County
562. Tuscola and Van Buren Counties
563. Washtenaw County
564. Wayne County (excluding the city of Detroit)
565. Wayne County, city of Detroit, wards 1-5
566. Wayne County, city of Detroit, wards 6-10

Minnesota.
567. Anoka, Becker, Benton, Blue Earth, Brown, Buchanan,
      Carver, Crow Wing, Morrison, Cass, and Itasca Counties

568. Dakota, Dodge, and Faribault Counties
569. Fillmore and Freeborn Counties
570. Goodhue and Hennepin Counties
571. Houston, Isanti, Jackson, Nobles, Pipestone, Kanabec, Mille Lacs, Aitkin, Lake, Le Sueur, Mahnomen, Martin, McLeod, and Meeker Counties
572. Monongalia, Mower, Murray, Nicollet, Olmstead, and Otter Tail Counties
573. Pine, Chisago, Ramsey, Renville, Pierce, and Rice Counties
574. St. Louis, Carlton, Scott, Sherburne, Sibley, and Stearns Counties
575. Steele, Todd, Pembina, Toombs, Breckenridge, Polk, Douglas, Wabasha, and Weseca Counties
576. Washington, Winona, and Wright Counties

Mississippi.
FREE SCHEDULES.
577. Adams, Amite, and Attala Counties
578. Bolivar, Calhoun, and Carroll Counties
579. Chickasaw and Choctaw Counties
580. Claiborne, Clarke, Coahoma, Copiah, and Covington Counties
581. De Soto, Franklin, Greene, and Harrison Counties
582. Hinds, Holmes, Issaquena, and Jackson Counties
583. Itawamba and Jasper Counties
584. Jefferson, Jones, Kemper, and Lawrence Counties
585. Lafayette and Lauderdale Counties
586. Leake, Lowndes, Madison, and Marion Counties
587. Marshall and Monroe Counties
588. Neshoba, Newton, and Noxubee Counties
589. Oktibbeha, Panola, Perry, and Pike Counties
590. Pontotoc and Rankin Counties
591. Scott, Simpson, Smith, and Tallahatchie Counties
592. Tippah, Tunica, and Warren Counties
593. Tishomingo and Wayne Counties
594. Wilkinson, Winston, Yalobusha, and Yazoo Counties

SLAVE SCHEDULES.
595. Adams, Amite, Attala, Bolivar, and Calhoun Counties
596. Carroll, Chickasaw, Choctaw, Claiborne, Clarke, and Coahoma Counties
597. Copiah, Covington, De Soto, Franklin, Greene, Harrison, and Hinds Counties
598. Holmes, Issaquena, Itawamba, and Jackson Counties
599. Jasper, Jefferson, Jones, Kemper, Lafayette, Lauderdale, and Lawrence Counties
600. Leake, Lowndes, and Madison Counties
601. Marion, Marshall, Monroe, Neshoba, and Newton Counties
602. Noxubee, Oktibbeha, Panola, Perry, Pike, and Pontotoc Counties
603. Rankin, Scott, Simpson, Smith, Tallahatchie, Tippah,

Tishomingo, Tunica, and Warren Counties
604. Wayne, Wilkinson, Winston, Yalobusha, and Yazoo Counties

Missouri.
FREE SCHEDULES.
605. Adair and Andrew Counties
606. Atchison, Audrain, and Barry Counties
607. Barton, Bates, and Benton Counties
608. Bollinger and Boone Counties
609. Buchanan County
610. Butler, Caldwell, and Callaway Counties
611. Camden and Cape Girardeau Counties
612. Carroll, Cass, and Carter Counties
613. Cedar, Chariton, and Christian Counties
614. Clark and Clay Counties
615. Clinton and Cole Counties
616. Cooper and Crawford Counties
617. Dade, Dallas, and Daviess Counties
618. De Kalb, Dent, Douglas, and Dunklin Counties
619. Franklin and Gasconade Counties
620. Gentry County
621. Greene and Grundy Counties
622. Harrison and Henry Counties
623. Hickory, Holt, and Howard Counties
624. Howell, Iron, and Jasper Counties
625. Jackson County
626. Jefferson and Johnson Counties
627. Knox and Laclede Counties
628. Lafayette and Lawrence Counties
629. Lewis and Lincoln Counties
630. Linn and Livingston Counties
631. Macon and Madison Counties
632. Maries and Marion Counties
633. McDonald, Mercer, and Miller Counties
634. Mississippi and Moniteau Counties
635. Monroe and Montgomery Counties
636. Morgan, New Madrid, and Newton Counties
637. Nodaway, Oregon, Osage, and Ozark Counties
638. Pemiscot, Perry, and Pettis Counties
639. Phelps and Pike Counties
640. Platte County
641. Polk, Pulaski, and Putnam Counties
642. Ralls and Randolph Counties
643. Ray, Reynolds, and Ripler Counties
644. St. Charles and St. Clair Counties
645. St. Francois, Ste. Genevieve, and Saline Counties
646. Schuyler and Scotland Counties
647. St. Louis County (part), city of St. Louis, ward 1
648. St. Louis County (part), city of St. Louis, ward 2
649. St. Louis County (part), city of St. Louis, ward 4
650. St. Louis County (part), city of St. Louis, ward 9

651. St. Louis County (part), city of St. Louis, ward 5
652. St. Louis County (part), city of St. Louis, ward 8
653. St. Louis County (part), city of St. Louis, ward 7
654. St. Louis County (part), city of St. Louis, ward 10
655. St. Louis County (part), city of St. Louis, wards 3 and 6
656. St. Louis County (part) (excluding the city of St. Louis)
657. Scott, Shannon, Shelby, and Stoddard Counties
658. Stone, Sullivan, Taney, and Texas Counties
659. Vernon, Warren, and Washington Counties
660. Wayne, Webster, and Wright Counties

SLAVE SCHEDULES.
661. Adair, Andrew, Atchison, Audrain, Bates, Benton, Bollinger, Boone, Buchanan, Butler, Caldwell, Callaway, Cape Girardeau, Carroll, Cass, Carter, Cedar, Chariton, Christian, Clark, Clay, Clinton, Cole, Cooper, Crawford, and Dade Counties
662. Dallas, Daviess, De Kalb, Dent, Dunklin, Franklin, Gasconade, Gentry, Greene, Grundy, Harrison, Henry, Hickory, Holt, Howard, Howell, Iron, Jackson, Jasper, Jefferson, Johnson, Knox, Laclede, and Lafayette Counties
663. Lawrence, Lewis, Linn, Lincoln, Livingston, Macon, Madison, Maries, Marion, McDonald, Mercer, Miller, Mississippi, Moniteau, Monroe, Montgomery, Morgan, New Madrid, Newton, Nodaway, Oregon, Osage, Ozark, Pemiscot, Perry, Pettis, Phelps, Pike, Platte, Polk, Pulaski, Putnam, Ralls, and Randolph Counties
664. Ray, Reynolds, Ripley, St. Charles, St. Clair, St. Francois, Ste. Genevieve, St. Louis, Saline, Schuyler, Scotland, Scott, Shannon, Shelby, Stoddard, Stone, Sullivan, Taney, Texas, Vernon, Warren, Washington, Wayne, Webster, and Wright Counties

Nebraska.
665. Entire territory

Nevada.
For Elko County, see St. Marys County, UT; for Douglas, Lyon, Ormsby, and Storey Counties, see Carson County, UT, on roll 1314.

New Hampshire.
666. Belknap County
667. Carroll County
668. Cheshire County
669. Coos County
670. Grafton County (part)
671. Grafton County (part)
672. Hillsboro County (part) (excluding the city of Manchester)
673. Hillsboro County (part) (excluding the city of Manchester)
674. City of Manchester (wards l-8)

675. Merrimack County (part), city of Concord
676. Merrimack County (part) (excluding the city of Concord)
677. Merrimack County (part) (excluding the city of Concord)
678. Rockingham County (part)
679. Rockingham County (part)
680. Strafford County
681. Sullivan County

New Jersey.
682. Atlantic County
683. Bergen County
684. Burlington County (part)
685. Burlington County (part)
686. Camden County
687. Cape May and Cumberland Counties
688. Essex County (part), city of Newark, wards 1-5, and 9
689. Essex County (part), city of Newark, wards 6-8, and 10-12
690. Essex County (part) (excluding the city of Newark)
691. Gloucester County
692. Hudson County (part), cities of Hudson and Hoboken
693. Hudson County (part), Jersey City
694. Hudson County (part) (excluding the cities of Hoboken, Hudson, and Jersey City)
695. Hunterdon County (part)
696. Hunterdon County (part)
697. Mercer County (part) (excluding the city of Trenton)
698. Mercer County (part), city of Trenton
699. Middlesex County (part)
700. Middlesex County (part)
701. Monmouth County (part)
702. Monmouth County (part)
703. Morris County (part)
704. Morris County (part)
705. Ocean County
706. Passaic County
707. Salem County
708. Somerset County
709. Sussex County
710. Union County
711. Warren County

New Mexico.
712. Arizona, Bernalillo, Dona Ana, and Rio Arriba Counties
713. San Miguel County
714. Santa Fe and Socorro Counties
715. Taos County
716. Santa Anna, Mora, and Valencia Counties

New York
717. Allegany County (part)
718. Allegany County (part)

719. Albany County (part), city of Albany, wards 1-7
720. Albany County (part), city of Albany, wards 8-10
721. Albany County (part) (excluding the city of Albany)
722. Albany County (part) (excluding the city of Albany)
723. Albany County (part) (excluding the city of Albany)
724. Broome County
725. Cattaraugus County (part)
726. Cattaraugus County (part)
727. Cayuga County (part), city of Auburn
728. Cayuga County (part) (excluding the city of Auburn)
729. Cayuga County (part) (excluding the city of Auburn)
730. Chemung County
731. Chautauqua County (part)
732. Chautauqua County (part)
733. Chenango County (part)
734. Chenango County (part)
735. Clinton County (part)
736. Clinton County (part)
737. Columbia County (part)
738. Columbia County (part)
739. Cortland County
740. Dutchess County (part)
741. Dutchess County (part)
742. Dutchess County (part)
743. Delaware County (part)
744. Delaware County (part)
745. Erie County (part), city of Buffalo, wards 1-3
746. Erie County (part), city of Buffalo, wards 4 and 5
747. Erie County (part), city of Buffalo, wards 6-8
748. Erie County (part), city of Buffalo, wards 9 and 10
749. Erie County (part), city of Buffalo, wards 11-13
750. Erie County (part) (excluding the city of Buffalo)
751. Erie County (part) (excluding the city of Buffalo)
752. Erie County (part) (excluding the city of Buffalo)
753. Essex County
754. Franklin County
755. Fulton County
756. Genesee County (part)
757. Genesee County (part)
758. Greene County
759. Hamilton and Herkimer (part) Counties
760. Herkimer County (part)
761. Jefferson County (part)
762. Jefferson County (part)
763. City of Brooklyn, wards 1 and 2
764. City of Brooklyn, wards 3 and 4
765. City of Brooklyn, ward 5
766. City of Brooklyn, ward 6
767. City of Brooklyn, wards 7 and 8
768. City of Brooklyn, ward 9
769. City of Brooklyn, ward 10

770. City of Brooklyn, ward 11
771. City of Brooklyn, ward 12
772. City of Brooklyn, ward 13
773. City of Brooklyn, wards 14 and 15
774. City of Brooklyn, wards 16 and 17
775. City of Brooklyn, wards 18 and 19
776. Kings County (part) (excluding the city of Brooklyn)
777. Lewis County
778. Livingston County (part)
779. Livingston County (part)
780. Madison County (part)
781. Madison County (part)
782. City of Rochester, wards 1-5
783. City of Rochester, wards 6-9
784. City of Rochester, wards 10-12
785. Monroe County (part) (excluding the city of Rochester)
786. Monroe County (part) (excluding the city of Rochester)
787. Montgomery County
788. New York City, ward 1
789. New York City, wards 2-4
790. New York City, ward 5
791. New York City, ward 6
792. New York City, ward 7, districts 1-3
793. New York City, ward 7, districts 4 and 5
794. New York City, ward 8, districts 1 and 2
795. New York City, ward 8, districts 3 and 4
796. New York City, ward 9, districts 2 and 4
797. New York City, ward 9, districts 1 and 3
798. New York City, ward 10
799. New York City, ward 11, districts 3, 4, and 6
800. New York City, ward 11, districts 2, 5, 9, and 10
801. New York City, ward 11, districts 1, 7, and 8
802. New York City, ward 12
803. New York City, ward 13
804. New York City, ward 14
805. New York City, ward 15
806. New York City, ward 16, districts 1, 4, and 5
807. New York City, ward 16, districts 2 and 3
808. New York City, ward 17, districts 5 and 6
809. New York City, ward 17, districts 2, 8, and 9
810. New York City, ward 17, districts 7 and 10
811. New York City, ward 17, districts 1, 3, and 4
812. New York City, ward 18, districts 5 and 6
813. New York City, ward 18, districts 3 and 4
814. New York City, ward 18, districts 1 and 2
815. New York City, ward 19; Blackwell Island
816. New York City, ward 20, districts 2, 4, 5, and 7
817. New York City, ward 20, districts 1, 3, and 6
818. New York City, ward 21, districts 3 and 5
819. New York City, ward 21, districts 1, 2, and 4
820. New York City, ward 22, districts 2 and 4

821. New York City, ward 22, districts 1 and 3
822. Niagara County (part)
823. Niagara County (part)
824. Oneida County (part) (excluding the city of Utica)
825. Oneida County (part) (excluding the city of Utica)
826. Oneida County (part) (excluding the city of Utica)
827. Oneida County (part), city of Utica
828. Onondaga County (part) (excluding the city of Syracuse)
829. Onondaga County (part) (excluding the city of Syracuse)
830. Onondaga County (part), city of Syracuse
831. Ontario County (part)
832. Ontario County (part)
833. Orange County (part)
834. Orange County (part)
835. Orange County (part)
836. Orleans County
837. Oswego County (part) (excluding the city of Oswego)
838. Oswego County (part) (excluding the city of Oswego)
839. Oswego County (part), city of Oswego
840. Otsego County (part)
841. Otsego County (part)
842. Putnam County
843. Queens County (part)
844. Queens County (part)
845. Queens County (part)
846. Rensselaer County (part), city of Troy, wards 1 -5
847. Rensselaer County (part), city of Troy, wards 6-10
848. Rensselaer County (part) (excluding the city of Troy)
849. Rensselaer County (part) (excluding the city of Troy)
850. Richmond County
851. Rockland County
852. St. Lawrence County (part)
853. St. Lawrence County (part)
854. St. Lawrence County (part)
855. St. Lawrence County (part)
856. Saratoga County (part)
857. Saratoga County (part)
858. Schenectady County
859. Schuyler County
860. Schoharie County
861. Seneca County
862. Steuben County (part)
863. Steuben County (part)
864. Suffolk County (part)
865. Suffolk County (part)
866. Sullivan County
867. Tioga County
868. Tompkins County
869. Ulster County (part)
870. Ulster County (part)
871. Ulster County (part)

872. Ulster County (part)
873. Warren County
874. Washington County (part)
875. Washington County (part)
876. Wayne County (part)
877. Wayne County (part)
878. Westchester County (part)
879. Westchester County (part)
880. Westchester County (part)
881. Westchester County (part)
882. Westchester County (part)
883. Wyoming County (part)
884. Wyoming County (part)
885. Yates County

North Carolina.

FREE SCHEDULES.

886. Alamance, Alexander, and Alleghany Counties
887. Anson, Ashe, and Beaufort Counties
888. Bertie, Bladen, and Brunswick Counties
889. Buncombe and Burke Counties
890. Cabarrus, Caldwell, Camden, and Carteret Counties
891. Caswell and Catawba Counties
892. Chatham and Cherokee Counties
893. Chowan, Cleveland, and Columbus Counties
894. Craven and Cumberland Counties
895. Currituck and Davidson Counties
896. Davie, Duplin, and Edgecombe Counties
897. Forsyth and Franklin Counties
898. Gaston, Gates, and Granville Counties
899. Greene and Halifax Counties
900. Guilford and Harnett Counties
901. Haywood and Henderson Counties
902. Hertford, Hyde, and Iredell Counties
903. Jackson, Johnston, and Jones Counties
904. Lenoir, Lincoln, McDowell, and Macon Counties
905. Madison, Martin, and Montgomery Counties
906. Mecklenburg and Moore Counties
907. Nash and New Hanover Counties
908. Northampton, Onslow, and Orange Counties
909. Pasquotank, Perquimans, and Person Counties
910. Pitt, Polk, and Randolph Counties
911. Richmond and Robeson Counties
912. Rockingham and Rowan Counties
913. Rutherford and Sampson Counties
914. Stanly, Stokes, and Surry Counties
915. Tyrrell and Union Counties
916. Wake and Warren Counties
917. Washington, Watauga, and Wayne Counties
918. Wilkes and Wilson Counties
919. Yadkin and Yancey Counties

SLAVE SCHEDULES.

920. Alamance, Alexander, Alleghany, Anson, Ashe, Beaufort, Bertie, Bladen, Brunswick, Buncombe, Burke, and Cabarrus Counties

921. Camden, Caldwell, Carteret, Caswell, Catawba, Chatham, Cherokee, Chowan, Cleveland, Columbus, Craven, and Cumberland Counties

922. Currituck, Davidson, Davie, Duplin, Edgecombe, Forsyth, Franklin, Gaston, and Gates Counties

923. Granville, Greene, Guilford, Halifax, Harnett, Haywood, Henderson, Hertford, Hyde, and Iredell Counties

924. Jackson, Johnston, Jones, Lenoir, Lincoln, Macon, Madison, Martin, McDowell, Mecklenburg, Montgomery, Moore, and Nash Counties

925. New Hanover, Northampton, Onslow, Orange, Pasquotank, Perquimans, Person, Pitt, Polk, and Randolph Counties

926. Richmond, Robeson, Rockingham, Rowan, Rutherford, Sampson, Stanly, Stokes, Surry, and Tyrrell Counties

927. Union, Wake, Warren, Washington, Watauga, Wayne, Wilkes, Wilson, Yadkin, and Yancey Counties

Ohio.

928. Adams County
929. Allen County
930. Ashland County
931. Auglaize County
932. Ashtabula County (part)
933. Ashtabula County (part)
934. Athens County
935. Carroll County
936. Belmont County (part)
937. Belmont County (part)
938. Brown County (part)
939. Brown County (part)
940. Butler County (part)
941. Butler County (part)
942. Champaign County
943. Clark County
944. Clermont County (part)
945. Clermont County (part)
946. Clinton County
947. Defiance County
948. Columbiana County (part)
949. Columbiana County (part)
950. Coshocton County
951. Crawford County
952. Cuyahoga County (part), city of Cleveland, wards 3-7
953. Cuyahoga County (part), city of Cleveland, wards 1, 2, 8-11
954. Cuyahoga County (part) (excluding the city of Cleveland)
955. Cuyahoga County (part) (excluding the city of Cleveland)
956. Darke County

957. Delaware County
958. Erie County
959. Fayette County
960. Fairfield County (part)
961. Fairfield County (part)
962. Franklin County (part) (excluding the city of Columbus)
963. Franklin County (part) (excluding the city of Columbus)
964. Franklin County (part), city of Columbus, wards 1-5
965. Fulton County
966. Gallia County
967. Geauga County
968. Greene County
969. Guernsey County
970. Hamilton County (part), city of Cincinnati, wards 1-3
971. Hamilton County (part), city of Cincinnati, wards 4 and 5
972. Hamilton County (part), city of Cincinnati, wards 6 and 7
973. Hamilton County (part), city of Cincinnati, wards 8 and 9
974. Hamilton County (part), city of Cincinnati, wards 10 and 11
975. Hamilton County (part), city of Cincinnati, ward 12
976. Hamilton County (part), city of Cincinnati, wards 13 and 14
977. Hamilton County (part), city of Cincinnati, ward 15
978. Hamilton County (part), city of Cincinnati, wards 16 and 17
979. Hamilton County (part) (excluding the city of Cincinnati)
980. Hamilton County (part) (excluding the city of Cincinnati)
981. Hamilton County (part) (excluding the city of Cincinnati)
982. Hancock County
983. Hardin County
984. Harrison County
985. Henry County
986. Highland County (part)
987. Highland County (part)
988. Hocking County
989. Holmes County
990. Huron County (part)
991. Huron County (part)
992. Jackson County
993. Jefferson County
994. Knox County (part)
995. Knox County (part)
996. Lake County
997. Lawrence County
998. Licking County (part)
999. Licking County (part)
1000. Logan County
1001. Lorain County (part)
1002. Lorain County (part)
1003. Lucas County
1004. Madison County
1005. Mahoning County
1006. Marion County
1007. Medina County

1008. Meigs County
1009. Mercer County
1010. Miami County (part)
1011. Miami County (part)
1012. Monroe County
1013. Montgomery County (part)
1014. Montgomery County (part)
1015. Montgomery County (part), city of Dayton, wards 1-6
1016. Morgan County
1017. Morrow County
1018. Muskingum County (part)
1019. Muskingum County (part)
1020. Noble County
1021. Ottawa and Paulding Counties
1022. Perry County
1023. Pickaway County
1024. Pike County
1025. Portage County
1026. Preble County
1027. Putnam County
1028. Richland County (part)
1029. Richland County (part)
1030. Ross County (part)
1031. Ross County (part)
1032. Sandusky County
1033. Scioto County
1034. Seneca County (part)
1035. Seneca County (part)
1036. Shelby County
1037. Stark County (part)
1038. Stark County (part)
1039. Summit County
1040. Trumbull County (part)
1041. Trumbull County (part)
1042. Tuscarawas County (part)
1043. Tuscarawas County (part)
1044. Union County
1045. Van Werk County
1046. Vinton County
1047. Warren County
1048. Washington County (part)
1049. Washington County (part)
1050. Wayne County (part)
1051. Wayne County (part)
1052. Williams County
1053. Wood County
1054. Wyandot County

Oregon.

1055. Benton, Coos, Clackamas, Clatsop, Columbia, Curry, Douglas, Jackson, Josephine, Lane, and Linn Counties

1056. Marion, Multnomah, Polk, Tillamook, Umpqua, Wasco, Washington, and Yamhill Counties

Pennsylvania.

1057. Adams County
1058. Allegheny County (part), city of Pittsburgh, wards 1-3
1059. Allegheny County (part), city of Pittsburgh, wards 4-6
1060. Allegheny County (part), city of Pittsburgh, wards 7-9
1061. Allegheny County (part)
1062. Allegheny County (part)
1063. Allegheny County (part)
1064. Allegheny County (part)
1065. Allegheny County (part)
1066. Allegheny County (part)
1067. Allegheny County (part), city of Allegheny, wards 1-3
1068. Allegheny County (part), city of Allegheny, ward 4
1069. Armstrong County (part)
1070. Armstrong County (part)
1071. Beaver County
1072. Bedford County
1073. Berks County (part)
1074. Berks County (part)
1075. Berks County (part)
1076. Berks County (part)
1077. Berks County (part), city of Reading
1078. Blair County
1079. Bradford County (part)
1080. Bradford County (part)
1081. Bradford County (part)
1082. Bucks County (part)
1083. Bucks County (part)
1084. Bucks County (part)
1085. Bucks County (part)
1086. Butler County (part)
1087. Butler County (part)
1088. Cambria County
1089. Carbon County
1090. Centre County
1091. Chester County (part)
1092. Chester County (part)
1093. Chester County (part)
1094. Chester County (part)
1095. Clarion County
1096. Clearfield County
1097. Clinton County
1098. Columbia County
1099. Crawford County (part)
1100. Crawford County (part)
1101. Cumberland County (part)
1102. Cumberland County (part)
1103. Dauphin County (part)

1104. Dauphin County (part)
1105. Delaware County
1106. Elk County
1107. Erie County (part)
1108. Erie County (part)
1109. Fayette County (part)
1110. Fayette (part) and Forest Counties
1111. Franklin County (part)
1112. Franklin County (part)
1113. Fulton County
1114. Greene County
1115. Huntingdon County
1116. Indiana County (part)
1117. Indiana County (part)
1118. Jefferson County
1119. Juniata County
1120. Lancaster County (part)
1121. Lancaster County (part)
1122. Lancaster County (part)
1123. Lancaster County (part)
1124. Lancaster County (part)
1125. Lancaster County (part)
1126. Lancaster County (part), city of Lancaster
1127. Lawrence County
1128. Lebanon County (part)
1129. Lebanon County (part)
1130. Lehigh County (part)
1131. Lehigh County (part)
1132. Luzerne County (part)
1133. Luzerne County (part)
1134. Luzerne County (part)
1135. Luzerne County (part)
1136. Lycoming County (part)
1137. Lycoming County (part)
1138. McKean County
1139. Mercer County (part)
1140. Mercer County (part)
1141. Mifflin County
1142. Monroe County
1143. Montgomery County (part)
1144. Montgomery County (part)
1145. Montgomery County (part)
1146. Montour County
1147. Northampton County (part)
1148. Northampton County (part)
1149. Northumberland County
1150. Perry County
1151. City of Philadelphia, ward 1
1152. City of Philadelphia, ward 2
1153. City of Philadelphia, ward 3
1154. City of Philadelphia, ward 4
1155. City of Philadelphia, ward 5
1156. City of Philadelphia, ward 6
1157. City of Philadelphia, ward 7
1158. City of Philadelphia, ward 8
1159. City of Philadelphia, ward 9
1160. City of Philadelphia, ward 10
1161. City of Philadelphia, ward 11
1162. City of Philadelphia, ward 12
1163. City of Philadelphia, ward 13
1164. City of Philadelphia, ward 14
1165. City of Philadelphia, ward 15
1166. City of Philadelphia, ward 16
1167. City of Philadelphia, ward 17
1168. City of Philadelphia, ward 18
1169. City of Philadelphia, ward 19 (part)
1170. City of Philadelphia, ward 19 (part)
1171. City of Philadelphia, ward 20
1172. City of Philadelphia, ward 21
1173. City of Philadelphia, ward 22
1174. City of Philadelphia, ward 23
1175. City of Philadelphia, ward 24
1176. Pike County
1177. Potter County
1178. Schuylkill County (part)
1179. Schuylkill County (part)
1180. Schuylkill County (part)
1181. Schuylkill County (part)
1182. Snyder County
1183. Somerset County
1184. Sullivan County
1185. Susquehanna County (part)
1186. Susquehanna County (part)
1187. Tioga County
1188. Union County
1189. Venango County
1190. Warren County
1191. Washington County (part)
1192. Washington County (part)
1193. Wayne County (part)
1194. Wayne County (part)
1195. Westmoreland County (part)
1196. Westmoreland County (part)
1197. Wyoming County
1198. York County (part)
1199. York County (part)
1200. York County (part)
1201. York County (part)

Rhode Island.
1202. Bristol County
1203. Kent County

1204. Newport County

1205. Providence County (part)

1206. Providence County (part)

1207. Providence County (part)

1208. Providence County (part), Providence City, ward 3

1209. Providence County (part), Providence City, wards 1, 6, and 7

1210. Providence County (part), Providence City, wards 2, 4, and 5

1211. Washington County

South Carolina.

FREE SCHEDULES.

1212. Abbeville and Anderson Districts

1213. Barnwell District

1214. Beaufort District

1215. Charleston District (part)

1216. Charleston District (part), city of Charleston, wards 1-8

1217. Chester, Chesterfield, and Clarendon Districts

1218. Colleton and Darlington Districts

1219. Edgefield, Fairfield, and Georgetown Districts

1220. Greenville District

1221. Horry, Kershaw, and Lancaster Districts

1222. Laurens and Lexington Districts

1223. Marion and Marlboro Districts

1224. Newberry and Orangeburg (Orangeburgh) Districts

1225. Pickens District

1226. Spartanburg District

1227. Richland, Sumter, and Union Districts

1228. Williamsburg and York Districts

SLAVE SCHEDULES.

1229. Abbeville, Anderson, and Barnwell Districts

1230. Darlington and Edgefield Districts

1231. Beaufort and Greens

1232. Charleston District

1233. Chester, Chesterfield, Kershaw, Lancaster, and Laurens Districts

1234. Clarendon and Colleton Districts

1235. Fairfield, Georgetown, Horry, and Lexington Districts

1236. Marion, Marlboro, Orangeburg, and Pickens Districts

1237. Newberry, Richland, and Spartanburg Districts

1238. Sumter, Union, Williamsburg, and York Districts

Tennessee.

FREE SCHEDULES.

1239. Anderson and Bedford Counties

1240. Benton, Bledsoe, and Campbell Counties

1241. Blount and Bradley Counties

1242. Cannon and Carter Counties

1243. Carroll and Cheatham Counties

1244. Claiborne, Cocke, and Cumberland Counties

1245. Coffee County

1246. Davidson County

1247. Decatur, De Kalb, and Dickson Counties

1248. Dyer and Fayette Counties

1249. Fentress and Franklin Counties

1250. Gibson and Grainger Counties

1251. Giles County

1252. Greene, Grundy, and Hancock Counties

1253. Hamilton and Hardeman Counties

1254. Hardin and Haywood Counties

1255. Hawkins County

1256. Henderson and Henry Counties

1257. Hickman and Humphreys Counties

1258. Jackson and Jefferson Counties

1259. Johnson and Knox Counties

1260. Lauderdale, Lawrence, and Lewis Counties

1261. Lincoln County

1262. McMinn and McNairy Counties

1263. Macon, Madison, and Marion Counties

1264. Maury County

1265. Marshall, Meigs, and Monroe Counties

1266. Montgomery and Morgan Counties

1267. Obion and Overton Counties

1268. Perry, Polk, and Rhea Counties

1269. Putnam and Roane Counties

1270. Robertson and Sevier Counties

1271. Rutherford, Scott, and Sequatchie Counties

1272. Smith and Stewart Counties

1273. Shelby County

1274. Warren County

1275. Sullivan and Sumner Counties

1276. Tipton and Union Counties

1277. Van Buren, Washington, and Wayne Counties

1278. Weakley County

1279. White and Williamson Counties

1280. Wilson County

SLAVE SCHEDULES.

1281. Anderson, Bedford, Benton, Blount, Bradley, Campbell, Cannon, Carroll, Carter, Cheatham, Claiborne, Cocke, Coffee, Cumberland, Davidson, Decatur, De Kalb, Dickson, Dyer, and Fentress Counties

1282. Fayette, Franklin, Gibson, Giles, Grainger, Greene, Grundy, Hamilton, Hancock, Hardeman, Hardin, and Hawkins Counties

1283. Haywood, Henderson, Henry, Hickman, Humphreys, Jackson, Jefferson, Johnson, Knox, Lauderdale, Lawrence, Lewis, Lincoln, McMinn, McNairy, and Macon Counties

1284. Madison, Marion, Marshall, Maury, Meigs, Monroe, Montgomery, Morgan, Obion, Overton, Perry, Polk, and Putnam Counties

1285. Rhea, Roane, Robertson, Rutherford, Scott, Sequatchie, Sevier, Shelby, Smith, Steward, and Sullivan Counties

1286. Sumner, Tipton, Union, Van Buren, Warren, Washington, Wayne, Weakley, White, Williamson, and Wilson Counties

Texas.

FREE SCHEDULES.

1287. Anderson, Angelina, Atascosa, Austin, and Bandera Counties

1288. Bastrop, Bell, and Bexar Counties

1289. Bowie, Bosque, Brazoria, Brazos, Brown, Burleson, Burnett, Caldwell, Calhoun, Comanche, and Cameron Counties

1290. Cass and Cherokee Counties

1291. Chambers, Collin, Colorado, Comal, and Cooke Counties

1292. Coryell, Dallas, Dawson. Denton. and De Witt Counties

1293. Eastland, Ellis, El Paso, Presidio, Encinal, Erath, Falls, and Fannin Counties

1294. Fayette, Fort Bend, Freestone, and Galveston Counties

1295. Gillespie, Goliad, Gonzales, Grayson, and Grimes Counties

1296. Guadalupe, Hamilton, Hardin, Harris, and Harrison Counties

1297. Hays, Henderson, Hidalgo, Hill, Hopkins, and Houston Counties

1298. Hunt, Jack, Jackson, Jasper, Jefferson, and Johnson Counties

1299. Karnes, Kaufman, Kerr, Kinney, Lamar, Lampasas, Lavaca, and Leon Counties

1300. Liberty, Limestone, Live Oak, Llano, McLennan, Madison, Marion, Mason, Matagorda, and Maverick Counties

1301. Medina, Milam, Montague, Clay, Montgomery, Nacogdoches, and Navarro Counties

1302. Newton, Nueces (part), Orange, Palo Pinto, Buchanan, Shackelford, Panola, and Parker Counties

1303. Polk, Red River, Refugio, Bee, and Robertson Counties

1304. Rusk, Sabine, San Augustine, San Patricio, Nueces (part), San Saba, and Shelby Counties

1305. Smith, Starr, and Titus Counties

1306. Travis, Trinity, Tyler, and Upshur Counties

1307. Uvalde, Van Zandt, Victoria, Walker, and Washington Counties

1308. Webb, Wharton, Williamson, Wise, Wood, Young, Trockmorton, Zapata, Zavala, and Frio Counties

SLAVE SCHEDULES.

1309. Anderson, Angelina, Atascosa, Austin, Bandera, Bastrop, Bell, Bexar, Bowie, Bosque, Brazoria, Brazos, Buchanan, Shackelford, Burleson, Burnet, Caldwell, Calhoun, Comanche, Cameron, Hidalgo, Cass, Chambers, Cherokee, Collin, Colorado, Comal, Cooke, Montague, Coryell, Dallas, Denton, De Witt, Ellis, El Paso, Presidio, Erath, and Falls Counties

1310. Fannin, Fayette, Fort Bend, Freestone, Galveston, Guadalupe, Gillespie, Goliad, Gonzales, Grayson, Grimes, Hamilton, Hardin, Harris, Harrison, Hays, Henderson, Hill, Hopkins, Houston, and Hunt Counties

1311. Jack, Jackson, Jasper, Jefferson, Johnson, Karnes, Kaufman, Kerr, Lamar, Lampasas, Lavaca, Leon, Liberty, Limestone, Llano, McLennan, Madison, Marion, Mason, Matagorda, Maverick, Medina, Milam, Montgomery, Nacogdoches, Navarro, Newton, Nueces, Live Oak, San Patricio, Orange, Palo Pinto, Panola, Parker, Polk, Red River, Refugio, and Bee Counties

1312. Robertson, Rusk, Sabine, San Augustine, San Saba, Shelby, Smith, Starr, Titus, Travis, Trinity, Tyler, Upshur, Uvalde, Van Zandt, Victoria, Walker, Washington, Wharton, Williamson, Wise, Wood, and Young Counties

Utah.

1313. Salt Lake, Great Salt Lake, Tooele, Green River, Summit, Davis, Weber, and Box Elder Counties

1314. Cache, Sanpete, Millard, Beaver, Iron, Juab, Utah, Washington, Shambie, Cedar, St. Marys, Humbolt (Humboldt), and Carson Counties and Slave Schedules

Vermont.

1315. Addison County

1316. Bennington County

1317. Caledonia County

1318. Grand Isle and Lamoille Counties

1319. Chittenden County

1320. Essex County

1321. Franklin County

1322. Orleans County

1323. Orange County

1324. Washington County

1325. Windham County

1326. Rutland County (part)

1327. Rutland County (part)

1328. Windsor County (part)

1329. Windsor County (part)

Virginia.

FREE SCHEDULES.

1330. Accomack County

1331. Albemarle and Alexandria Counties

1332. Alleghany, Amelia, Amherst, and Appomattox Counties

1333. Augusta County

1334. Barbour and Bath Counties

1335. Bedford and Berkeley Counties

1336. Boone, Botetourt, and Braxton Counties

1337. Brooke, Brunswick, Buchanan, and Buckingham Counties

1338. Cabell and Campbell Counties

1339. Caroline and Carroll Counties

1340. Calhoun, Clay, Charles City, Charlotte, and Chesterfield Counties
1341. Clarke, Craig, Culpeper, and Cumberland Counties
1342. Dinwiddie and Doddridge Counties
1343. Elizabeth City, Essex, and Fairfax Counties
1344. Fauquier and Fayette Counties
1345. Floyd, Fluvanna, Giles, and Gilmer Counties
1346. Franklin County
1347. Frederick, Gloucester, and Goochland Counties
1348. Grayson and Greenbrier Counties
1349. Greene, Greensville, Halifax, and Hancock Counties
1350. Hampshire and Hanover Counties
1351. Hardy and Harrison Counties
1352. Henrico County, city of Richmond, wards 1 and 2
1353. Henrico County, city of Richmond, ward 3, eastern division and western subdivision
1354. Henry, Highland, Isle of Wight, and Jackson Counties
1355. James City and Jefferson Counties
1356. Kanawha and King George Counties
1357. King and Queen, King William, Lancaster, and Lee Counties
1358. Lewis and Logan Counties
1359. Loudoun, Louisa, and Lunenburg Counties
1360. Madison and Marshall Counties
1361. Marion and Mason Counties
1362. Mathews, McDowell, Mecklenburg, and Mercer Counties
1363. Middlesex, Montgomery, and Monroe Counties
1364. Monongalia and Morgan Counties
1365. Nansemond, Nelson, New Kent, and Nicholas Counties
1366. Norfolk County
1367. Northampton, Northumberland, and Nottoway Counties
1368. Ohio County
1369. Orange, Page, and Patrick Counties
1370. Pendleton and Pittsylvania Counties
1371. Pleasants, Pocahontas, Powhatan, and Prince Edward Counties
1372. Preston and Prince George Counties
1373. Prince William, Princess Anne, Pulaski, Putnam, and Raleigh Counties
1374. Randolph, Rappahannock, Richmond, and Ritchie Counties
1375. Roane, Roanoke, and Stafford Counties
1376. Russell and Scott Counties
1377. Shenandoah and Smyth Counties
1378. Rockbridge County
1379. Rockingham and Surry Counties
1380. Southampton, Spotsylvania, and Sussex Counties
1381. Taylor, Tazewell, Tucker, and Warren Counties
1382. Tyler, Upshur, and Warwick Counties
1383. Washington, Wayne, Webster, and Westmoreland Counties

1384. Wetzel, Wirt, Wise, and Wood Counties
1385. Wyoming, Wythe, and York Counties

SLAVE SCHEDULES.
1386. Accomack, Albemarle, Alleghany, Amelia, Amherst, and Appomattox Counties
1387. Augusta, Barbour, Bath, Bedford, Berkeley, Boone, Botetourt, Braxton, Brooke, Brunswick, Buchanan, Buckingham, Cabell, and Calhoun Counties
1388. Campbell, Caroline, Carroll, Charles City, Charlotte, and Chesterfield Counties
1389. Clarke, Clay, Craig, Culpeper, Cumberland, Dinwiddie, Doddridge, Elizabeth City, Essex, and Fairfax Counties
1390. Fauquier, Fayette, Floyd, Fluvanna, Franklin, Frederick, Giles, Gilmer, Gloucester, Goochland, Grayson, Greenbrier, and Greene Counties
1391. Greensville, Halifax, Hampshire, Hanover, Hardy, Harrison, Henry, Highland, Isle of Wight, and Jackson Counties
1392. Henrico, James City, Jefferson, Kanawha, King George, King and Queen, and King William Counties
1393. Lancaster, Lee, Lewis, Logan, Loudoun, Louisa, Lunenburg, Madison, Marion, Marshall, Mason, and Mathews Counties
1394. Mecklenburg, Mercer, Middlesex, Monongalia, Monroe, Montgomery, Morgan, Nansemond, Nelson, New Kent, Nicholas, and Norfolk Counties
1395. Northampton, Northumberland, Nottoway, Ohio, Orange, Page, Patrick, Pendleton, Pittsylvania, Pleasants, Pocahontas, and Powhatan Counties
1396. Preston, Prince Edward, Prince George, Prince William, Princess Anne, Pulaski, Putnam, Raleigh, Randolph, Rappahannock, Richmond, Ritchie, Roane, Roanoke, Rockbridge, Rockingham, Russell, Scott, Shenandoah, and Smyth Counties
1397. Southampton, Spotsylvania, Stafford, Surry, Sussex, Tazewell, Tucker, Tyler, Upshur, Warwick, Warren, Washington, Wayne, Webster, Westmoreland, Wetzel, Wirt, Wise, Wood, Wyoming, Wythe, and York Counties

Washington.
1398. Island, Whatcom, Clallam, Kitsap, Jefferson, Klickitat, Pacific, Chehalis, Clark, Cowlitz, Skamania, Spokane, Snohomish, Thurston, Lewis, Pierce, King, and Walla Walla Counties

Wisconsin.
1399. Adams and Bad Ax Counties
1400. Brown, Buffalo, and Calumet Counties
1401. Ashland, Chippewa, Clark, and Columbia Counties
1402. Crawford, Door, and Douglas Counties
1403. Dane County (part)

1404. Dane County (part)
1405. Dodge County (part)
1406. Dodge County (part)
1407. Dunn, Eau Claire, and Fond du Lac (part), Counties
1408. Fond du Lac County (part)
1409. Grant County
1410. Green Lake County
1411. Green County
1412. Iowa and Jackson Counties
1413. Jefferson County
1414. Juneau County
1415. Kenosha and Kewaunee Counties
1416. Lafayette and La Pointe Counties
1417. La Crosse County
1418. Manitowoc and Marathon Counties
1419. Marquette County
1420. Milwaukee County (part)
1421. City of Milwaukee, wards 1 and 7
1422. City of Milwaukee, wards 2, 3, and 4
1423. City of Milwaukee, wards 5, 6,8, and 9
1424. Monroe, Oconto, and Outagamie Counties
1425. Ozaukee County
1426. Pepin, Pierce, and Portage Counties
1427. Racine County
1428. Richland, Saint Croix, Polk, Burnett, and Dallas Counties
1429. Sauk and Shawano Counties
1430. Rock County (part)
1431. Rock County (part)
1432. Sheboygan County
1433. Waupaca County
1434. Trempealeau and Walworth Counties
1435. Waushara County
1436. Waukesha County
1437. Winnebago and Wood Counties
1438. Washington County

Ninth Census of the United States, 1870. M593. 1,748 rolls.

Alabama.

1. Autauga, Baker, and Baldwin Counties
2. Barbour and Bibb Counties
3. Blount County
4. Bullock County
5. Butler and Calhoun Counties
6. Chambers County
7. Cherokee and Choctaw Counties
8. Clarke and Clay Counties
9. Cleburne and Coffee Counties
10. Colbert and Conecuh Counties
11. Coosa and Covington Counties

12. Crenshaw and Dale Counties
13. Dallas County (part)
14. Dallas County (part)
15. De Kalb, Elmore, and Escambia Counties
16. Etowah, Fayette, and Franklin Counties
17. Geneva and Greene Counties
18. Hale County
19. Henry County
20. Jackson County
21. Jefferson and Lauderdale Counties
22. Lawrence County
23. Lee County
24. Limestone County
25. Lowndes County
26. Macon County (part)
27. Macon (part) and Madison Counties
28. Marengo County
29. Marion and Marshall Counties
30. Mobile County (excluding the city of Mobile)
31. City of Mobile
32. Monroe and Morgan Counties
33. Perry County
34. Montgomery County (excluding the city of Montgomery)
35. City of Montgomery
36. Pickens County
37. Pike and Randolph Counties
38. Russell County
39. Sanford and Shelby Counties
40. St. Clair and Sumpter Counties
41. Talladega County
42. Tallapoosa County
43. Tuscaloosa County
44. Walker and Washington Counties
45. Wilcox and Winston Counties

Arizona.

46. Entire territory

Arkansas.

47. Arkansas, Ashley, and Benton Counties
48. Boone, Bradley, and Calhoun Counties
49. Carroll, Chicot, and Clark Counties
50. Columbia and Conway Counties
51. Craighead, Crawford, and Crittenden Counties
52. Cross, Dallas, Desha, and Drew Counties
53. Franklin, Fulton, and Grant Counties
54. Greene, Hempstead, and Hot Springs Counties
55. Independence and Izard Counties
56. Jackson and Jefferson Counties
57. Johnson and Lafayette Counties
58. Lawrence, Little River, Madison, Marion, and Mississippi

Counties

59. Monroe, Montgomery, Newton, Ouachita, and Perry Counties
60. Phillips, Pike, and Poinsett Counties
61. Polk, Pope, and Prairie Counties
62. Pulaski County
63. Randolph, Saline, and Scott Counties
64. Searcy, Sebastian, and Sevier Counties
65. Sharp, St. Francis, and Union Counties
66. Van Buren and Washington Counties
67. White, Woodruff, and Yell Counties

California.

68. Alameda County
69. Alpine and Amador Counties
70. Butte and Calaveras Counties
71. Colusa, Contra Costa, and Del Norte Counties
72. El Dorado, Fresno, and Humboldt Counties
73. Inyo, Kern, Klamath, Lake, Lassen, and Los Angeles Counties
74. Mann, Marin, Mariposa, Mendocino, Merced, Mono, and Monterey Counties
75. Napa and Nevada Counties
76. Placer County
77. Plumas and Sacramento Counties
78. San Bernardino and San Diego Counties
79. City of San Francisco, wards 1-3
80. City of San Francisco, ward 4
81. City of San Francisco, wards 5-7
82. City of San Francisco, ward 8
83. City of San Francisco, wards 9 and 10
84. City of San Francisco, ward 11
85. City of San Francisco, ward 12
86. San Joaquin County
87. San Luis Obispo, San Mateo, and Santa Barbara Counties
88. Santa Clara County
89. Santa Cruz, Shasta, Sierra, and Siskiyou Counties
90. Solano County
91. Sonoma County
92. Stanislaus, Sutter, Tehama, Trinity, and Tulare Counties
93. Tuolumne, Yolo, and Yuba Counties

Colorado.

94. Arapahoe, Bent, Boulder, Clear Creek, Summit (part), Conejos, Costilla, Douglas, and El Paso Counties
95. Fremont, Gilpin, Greenwood, Huerfano, Jefferson, Lake, Larimer, Las Animas, Pueblo, Saguache, Summit (part), and Weld Counties

Connecticut.

96. Fairfield (part) County

97. Fairfield (part) County
98. Fairfield (part) County
99. Fairfield (part) County
100. City of Hartford, wards 1-3
101. City of Hartford, wards 4-6
102. Hartford County (part)(excluding the city of Hartford)
103. Hartford County (part) (excluding the city of Hartford)
104. Hartford County (part) (excluding the city of Hartford)
105. Litchfield County (part)
106. Litchfield County (part)
107. Middlesex County (part)
108. Middlesex County (part)
109. City of New Haven, wards 1-3
110. City of New Haven, wards 4-8
111. New Haven County (part) (excluding the city of New Haven)
112. New Haven County (part) (excluding the city of New Haven)
113. New London County (part)
114. New London County (part)
115. Tolland County
116. Windham County (part)
117. Windham County (part)

Dakota.

118. Entire territory

Delaware.

119. Kent County
120. New Castle County (excluding the city of Wilmington)
121. City of Wilmington
122. Sussex County

District of Columbia.

123. Wards 1 and 2
124. Wards 3 and 4
125. Wards 5 and 6
126. Ward 7
127. Georgetown, east of 7th Street, and west part

Florida.

128. Alachua, Baker, Bradford, Brevard, Calhoun, Clay, and Columbia Counties
129. Dade, Duval, Escambia, Franklin, and Gadsden Counties
130. Hamilton, Hernando, Hillsborough, Holmes, and Jackson Counties
131. Jefferson, Lafayette, Leon, Levy, and Liberty Counties
132. Madison, Manatee, Marion, Monroe, and Nassau Counties
133. Orange, Polk, Putnam, Santa Rosa, St. Johns, Sumter, Suwanee, Taylor, Volusia, Wakulla, Walton, and Washington Counties

Georgia.

134. Appling, Baker, Baldwin, and Banks Counties
135. Bartow and Berrien Counties
136. Bibb County
137. Brooks, Bryan, and Bulloch Counties
138. Burke, Butts, and Calhoun Counties
139. Camden, Campbell, and Carroll Counties
140. Catoosa, Charlton, and Chatham (excluding the city of Savannah) Counties
141. City of Savannah
142. Chattahoochee and Chattooga Counties
143. Cherokee and Clarke Counties
144. Clay, Clayton, Clinch, Cobb, Coffee, and Colquitt Counties
145. Columbia and Coweta Counties
146. Crawford, Dade, Dawson, and Decatur Counties
147. De Kalb, Dooly, and Dougherty Counties
148. Early, Echols, Effingham, Elbert, Emanuel, and Fannin Counties
149. Fayette and Floyd Counties
150. Forsyth and Franklin Counties
151. Fulton County
152. Gilmer, Glascock, and Glynn Counties
153. Gordon and Greene Counties
154. Gwinnett and Habersham Counties
155. Hall and Hancock Counties
156. Haralson and Harris Counties
157. Hart, Heard, and Henry Counties
158. Houston and Irwin Counties
159. Jackson and Jasper Counties
160. Jefferson, Johnson, and Jones Counties
161. Laurens and Lee Counties
162. Liberty and Lincoln Counties
163. Lowndes, Lumpkin, and Macon Counties
164. Madison, Marion, and McIntosh Counties
165. Meriwether, Miller, and Milton Counties
166. Mitchell, Monroe, and Montgomery Counties
167. Morgan, Murray, and Muscogee Counties
168. Newton, Oglethorpe, and Paulding Counties
169. Pickens, Pierce, and Pike Counties
170. Polk and Pulaski Counties
171. Putnam, Quitman, Rabun, and Randolph Counties
172. Richmond County
173. Schley, Screven, and Spalding Counties
174. Stewart, and Sumter Counties
175. Talbot, Taliaferro, and Tattnall Counties
176. Taylor, Telfair, and Terrell Counties
177. Thomas and Towns Counties
178. Troup and Twiggs Counties
179. Union and Upson Counties
180. Walker and Walton Counties
181. Ware and Warren Counties
182. Washington, Wayne, and Webster Counties
183. White, Whitfield, and Wilcox Counties
184. Wilkes, Wilkinson, and Worth Counties

Idaho.

185. Entire territory

Illinois.

186. Adams County (part)
187. Adams County (part)
188. Alexander and Bond Counties
189. Boone and Brown Counties
190. Bureau County
191. Calhoun and Carroll Counties
192. Cass County
193. Champaign County
194. Christian County
195. Clark County
196. Clay and Clinton Counties
197. Coles County
198. City of Chicago, wards 1 and 2
199. City of Chicago, ward 3
200. City of Chicago, wards 4 and 5
201. City of Chicago, ward 6
202. City of Chicago, ward 7
203. City of Chicago, ward 8
204. City of Chicago, ward 9
205. City of Chicago, ward 10
206. City of Chicago, wards 11 and 12
207. City of Chicago, wards 13 and 14
208. City of Chicago, ward 15
209. City of Chicago, wards 16 and 17
210. City of Chicago, ward 18
211. City of Chicago, wards 19 and 20
212. Cook County (part) (excluding the city of Chicago)
213. Cook County (part) (excluding the city of Chicago)
214. Crawford and Cumberland Counties
215. De Kalb County
216. De Witt and Douglas Counties
217. Du Page County
218. Edgar County
219. Edwards and Effingham Counties
220. Fayette County
221. Ford and Franklin Counties
222. Fulton County (part)
223. Fulton County (part)
224. Gallatin and Greene Counties
225. Grundy and Hamilton Counties
226. Hancock County (part)
227. Hancock County (part)

228. Hardin and Henderson Counties
229. Henry County (part)
230. Henry County (part)
231. Iroquois County
232. Jackson and Jasper Counties
233. Jefferson and Jersey Counties
234. Jo Daviess County
235. Johnson County
236. Kane County (part)
237. Kane County (part)
238. Kankakee County
239. Kendall County
240. Knox County (part)
241. Knox County (part)
242. Lake County
243. La Salle County (part)
244. La Salle County (part)
245. Lawrence County
246. Lee County
247. Livingston County
248. Logan County
249. Macon County
250. Macoupin County
251. Madison County (part)
252. Madison County (part)
253. Marion County
254. Marshall County
255. Mason and Massac Counties
256. McDonough County
257. McHenry County
258. McLean County (part)
259. McLean County (part)
260. Menard and Mercer Counties
261. Monroe County
262. Montgomery County
263. Morgan County
264. Moultrie County
265. Ogle County
266. Peoria County (excluding the city of Peoria)
267. City of Peoria and Peoria County (part) (excluding the city of Peoria)
268. Perry and Piatt Counties
269. Pike County
270. Pope County
271. Pulaski and Putnam Counties
272. Randolph and Richland Counties
273. Rock Island County
274. Saline County
275. Stephenson County
276. Schuyler and Scott Counties
277. Shelby County

278. Stark County
279. St. Clair County (part)
280. St. Clair County (part)
281. Sangamon County (part)
282. Sangamon County (part)
283. Tazewell County
284. Union County
285. Vermilion County
286. Wabash and Warren Counties
287. Washington County
288. Wayne County
289. White County
290. Whiteside County
291. Will County (part)
292. Will County (part)
293. Williamson County
294. Winnebago County
295. Woodford County

Indiana.
296. Adams County
297. Allen County (part)
298. Allen County (part)
299. Bartholomew and Benton Counties
300. Blackford and Boone Counties
301. Brown and Carroll Counties
302. Cass County
303. Clark County
304. Clay County
305. Clinton County
306. Crawford and Daviess Counties
307. Dearborn County
308. Decatur County
309. De Kalb County
310. Delaware and Dubois Counties
311. Elkhart County
312. Fayette County
313. Floyd County
314. Fountain County
315. Franklin County
316. Fulton and Gibson Counties
317. Grant County
318. Greene County
319. Hamilton County
320. Hancock County
321. Harrison County
322. Hendricks County
323. Henry County
324. Howard County
325. Huntington County
326. Jackson and Jasper Counties

327. Jay County
328. Jefferson County
329. Jennings County
330. Johnson County
331. Knox County
332. Kosciusko County
333. Lagrange and Lake Counties
334. La Porte County
335. Lawrence County
336. Madison County
337. Marion County (excluding the city of Indianapolis)
338. City of Indianapolis (second enumeration), wards 1-4
339. City of Indianapolis (second enumeration), wards 5-9
340. City of Indianapolis (first enumeration), wards 1-4
341. City of Indianapolis (first enumeration), wards 5-9
342. Marshall and Martin Counties
343. Miami County
344. Monroe County
345. Montgomery County
346. Morgan County
347. Newton, Noble, and Ohio Counties
348. Orange and Owen Counties
349. Parke County
350. Perry and Pike Counties
351. Porter County
352. Posey and Pulaski Counties
353. Putnam County
354. Randolph County
355. Ripley County
356. Rush County
357. Scott and Shelby Counties
358. Spencer County
359. Starke and Steuben Counties
360. St. Joseph County
361. Sullivan and Switzerland Counties
362. Tippecanoe County
363. Tipton and Union Counties
364. Vanderburgh County
365. Vermillion County
366. Vigo County
367. Wabash County
368. Warren and Warrick Counties
369. Washington County
370. Wayne County (part)
371. Wayne County (part)
372. Wells County
373. White and Whitley Counties

Iowa.

374. Adair, Adams, and Allamakee Counties
375. Appanoose and Audubon Counties

376. Benton County
377. Black Hawk County
378. Boone and Bremer Counties
379. Buchanan, Buena Vista, and Butler Counties
380. Calhoun, Carroll, Cass, and Cedar Counties
381. Cerro Gordo, Cherokee, and Chickasaw Counties
382. Clarke and Clay Counties
383. Clayton County
384. Clinton County (part)
385. Clinton (part), Crawford, and Dallas Counties
386. Davis and Decatur Counties
387. Delaware County
388. Des Moines and Dickinson Counties
389. Dubuque County (part)
390. Dubuque County (part)
391. Emmet and Fayette Counties
392. Floyd, Franklin, and Fremont Counties
393. Greene, Grundy, and Guthrie Counties
394. Hamilton, Hancock, and Hardin Counties
395. Harrison and Henry Counties
396. Howard, Humboldt, Ida, and Iowa Counties
397. Jackson County
398. Jasper County
399. Jefferson County
400. Johnson County
401. Jones County
402. Keokuk and Kossuth Counties
403. Lee County (part)
404. Lee County (part)
405. Linn County
406. Louisa, Lucas, Lyon, and Osceola Counties
407. Madison County
408. Mahaska County
409. Marion County
410. Marshall County
411. Mills and Mitchell Counties
412. Monona and Monroe Counties
413. Montgomery and Muscatine Counties
414. O'Brien and Page Counties
415. Palo Alto, Plymouth, Pocahontas, and Polk Counties
416. Pottawattamie County
417. Poweshiek, Ringgold, and Sac Counties
418. Scott County (part)
419. Scott County (part)
420. Shelby, Sioux, Story, and Tama Counties
421. Taylor, Union, and Van Buren Counties
422. Wapello County
423. Warren County
424. Washington County
425. Wayne and Webster Counties
426. Winnebago and Winneshiek Counties

427. Woodbury, Worth, and Wright Counties

Kansas.

428. Allen, Anderson, and Atchison Counties
429. Barton, Bourbon, Brown, and Butler Counties
430. Chase, Cherokee, Clay, and Cloud Counties
431. Coffey, Cowley, Crawford, and Davis Counties
432. Dickinson and Doniphan Counties
433. Douglas County
434. Ellis, Ellsworth, Ford, Franklin, Greenwood, and Howard Counties
435. Jackson, Jefferson, Jewell, and Johnson Counties
436. Labette County
437. Leavenworth County
438. Lincoln, Linn, Lyon, Marion, and Marshall Counties
439. McPherson, Miami, Mitchell, Montgomery, and Morris Counties
440. Nemaha, Neosho, Ness, and Osage Counties
441. Osborne, Ottawa, Pawnee, Pottawatomie, Republic, Rice, Riley, and Russell Counties
442. Saline, Sedgwick, Shawnee, Smith, Sumner, Trego, Wabaunsee, Wallace, and Washington Counties
443. Wilson, Woodson, and Wyandotte Counties

Kentucky.

444. Adair, Allen, and Anderson Counties
445. Ballard and Barren Counties
446. Bath and Boone Counties
447. Bourbon County
448. Boyd and Boyle Counties
449. Bracken and Breathitt Counties
450. Breckinridge and Bullitt Counties
451. Butler and Caldwell Counties
452. Calloway County
453. Campbell County
454. Carroll, Carter, and Casey Counties
455. Christian County
456. Clark and Clay Counties
457. Clinton and Crittenden Counties
458. Cumberland and Daviess Counties
459. Edmonson, Elliott, and Estill Counties
460. Fayette County
461. Fleming and Floyd Counties
462. Franklin, Fulton, and Gallatin Counties
463. Garrard and Grant Counties
464. Graves County
465. Grayson and Green Counties
466. Greenup and Hancock Counties
467. Hardin County
468. Harlan, Harrison, and Hart Counties
469. Henderson County

470. Henry and Hickman Counties
471. Hopkins and Jackson Counties
472. Jefferson County (excluding the city of Louisville)
473. City of Louisville, wards 1-3
474. City of Louisville, wards 4-6
475. City of Louisville, wards 7-10
476. City of Louisville, wards 11-12
477. Jessamine, Johnson, and Josh Bell Counties
478. Kenton County (part)
479. Kenton County (part)
480. Knox, Larue, Laurel, and Lawrence Counties
481. Lee, Letcher, and Lewis Counties
482. Lincoln and Livingston Counties
483. Logan County
484. Lyon, Madison, and Magoffin Counties
485. Marion and Marshall Counties
486. Mason County
487. McCracken, McLean, and Meade Counties
488. Menifee and Mercer Counties
489. Metcalfe, Monroe, and Montgomery Counties
490. Morgan and Muhlenberg Counties
491. Nelson and Nicholas Counties
492. Ohio County
493. Oldham and Owen Counties
494. Owsley, Pendleton, and Perry Counties
495. Pike and Powell Counties
496. Pulaski and Robertson Counties
497. Rockcastle, Rowan, Russell, and Scott Counties
498. Shelby County
499. Simpson, Spencer, and Taylor Counties
500. Todd County
501. Trigg, Trimble, and Union Counties
502. Warren and Washington Counties
503. Wayne and Webster Counties
504. Whitley, Wolfe, and Woodford Counties

Louisiana.

505. Ascension and Assumption Parishes
506. Avoyelles Parish
507. Bienville and Bossier Parishes
508. Caddo Parish
509. Calcasieu, Caldwell, Cameron, Carroll, and Catahoula Parishes
510. Claiborne Parish
511. Concordia and De Soto Parishes
512. East Baton Rouge and East Feliciana Parishes
513. Franklin, Grant, and Iberia Parishes
514. Iberville and Jackson Parishes
515. Jefferson Parish
516. Lafayette and Lafourche Parishes
517. Livingston, Madison, and Morehouse Parishes

518. Natchitoches Parish
519. City of New Orleans, wards 1 and 2
520. City of New Orleans, ward 3
521. City of New Orleans, wards 4 and 5
522. City of New Orleans, wards 6 and 7
523. City of New Orleans, wards 8 and 9
524. City of New Orleans, wards 10 and 11
525. City of New Orleans, wards 12-14
526. Ouachita and Plaquemines Parishes
527. Pointe Coupee Parish
528. Rapides, Richland, Sabine, and St. Bernard Parishes
529. St. Charles, St. Helena, St. James, and St. John the Baptist Parishes
530. St. Landry Parish
531. St. Martin and St. Mary Parishes
532. St. Tammany, Tangipahoa and Tensas Parishes
533. Terrebonne Parish
534. Union and Vermilion Parishes
535. Washington, West Baton Rouge, West Feliciana, and Winn Parishes

Maine.
536. Androscoggin County (part)
537. Androscoggin County (part)
538. Aroostook County
539. Cumberland County (part) (excluding the city of Portland)
540. Cumberland County (part) (excluding the city of Portland)
541. City of Portland, wards 1-7, and city of Portland Islands
542. Cumberland County (part) (excluding the city of Portland)
543. Franklin County
544. Hancock County (part)
545. Hancock County (part)
546. Kennebec County (part)
547. Kennebec County (part)
548. Knox County
549. Lincoln County
550. Oxford County (part)
551. Oxford County (part)
552. Penobscot County (part)
553. Penobscot County (part)
554. Penobscot County (part)
555. Penobscot County (part)
556. Piscataquis County
557. Sagadahoc County
558. Somerset County (part)
559. Somerset County (part)
560. Waldo County (part)
561. Waldo County (part)
562. Washington County (part)
563. Washington County (part)
564. York County (part)
565. York County (part)

Maryland.
566. Allegany County (part)
567. Allegany County (part)
568. Anne Arundel County
569. Baltimore County (part) (excluding the city of Baltimore)
570. Baltimore County (part) (excluding the city of Baltimore)
571. City of Baltimore, wards 1 and 2
572. City of Baltimore, ward 3
573. City of Baltimore, wards 4 and 5
574. City of Baltimore, wards 6 and 7
575. City of Baltimore, wards 8-10
576. City of Baltimore, wards 11 and 12
577. City of Baltimore, wards 13 and 14
578. City of Baltimore, wards 15 and 16
579. City of Baltimore, wards 17 and 18
580. City of Baltimore, wards 19 and 20
581. Calvert and Caroline Counties
582. Carroll County
583. Cecil County
584. Charles County
585. Dorchester County
586. Frederick County (part)
587. Frederick County (part)
588. Harford County
589. Howard County
590. Kent County
591. Montgomery County
592. Prince Georges County
593. Queen Annes County
594. St. Mary's County
595. Somerset and Talbot Counties
596. Washington County (part)
597. Washington County (part)
598. Wicomico County
599. Worcester County

Massachusetts.
600. Barnstable County
601. Berkshire County (part)
602. Berkshire County (part)
603. Bristol County (part)
604. Bristol County (part)
605. Bristol County (part)
606. Bristol (part) and Dukes Counties
607. Essex County (part) (excluding the cities of Lawrence, Lynn, and Salem)
608. Essex County (part) (excluding the cities of Lawrence, Lynn, and Salem)
609. City of Lawrence

610. City of Lynn

611. Essex County (part) (excluding the cities of Lawrence, Lynn, and Salem)

612. Essex County (part) (excluding the cities of Lawrence, Lynn, and Salem)

613. City of Salem

614. Essex County (part) (excluding the cities of Lawrence, Lynn, and Salem)

615. Franklin County

616. Hampden County (part) (excluding the city of Springfield)

617. Hampden County (part) (excluding the city of Springfield)

618. City of Springfield

619. Hampden County (part) (excluding the city of Springfield)

620. Hampshire County (part)

621. Hampshire County (part)

622. Middlesex County (part) (excluding the cities of Cambridge and Lowell)

623. City of Cambridge, wards 1 and 2

624. City of Cambridge, wards 3-5

625. Middlesex County (part) (excluding the cities of Cambridge and Lowell)

626. Middlesex County (part) (excluding the cities of Cambridge and Lowell)

627. City of Lowell, wards 1 and 2

628. City of Lowell, wards 3-6

629. Middlesex County (part) (excluding the cities of Cambridge and Lowell)

630. Middlesex County (part) (excluding the cities of Cambridge and Lowell)

631. Middlesex County (part) (excluding the cities of Cambridge and Lowell)

632. Middlesex County (part) (excluding the cities of Cambridge and Lowell)

633. Middlesex County (part) (excluding the cities of Cambridge and Lowell)

634. Nantucket and Norfolk (part) Counties

635. Norfolk County (part)

636. Norfolk County (part)

637. Norfolk County (part)

638. Plymouth County (part)

639. Plymouth County (part)

640. City of Boston, ward 1

641. City of Boston, ward 2

642. City of Boston, wards 3 and 4

643. City of Boston, wards 5 and 6

644. City of Boston, ward 7

645. City of Boston, wards 8 and 9

646. City of Boston, ward 10

647. City of Boston, wards 11 and 12

648. City of Boston, wards 13 and 14

649. City of Boston, wards 15 and 16

650. Suffolk (excluding the city of Boston) County

651. Worcester County (part) (excluding the city of Worcester)

652. Worcester County (part) (excluding the city of Worcester)

653. Worcester County (part) (excluding the city of Worcester)

654. Worcester County (part) (excluding the city of Worcester)

655. Worcester County (part) (excluding the city of Worcester)

656. Worcester County (part) (excluding the city of Worcester)

657. Worcester County (part) (excluding the city of Worcester)

658. City of Worcester, wards 1-4

659. City of Worcester, wards 5-8

Michigan.

660. Alcona and Allegan Counties

661. Alpena, Antrim, and Barry Counties

662. Bay and Benzie Counties

663. Berrien County (part)

664. Berrien County (part)

665. Branch County

666. Calhoun County (part)

667. Calhoun County (part)

668. Cass County

669. Charlevoix, Cheboygan, Chippewa, Clare, and Clinton Counties

670. Delta, Eaton, and Emmet Counties

671. Genesee County

672. Grand Traverse and Gratiot Counties

673. Hillsdale County

674. Houghton and Huron Counties

675. Ingham County

676. Ionia County

677. Iosco and Isabella Counties

678. Jackson County (part)

679. Jackson County (part)

680. Kalamazoo and Kalkaska Counties

681. Kent County (part)

682. Kent County (part)

683. Keweenaw and Lake Counties

684. Lapeer and Leelanau Counties

685. Lenawee County (part)

686. Lenawee County (part)

687. Livingston and Mackinac Counties

688. Macomb County

689. Manistee, Manitou, Marquette, and Mason Counties

690. Mecosta, Menominee, Midland, and Missaukee Counties

691. Monroe County

692. Montcalm and Muskegon Counties

693. Newaygo County

694. Oakland County (part)

695. Oakland County (part)

696. Oceana, Ogemaw, Ontonagon, Osecola, and Oscoda Counties

697. Ottawa and Presque Isle Counties
698. St. Clair County (part)
699. St. Clair County (part)
700. St. Joseph County
701. Saginaw County (part)
702. Saginaw County (part)
703. Sanilac and Schoolcraft Counties
704. Shiawassee County
705. Tuscola County
706. Van Buren County
707. Washtenaw County (part)
708. Washtenaw County (part)
709. Wayne County (part) (excluding the city of Detroit)
710. Wayne County (part) (excluding the city of Detroit)
711. Wexford County
712. City of Detroit, wards 1-5
713. City of Detroit, ward 6
714. City of Detroit, wards 7 and 8
715. City of Detroit, wards 9 and 10

Minnesota.

(See T132 at the end of the 1870 listings for other counties.)
716. Stearns, Steele, Stevens, and St. Louis Counties
717. Todd, Wabasha, Wadena, and Waseca Counties
718. Washington, Watonwan, and Wilken Counties
719. Winona and Wright Counties

Mississippi.

720. Adams and Alcorn Counties
721. Amite County
722. Attala, Bolivar, and Calhoun Counties
723. Carroll County
724. Chickasaw County
725. Choctaw County
726. Claiborne and Clarke Counties
727. Coahoma, Copiah, and Covington Counties
728. De Soto County
729. Franklin, Greene, Grenada, Hancock, and Harrison Counties
730. Hinds County
731. Holmes and Issaquena Counties
732. Itawamba, Jackson, and Jasper Counties
733. Jefferson, Jones, and Kemper Counties
734. Lafayette County
735. Lauderdale and Lawrence Counties
736. Leake and Lee Counties
737. Lincoln County
738. Lowndes County
739. Madison and Marion Counties
740. Marshall County
741. Monroe and Neshoba Counties
742. Newton County

743. Noxubee County
744. Oktibbcha County
745. Perry and Pike Counties
746. Pontotoc and Prentiss Counties
747. Panola County
748. Rankin, Scott, and Simpson Counties
749. Smith, Sunflower, and Tallahatchie Counties
750. Tippah and Tishomingo Counties
751. Tunica and Warren Counties
752. Washington and Wayne Counties
753. Wilkinson and Winston Counties
754. Yalobusha and Yazoo Counties

Missouri.

755. Adair and Andrew Counties
756. Atchison and Audrain Counties
757. Barry and Barton Counties
758. Bates County
759. Benton and Bollinger Counties
760. Boone County
761. Buchanan County (part)
762. Buchanan County (part)
763. Butler and Caldwell Counties
764. Callaway and Camden Counties
765. Cape Girardeau County
766. Carroll and Carter Counties
767. Cass County
768. Cedar and Chariton Counties
769. Christian and Clark Counties
770. Clay County
771. Clinton and Cole Counties
772. Cooper and Crawford Counties
773. Dade, Dallas, and Daviess Counties
774. De Kalb, Dent, Douglas, and Dunklin Counties
775. Franklin County
776. Gasconade and Gentry Counties
777. Greene and Grundy Counties
778. Harrison and Henry Counties
779. Hickory and Holt Counties
780. Howard, Howell, and Iron Counties
781. Jackson County (excluding Kansas City)
782. Kansas City
783. Jasper and Jefferson Counties
784. Johnson County
785. Knox County
786. Laclede and Lafayette Counties
787. Lawrence and Lewis Counties
788. Lincoln and Linn Counties
789. Livingston County
790. Macon and Madison Counties
791. Maries and Marion Counties

792. McDonald, Mercer, Miller, and Mississippi Counties
793. Moniteau and Monroe Counties
794. Montgomery, Morgan, and New Madrid Counties
795. Newton and Nodaway Counties
796. Oregon, Osage, Ozark, Pemiscot, and Perry Counties
797. Pettis and Phelps Counties
798. Pike County
799. Platte County
800. Polk County
801. Pulaski and Putnam Counties
802. Ralls and Randolph Counties
803. Ray, Reynolds, and Ripley Counties
804. Saline and Schuyler Counties
805. Scotland, Scott, and Shannon Counties
806. Shelby and St. Charles Counties
807. St. Clair, Ste. Genevieve, and St. Francois Counties
808. St. Louis County (part) (excluding the city of St. Louis)
809. St. Louis County (part) (excluding the city of St. Louis)
810. City of St. Louis, subdivisions 3 and 2 (ward 1)
811. City of St. Louis, ward 2
812. City of St. Louis, ward 3
813. City of St. Louis, ward 4
814. City of St. Louis, ward 5 (part)
815. City of St. Louis, ward 5 (part)
816. City of St. Louis, ward 6
817. City of St. Louis, ward 7
818. City of St. Louis, ward 8
819. City of St. Louis, ward 9
820. City of St. Louis, ward 10
821. City of St. Louis, ward 11
822. City of St. Louis, ward 12
823. Stoddard, Stone, Sullivan, and Taney Counties
824. Texas, Vernon, and Warren Counties
825. Washington and Wayne Counties
826. Webster, Worth, and Wright Counties

Montana.
827. Entire territory

Nebraska.
828. Black Bird, Buffalo, Burt, Butler, Cass, Cedar, Cheyenne, Clay, Colfax, Cuming, Dakota, Dawson, Dixon, Dodge, and Gage Counties
829. Douglas, Fillmore, Gage, Pawnee Reservation, and Adams Counties
830. Hall, Hamilton, Jefferson, Johnson, Kearney, Lancaster, L'Eau qui Court, Lincoln, Madison, and Merrick Counties; and Winnebago Indian Reservation
831. Nemaha, Nuckolls, and Otoe Counties
832. Pawnee, Pierce, Platte, Polk, Richardson, and Saline Counties

833. Sarpy, Saunders, Seward, Stanton, Washington, Wayne, and York Counties

Nevada.
834. Churchill, Douglas, Elko, Esmeralda, Humboldt, Lander, Lincoln, Lyon, Nye, and Ormsby Counties
835. Storey, Washoe, and White Pine Counties

New Hampshire.
836. Belknap County
837. Carroll County
838. Cheshire County
839. Coos County
840. Grafton County (part)
841. Grafton County (part)
842. Hillsboro County (part) (excluding the city of Manchester)
843. City of Manchester
844. Hillsboro County (part) (excluding the city of Manchester)
845. Merrimack County (part)
846. Merrimack County (part)
847. Rockingham County (part)
848. Rockingham County (part)
849. Strafford County
850. Sullivan County

New Jersey.
851. Atlantic County
852. Bergen County
853. Burlington County (part)
854. Burlington County (part)
855. Camden County (part)
856. Camden County (part)
857. Burlington County (part)
858. Cape May County
859. Cumberland County
860. Essex County (part) (excluding the city of Newark)
861. Essex County (part) (excluding the city of Newark)
862. Gloucester County
863. Hudson County (part) (excluding Jersey City and the city of Hoboken)
864. City of Hoboken
865. Hudson County (part) (excluding Jersey City and the city of Hoboken)
866. Jersey City, wards 1-5
867. Jersey City, wards 6-10
868. Jersey City, wards 11-16
869. Hunterdon County (part)
870. Hunterdon County (part)
871. Mercer County (part)
872. Mercer County (part)
873. Middlesex County (part)

874. Middlesex County (part)
875. Monmouth County (part)
876. Monmouth County (part)
877. Morris County (part)
878. Morris County (part)
879. City of Newark, wards 1-3
880. City of Newark, wards 4-6
881. City of Newark, wards 7-10
882. City of Newark, wards 11-13
883. Ocean County
884. Passaic County (part) (excluding the city of Paterson)
885. City of Paterson
886. Passaic County (part) (excluding the city of Paterson)
887. Salem County
888. Somerset County
889. Sussex County
890. Union County (part)
891. Union County (part)
892. Warren County

New Mexico.
893. Bernalillo, Colfax, Dona Ana, and Grant Counties
894. Lincoln, Mora, and Rio Arriba Counties
895. San Miguel and Santa Ana Counties
896. Santa Fe, Socorro, and Taos Counties
897. Valencia County

New York.
898. City of Albany, wards 1-6
899. City of Albany, wards 7-9
900. City of Albany, ward 10
901. Albany County (part) (excluding the city of Albany)
902. Albany County (part) (excluding the city of Albany)
903. Albany County (part) (excluding the city of Albany)
904. Allegany County (part)
905. Allegany County (part)
906. Broome County (part)
907. Broome County (part)
908. Cattaraugus County (part)
909. Cattaraugus County (part)
910. Cayuga County (part)
911. Cayuga County (part)
912. Chautauqua County (part)
913. Chautauqua County (part)
914. Chemung County (part)
915. Chemung County (part)
916. Chenango County (part)
917. Chenango County (part)
918. Clinton County (part)
919. Clinton County (part)
920. Columbia County (part)
921. Columbia County (part)
922. Cortland County
923. Delaware County (part)
924. Delaware County (part)
925. Dutchess County (part) (excluding the city of Poughkeepsie)
926. Dutchess County (part) (excluding the city of Poughkeepsie)
927. City of Poughkeepsie
928. Dutchess County (part) (excluding the city of Poughkeepsie)
929. Erie County (part) (excluding the city of Buffalo)
930. Erie County (part) (excluding the city of Buffalo)
931. Erie County (part) (excluding the city of Buffalo)
932. City of Buffalo, wards 1-3
933. City of Buffalo, wards 4-5
934. City of Buffalo, wards 6-8
935. City of Buffalo, wards 9-13
936. Essex County
937. Franklin County
938. Fulton County
939. Genesee County
940. Greene County
941. Hamilton County
942. Herkimer County (part)
943. Herkimer County (part)
944. Jefferson County (part)
945. Jefferson County (part)
946. City of Brooklyn, wards 1-3
947. City of Brooklyn, wards 4 and 5
948. City of Brooklyn, ward 6
949. City of Brooklyn, ward 7
950. City of Brooklyn, wards 8 and 9
951. City of Brooklyn, ward 10
952. City of Brooklyn, ward 11
953. City of Brooklyn, ward 12
954. City of Brooklyn, ward 13
955. City of Brooklyn, ward 14
956. City of Brooklyn, ward 15
957. City of Brooklyn, ward 16
958. City of Brooklyn, wards 17 and 18
959. City of Brooklyn, ward 19
960. City of Brooklyn, ward 20
961. City of Brooklyn, ward 21
962. City of Brooklyn, ward 22
963. Kings County (excluding the city of Brooklyn)
964. Lewis County
965. Livingston County (part)
966. Livingston County (part)
967. Madison County (part)
968. Madison County (part)
969. City of Rochester, wards 1-8
970. City of Rochester, wards 9-14
971. Monroe County (part) (excluding the city of Rochester)

972. Monroe County (part) (excluding the city of Rochester)

973. Monroe County (part) (excluding the city of Rochester)

974. Montgomery County

975. New York City (first enumeration), wards 1 and 2

976. New York City (first enumeration), wards 3 and 4

977. New York City (first enumeration), ward 5

978. New York City (first enumeration), ward 6

979. New York City (first enumeration), ward 7, election districts 1-5

980. New York City (first enumeration), ward 7, election districts 6-11

981. New York City (first enumeration), ward 8

982. New York City (first enumeration), ward 9, election districts 1-7

983. New York City (first enumeration), ward 9, election districts 8-16

984. New York City (first enumeration), ward 10, election districts 1-7

985. New York City (first enumeration), ward 10, election districts 8-12

986. New York City (first enumeration), ward 11, election districts 1-5

987. New York City (first enumeration), ward 11, election districts 6-13

988. New York City (first enumeration), ward 11, election districts 14-25

989. New York City (first enumeration), ward 12, election districts 1-9

990. New York City (first enumeration), ward 12, election districts 10-18

991. New York City (first enumeration), ward 13

992. New York City (first enumeration), ward 14

993. New York City (first enumeration), ward 15, election districts 1-4

994. New York City (first enumeration), ward 15, election districts 5-11

995. New York City (first enumeration), ward 16, election districts 1-8

996. New York City (first enumeration), ward 16, election districts 9-18

997. New York City (first enumeration), ward 17, election districts 1-7

998. New York City (first enumeration), ward 17, election districts 8-15

999. New York City (first enumeration), ward 17, election districts 16-22

1000. New York City (first enumeration), ward 17, election districts 23-28

1001. New York City (first enumeration), ward 18, election districts 1-10

1002. New York City (first enumeration), ward 18, election districts 11-24

1003. New York City (first enumeration), ward 19, election districts 1-11

1004. New York City (first enumeration), ward 19, election districts 12-19

1005. New York City (first enumeration), ward 19, election districts 20-31

1006. New York City (first enumeration), ward 20, election districts 1-4

1007. New York City (first enumeration), ward 20, election districts 5-12

1008. New York City (first enumeration), ward 20, election districts 13-22

1009. New York City (first enumeration), ward 21, election districts 1-16

1010. New York City (first enumeration), ward 21, election districts 17-21

1011. New York City (first enumeration), ward 22, election districts 1-3

1012. New York City (first enumeration), ward 22, election districts 4-10

1013. New York City (first enumeration), ward 22, election districts 11-17

1014. New York City (second enumeration), wards 1-3

1015. New York City (second enumeration), ward 4

1016. New York City (second enumeration), ward 5

1017. New York City (second enumeration), ward 6

1018. New York City (second enumeration), ward 7, election districts 1-7

1019. New York City (second enumeration), ward 7, election districts 8-15

1020. New York City (second enumeration), ward 8, election districts 1-12

1021. New York City (second enumeration), ward 8, election districts 13-23

1022. New York City (second enumeration), ward 9, election districts 1-10

1023. New York City (second enumeration), ward 9, election districts 11-20

1024. New York City (second enumeration), ward 10, election districts 1-7

1025. New York City (second enumeration), ward 10, election districts 8-14

1026. New York City (second enumeration), ward 11, election districts 1-7

1027. New York City (second enumeration), ward 11, election districts 8-13

1028 New York City (second enumeration), ward 11, election districts 14-25

1029. New York City (second enumeration), ward 12, election districts 1-10

1030. New York City (second enumeration), ward 12, election districts 11-19

1031. New York City (second enumeration), ward 13

1032. New York City (second enumeration), ward 14

1033. New York City (second enumeration), ward 15

1034. New York City (second enumeration), ward 16, election districts 1-10

1035. New York City (second enumeration), ward 16, election districts 11-16

1036. New York City (second enumeration), ward 17, election districts 1-10

1037. New York City (second enumeration), ward 17, election districts 11-17

1038. New York City (second enumeration), ward 17, election districts 18-22

1039. New York City (second enumeration), ward 17, election districts 23-28

1040. New York City (second enumeration), ward 18, election districts 1-15

1041. New York City (second enumeration), ward 18, election districts 16-23

1042. New York City (second enumeration), ward 19, election districts 1-9

1043. New York City (second enumeration), ward 19, election districts 10-14

1044 New York City (second enumeration), ward 19, election districts 15-23

1045. New York City (second enumeration), ward 19, election districts 24-31

1046. New York City (second enumeration), ward 20, election districts 1-8

1047. New York City (second enumeration), ward 20, election districts 9-15

1048. New York City (second enumeration), ward 20, election districts 16-22

1049. New York City (second enumeration), ward 21, election districts 1-11

1050. New York City (second enumeration), ward 21, election districts 12-21

1051. New York City (second enumeration), ward 22, election districts 1-9

1052. New York City (second enumeration), ward 22, election districts 10-17

1053. New York City (second enumeration), ward 22, election districts 18-22

1054. Niagara County (part)

1055. Niagara County (part)

1056. City of Utica

1057. Oneida County (part) (excluding the city of Utica)

1058. Oneida County (part) (excluding the city of Utica)

1059. Oneida County (part) (excluding the city of Utica)

1060. Onondaga County (part) (excluding the city of Syracuse)

1061. Onondaga County (part) (excluding the city of Syracuse)

1062. City of Syracuse, wards 1-5

1063. City of Syracuse, wards 6-8

1064. Onondaga County (part) (excluding the city of Syracuse)

1065. Ontario County (part)

1066. Ontario County (part)

1067. Orange County (part) (excluding the city of Newburgh)

1068. Orange County (part) (excluding the city of Newburgh)

1069. City of Newburgh

1070. Orange County (part) (excluding the city of Newburgh)

1071. Orleans County

1072. Oswego County (part)

1073. Oswego County (part)

1074. Oswego County (part)

1075. Otsego County (part)

1076. Otsego County (part)

1077. Putnam County

1078. City of Flushing

1079. Queens County (part) (excluding the city of Flushing)

1080. Queens County (part) (excluding the city of Flushing)

1081. Queens County (part) (excluding the city of Flushing)

1082. Rensselaer County (part) (excluding the city of Troy)

1083. Rensselaer County (part) (excluding the city of Troy)

1084. City of Troy, wards 1-7

1085. City of Troy, wards 8-10

1086. Richmond County

1087. Rockland County

1088. Saratoga County (part)

1089. Saratoga County (part)

1090. Schenectady County

1091. Schoharie County

1092. Schuyler County

1093. Seneca County

1094. Steuben County (part)

1095. Steuben County (part)

1096. Steuben County (part)

1097. St. Lawrence County (part)

1098. St. Lawrence County (part)

1099. St. Lawrence County (part)

1100. Suffolk County (part)

1101. Suffolk County (part)

1102. Sullivan County

1103. Tioga County

1104. Tompkins County

1105. Ulster County (part)

1106. Ulster County (part)

1107. Ulster County (part)

1108. Ulster County (part)

1109. Warren County

1110. Washington County (part)

1111. Washington County (part)
1112. Wayne County (part)
1113. Wayne County (part)
1114. Westchester County (part)
1115. Westchester County (part)
1116. Westchester County (part)
1117. Westchester County (part)
1118. Westchester County (part)
1119. Wyoming County
1120. Yates County

North Carolina.

1121. Alamance, Alexander, and Alleghany Counties
1122. Anson and Ashe Counties
1123. Beaufort and Bertie Counties
1124. Bladen County
1125. Brunswick and Buncombe Counties
1126. Burke and Cabarrus Counties
1127. Caldwell, Camden, and Carteret Counties
1128. Caswell and Catawba Counties
1129. Chatham County
1130. Cherokee, Chowan, and Clay Counties
1131. Cleveland and Columbus Counties
1132. Craven County
1133. Cumberland, Currituck, and Dare Counties
1134. Davidson County
1135. Davie and Duplin Counties
1136. Edgecombe County
1137. Forsyth and Franklin Counties
1138. Gaston County
1139. Gates and Granville Counties
1140. Greene and Guilford Counties
1141. Halifax County
1142. Harnett and Haywood Counties
1143. Henderson, Hertford, and Hyde Counties
1144. Iredell and Jackson Counties
1145. Johnston and Jones Counties
1146. Lenoir, Lincoln, and Macon Counties
1147. Madison, Martin, and McDowell Counties
1148. Mecklenburg County
1149. Mitchell, Montgomery, and Moore Counties
1150. Nash County
1151. New Hanover County
1152. Northampton County
1153. Onslow and Orange Counties
1154. Pasquotank, Perquimans, and Person Counties
1155. Pitt and Polk Counties
1156. Randolph and Richmond Counties
1157. Robeson and Rockingham Counties
1158. Rowan County
1159. Rutherford and Sampson Counties

1160. Stanly and Stokes Counties
1161. Surry, Transylvania, Tyrell, and Union Counties
1162. Wake County (part)
1163. Wake County (part)
1164. Warren, Washington, and Watauga Counties
1165. Wayne and Wilkes Counties
1166. Wilson, Yadkin, and Yancy Counties

Ohio.

1167. Adams County
1168. Allen County
1169. Ashland County
1170. Ashtabula County
1171. Athens County
1172. Auglaize County
1173. Belmont County (part)
1174. Belmont County (part)
1175. Brown County
1176. Butler County (part)
1177. Butler County (part)
1178. Carroll County
1179. Champaign County
1180. Clark County
1181. Clermont County
1182. Clinton County
1183. Columbiana County (part)
1184. Columbiana County (part)
1185. Coshocton County
1186 Crawford County
1187. Cuyahoga County (part) (excluding the city of Cleveland)
1188. City of Cleveland, wards 1-3
1189. City of Cleveland, wards 4-5
1190. City of Cleveland, wards 6 and 7
1191. City of Cleveland, wards 8-10
1192. City of Cleveland, wards 11-15, and Dover and East Cleveland
1193. Cuyahoga county (part) (excluding the city of Cleveland)
1194. Darke County
1195. Defiance County
1196. Delaware County
1197. Erie County
1198. Fairfield County
1199. Fayette County
1200. Franklin County (excluding the city of Columbus)
1201. City of Columbus
1202. Fulton County
1203. Gallia County
1204. Geauga County
1205. Greene County
1206. Guernsey County
1207. Hamilton County (part) (excluding the city of Cincinnati)

1208. Hamilton County (part) (excluding the city of Cincinnati)
1209. City of Cincinnati, wards 1-3
1210. City of Cincinnati, wards 4-6
1211. City of Cincinnati, wards 7 and 8
1212. City of Cincinnati, wards 9-11
1213. City of Cincinnati, wards 12 and 13
1214. City of Cincinnati, wards 14 and 15
1215. City of Cincinnati, wards 16 and 17
1216. City of Cincinnati, ward 18
1217. City of Cincinnati, wards 19-24
1218. Hancock County
1219. Hardin County
1220. Harrison County
1221. Henry County
1222. Highland County
1223. Hocking County
1224. Holmes County
1225. Huron County
1226. Jackson County
1227. Jefferson County (part)
1228. Jefferson County (part)
1229. Knox County
1230. Lake County
1231. Lawrence County
1232. Licking County (part)
1233. Licking County (part)
1234. Logan County
1235. Lorain County
1236. Lucas County (excluding the city of Toledo)
1237. City of Toledo
1238. Madison County
1239. Mahoning County
1240. Marion County
1241. Medina County
1242. Meigs County
1243. Mercer County
1244. Miami County
1245. Monroe County
1246. Morgan County
1247. Morrow County
1248. Montgomery County (excluding the city of Dayton)
1249. City of Dayton
1250. Muskingum County (part)
1251. Muskingum County (part)
1252. Noble County
1253. Ottawa County
1254. Paulding County
1255. Perry County
1256. Pickaway County
1257. Pike County
1258. Portage County

1259. Preble County
1260. Putnam County
1261. Richland County
1262. Ross County (part)
1263. Ross County (part)
1264. Sandusky County
1265. Scioto County
1266. Seneca County
1267. Shelby County
1268. Stark County (part)
1269. Stark County (part)
1270. Summit County
1271. Trumbull County (part)
1272. Trumbull County (part)
1273. Tuscarawas County
1274. Union County
1275. Van Wert County
1276. Vinton County
1277. Warren County
1278. Washington County (part)
1279. Washington County (part)
1280. Wayne County (part)
1281. Wayne County (part)
1282. Williams County
1283. Wood County
1284. Wyandot County

Oregon.
1285. Baker, Benton, Clackamas, Clatsop, Columbia, Coos, Curry, and Douglas Counties
1286. Grant, Jackson, Josephine, Lane, and Linn Counties
1287. Marion, Multnomah, Polk, and Tillamook Counties
1288. Umatilla, Union, Wasco, Washington, and Yamhill Counties

Pennsylvania.
1289. Adams County
1290. City of Allegheny, wards 1-3
1291. City of Allegheny, wards 4-8
1292. Allegheny County (part) (excluding the cities of Allegheny and Pittsburgh)
1293. Allegheny County (part) (excluding the cities of Allegheny and Pittsburgh)
1294. Allegheny County (part) (excluding the cities of Allegheny and Pittsburgh)
1295. City of Pittsburgh, wards 1-5
1296. City of Pittsburgh, wards 6-10
1297. City of Pittsburgh, wards 11-16
1298. City of Pittsburgh, wards 16-23
1299. Allegheny County (part) (excluding the cities of Allegheny and Pittsburgh)
1300. Armstrong County (part)

1301. Armstrong County (part)
1302. Beaver County (part)
1303. Beaver County (part)
1304. Bedford County
1305. Berks County (part) (excluding the city of Reading)
1306. Berks County (part) (excluding the city of Reading)
1307. City of Reading
1308. Berks County (part) (excluding the city of Reading)
1309. Blair County (part)
1310. Blair County (part)
1311. Bradford County (part)
1312. Bradford County (part)
1313. Bucks County (part)
1314. Bucks County (part)
1315. Butler County (part)
1316. Butler County (part)
1317. Cambria County (part)
1318. Cambria County (part)
1319. Cameron County
1320. Carbon County
1321. Centre County (part)
1322. Centre County (part)
1323. Chester County (part)
1324. Chester County (part)
1325. Chester County (part)
1326. Clarion County
1327. Clearfield County
1328. Clinton County
1329. Columbia County
1330. Crawford County (part)
1331. Crawford County (part)
1332. Cumberland County (part)
1333. Cumberland County (part)
1334. Dauphin County (part)
1335. Dauphin County (part)
1336. Delaware County (part)
1337. Delaware County (part)
1338. Elk County
1339. Erie County (part) (excluding the city of Erie)
1340. City of Erie
1341. Erie County (part) (excluding the city of Erie)
1342. Fayette County (part)
1343. Fayette County (part)
1344. Forest County
1345. Franklin County (part)
1346. Franklin County (part)
1347. Fulton County
1348. Greene County
1349. Huntingdon County
1350. Indiana County (part)
1351. Indiana County (part)

1352. Jefferson County
1353. Juniata County
1354. Lancaster County (part)
1355. Lancaster County (part)
1356. Lancaster County (part)
1357. Lancaster County (part)
1358. Lancaster County (part)
1359. Lancaster County (part)
1360. Lawrence County
1361. Lebanon County
1362. Lehigh County (part)
1363. Lehigh County (part)
1364. Luzerne County (part) (excluding the city of Scranton)
1365. Luzerne County (part) (excluding the city of Scranton)
1366. Luzerne County (part) (excluding the city of Scranton)
1367. Luzerne County (part) (excluding the city of Scranton)
1368. City of Scranton
1369. Luzerne County (part) (excluding the city of Scranton)
1370. Lycoming County (part)
1371. Lycoming County (part)
1372. McKean County
1373. Mercer County (part)
1374. Mercer County (part)
1375. Mifflin County
1376. Monroe County
1377. Montgomery County (part)
1378. Montgomery County (part)
1379. Montgomery County (part)
1380. Montour County
1381. Northampton County (part)
1382. Northampton County (part)
1383. Northampton County (part)
1384. Northumberland County (part)
1385. Northumberland County (part)
1386. Perry County
1387. City of Philadelphia (first enumeration), ward 1
1388. City of Philadelphia (first enumeration), ward 2
1389. City of Philadelphia (first enumeration), ward 3
1390. City of Philadelphia (first enumeration), ward 4
1391. City of Philadelphia (first enumeration), wards 5 and 6
1392. City of Philadelphia (first enumeration), ward 7
1393. City of Philadelphia (first enumeration), ward 8
1394. City of Philadelphia (first enumeration), ward 9
1395. City of Philadelphia (first enumeration), ward 10
1396. City of Philadelphia (first enumeration), wards 11 and 12
1397. City of Philadelphia (first enumeration), ward 13
1398. City of Philadelphia (first enumeration), ward 14
1399. City of Philadelphia (first enumeration), ward 15, election districts 43-45
1400. City of Philadelphia (first enumeration), ward 15, election

districts 46 and 47

1401. City of Philadelphia (first enumeration), ward 16

1402. City of Philadelphia (first enumeration), ward 17

1403. City of Philadelphia (first enumeration), ward 18

1404. City of Philadelphia (first enumeration), ward 19, election districts 57 and 58

1405. City of Philadelphia (first enumeration), ward 19, election districts 59-61

1406. City of Philadelphia (first enumeration), ward 20, election districts 62-65

1407. City of Philadelphia (first enumeration), ward 20, election districts 66-68

1408. City of Philadelphia (first enumeration), ward 22

1409. City of Philadelphia (first enumeration), ward 21

1410. City of Philadelphia (first enumeration), ward 23

1411. City of Philadelphia (first enumeration), ward 24

1412. City of Philadelphia (first enumeration), ward 25

1413. City of Philadelphia (first enumeration), ward 26, election districts 84 and 85

1414. City of Philadelphia (first enumeration), ward 26, election districts 86 and 88

1415. City of Philadelphia (second enumeration), ward 1

1416. City of Philadelphia (second enumeration), ward 2

1417. City of Philadelphia (second enumeration), ward 3

1418. City of Philadelphia (second enumeration), ward 4

1419. City of Philadelphia (second enumeration), wards 5 and 6

1420. City of Philadelphia (second enumeration), ward 7

1421. City of Philadelphia (second enumeration), ward 8

1422. City of Philadelphia (second enumeration), ward 9

1423. City of Philadelphia (second enumeration), ward 10

1424. City of Philadelphia (second enumeration), wards 11 and 12

1425. City of Philadelphia (second enumeration), ward 13

1426. City of Philadelphia (second enumeration), ward 14

1427. City of Philadelphia (second enumeration), ward 15, election districts 45-47

1428. City of Philadelphia (second enumeration), ward 15, election districts 43 and 44

1429. City of Philadelphia (second enumeration), ward 16

1430. City of Philadelphia (second enumeration), ward 17

1431. City of Philadelphia (second enumeration), ward 18

1432. City of Philadelphia (second enumeration), ward 19, election districts 57-59

1433. City of Philadelphia (second enumeration), ward 19, election districts 60 and 61

1434. City of Philadelphia (second enumeration), ward 20, election districts 65-68

1435. City of Philadelphia (second enumeration), ward 20, election districts 62-64

1436. City of Philadelphia (second enumeration), ward 21

1437. City of Philadelphia (second enumeration), ward 22

1438. City of Philadelphia (second enumeration), ward 23

1439. City of Philadelphia (second enumeration), ward 24

1440. City of Philadelphia (second enumeration), ward 25

1441. City of Philadelphia (second enumeration), ward 26, election districts 84-86

1442. City of Philadelphia (second enumeration), ward 26, election districts 87 and 88

1443. City of Philadelphia (second enumeration), ward 27

1444. City of Philadelphia (second enumeration), ward 28

1445. City of Philadelphia (first enumeration), wards 27-28

1446. Pike and Potter Counties

1447. Schuylkill County (part)

1448. Schuylkill County (part)

1449. Schuylkill County (part)

1450. Schuylkill County (part)

1451. Snyder County

1452. Somerset County

1453. Sullivan County

1454. Susquehanna County (part)

1455. Susquehanna County (part)

1456. Tioga County (part)

1457. Tioga County (part)

1458. Union County

1459. Venango County (part)

1460. Venango County (part)

1461. Warren County

1462. Washington County (part)

1463. Washington County (part)

1464. Wayne County

1465. Westmoreland County (part)

1466. Westmoreland County (part)

1467. Wyoming County

1468. York County (part)

1469. York County (part)

1470. York County (part)

Rhode Island.

1471. Bristol and Kent Counties

1472. Newport County

1473. Washington County

1474. Providence County (part) (excluding the town of North Providence and city of Providence)

1475. Providence County (part) (excluding the town of North Providence and city of Providence)

1476. Town of North Providence

1477. Providence County (part) (excluding the town of North Providence and city of Providence)

1478. City of Providence, wards 1-4

1479. City of Providence, wards 5-7

1480. City of Providence, wards 8 and 9

South Carolina.

1481. Abbeville County
1482. Anderson County
1483. Barnwell County (part)
1484. Barnwell County (part)
1485. Beaufort County
1486. City of Charleston, wards 1-4
1487. City of Charleston, wards 5-8
1488. Charleston County (part) (excluding the city of Charleston)
1489. Charleston County (part) (excluding the city of Charleston)
1490. Chester County
1491. Chesterfield and Clarendon Counties
1492. Colleton County
1493. Darlington County
1494. Edgefield County (part)
1495. Edgefield County (part)
1496. Fairfield County
1497. Georgetown County
1498. Greenville County
1499. Horry and Kershaw Counties
1500. Lancaster County
1501. Laurens County
1502. Lexington County
1503. Marion County
1504. Marlboro and Newberry Counties
1505. Oconee County
1506. Orangeburg and Pickens Counties
1507. Richland County
1508. Spartanburg County
1509. Sumter County
1510. Union County
1511. Williamsburg County
1512. York County

Tennessee.

1513. Anderson County
1514. Bedford and Benton Counties
1515. Bledsoe, Blount, and Bradley Counties
1516. Campbell and Cannon Counties
1517. Carroll County
1518. Carter, Cheatham, and Claiborne Counties
1519. Cocke County
1520. Coffee and Cumberland Counties
1521. Davidson County, districts 2-16
1522. Davidson County, districts 17-25
1523. City of Nashville
1524. Decatur, De Kalb, and Dickson Counties
1525. Dyer County
1526. Fayette and Fentress Counties

1527. Franklin County
1528. Gibson County
1529. Giles County
1530. Grainger County
1531. Greene County
1532. Grundy and Hamilton Counties
1533. Hancock and Hardeman Counties
1534. Hardin County
1535. Hawkins County
1536. Haywood County
1537. Henderson County
1538. Henry and Hickman Counties
1539. Humphreys and Jackson Counties
1540. Jefferson and Johnson Counties
1541. Knox County
1542. Lake and Lauderdale Counties
1543. Lawrence and Lewis Counties
1544. Lincoln County
1545. Macon and Madison Counties
1546. Marion and Marshall Counties
1547. Maury County, districts 1-12
1548. Maury County, districts 13-25
1549. McMinn, McNairy, and Meigs Counties
1550. Monroe County
1551. Montgomery County
1552. Morgan and Obion Counties
1553. Overton and Perry Counties
1554. Polk, Putnam, and Rhea Counties
1555. Roane County
1556. Robertson County
1557. Rutherford County (part)
1558. Rutherford County (part)
1559. Scott, Sequatchie, and Sevier Counties
1560. Shelby County, districts 1-9
1561. Shelby County, districts 10-17
1562. City of Memphis, wards 1-6
1563. City of Memphis, wards 7-10
1564. Smith and Stewart Counties
1565. Sullivan County
1566. Sumner County
1567. Tipton, Union, and Van Buren Counties
1568. Warren and Washington Counties
1569. Wayne County
1570. Weakley and White Counties
1571. Williamson County
1572. Wilson County

Texas.

1573. Anderson, Angelina, Atascosa, and Frio Counties
1574. Austin, Bandera, Bastrop, and Bee Counties
1575. Bell and Bexar Counties

1576. Blanco, Bosque, Bowie, and Brazoria Counties

1577. Brazos, Brown, Burleson, Burnet, Caldwell, and Calhoun Counties

1578. Cameron, Chambers, and Cherokee Counties

1579. Coleman and Collin Counties

1580. Colorado, Comal, Commanche, and Cooke Counties

1581. Coryell and Dallas Counties

1582. Davis, Denton, and De Witt Counties

1583. Eastland, Ellis, El Paso, Encinal, and Erath Counties

1584. Falls and Fannin Counties

1585. Fayette and Fort Bend Counties

1586. Freestone and Galveston Counties

1587. Gillespie, Goliad, and Gonzales Counties

1588. Grayson and Grimes Counties

1589. Guadalupe, Hamilton, Hardin, and Harris Counties

1590. Harrison and Hays Counties

1591. Henderson, Hidalgo, and Hill Counties

1592. Hood, Hopkins, and Houston Counties

1593. Hunt, Jack, Jackson, Jasper, Jefferson, and Johnson Counties

1594. Karnes, Kaufman, Kendall, Kerr, Kimble, Menard, Kinney, and Lamar Counties

1595. Lampasas and Lavaca Counties

1596. Leon, Liberty, Limestone, and Live Oak Counties

1597. McMullen, La Salle, Llano, Madison, Marion, Mason, Matagorda, Maverick, Uvalde, and Zavala Counties

1598. McCulloch, McLennan, Medina, and Milan Counties

1599. Montague, Montgomery, and Nacogdoches Counties

1600. Navarro, Newton, Nueces, Duval, and Orange Counties

1601. Panola, Parker, Palo Pinto?, Polk, and Presidio Counties

1602. Red River, Refugio, and Robertson Counties

1603. Rusk County

1604. Sabine, San Augustine, San Patricio, San Saba, Shackelford, and Shelby Counties

1605. Smith, Starr, Stephens, and Tarrant Counties

1606. Titus, Travis, Trinity, and Tyler Counties

1607. Upshur, Van Zandt, Victoria, and Walker Counties

1608. Washington and Webb Counties

1609. Wharton, Williamson, Wilson, Wise, Wood, Young, and Zapata Counties

Utah.

1610. Beaver, Box Elder, Cache, Davis, Iron, and Juab Counties

1611. Millard, Morgan, Piute, Rich, Rio Virgin, Kane, and Salt Lake Counties

1612. Sanpete, Sevier, Summit, Tooele, and Utah Counties

1613. Wasatch, Washington, and Weber Counties

Vermont.

1614. Addison County

1615. Bennington County

1616. Caledonia County

1617. Chittenden County (part)

1618. Chittenden County (part)

1619. Essex County

1620. Franklin County

1621. Grand Isle and Lamoille Counties

1622. Orange County

1623. Orleans County

1624. Rutland County (part)

1625. Rutland County (part)

1626. Washington County

1627. Windham County

1628. Windsor County (part)

1629. Windsor County (part)

Virginia.

1630. Accomack County

1631. Albemarle County

1632. Alexandria and Alleghany Counties

1633. Amelia, Amherst, and Appomattox Counties

1634. Augusta County

1635. Bath and Bedford Counties

1636. Bland and Botetourt Counties

1637. Brunswick, Buchanan, and Buckingham Counties

1638. Campbell County

1639. Caroline, Carroll, and Charles City Counties

1640. Charlotte and Chesterfield Counties

1641. Clarke, Craig, and Culpeper Counties

1642. Cumberland County

1643. Dinwiddie County

1644. Elizabeth City and Essex Counties

1645. Fairfax and Fauquier Counties

1646. Floyd and Fluvanna Counties

1647. Franklin County

1648. Frederick, Giles, and Gloucester Counties

1649. Goochland, Grayson, Greene, and Greensville Counties

1650. Halifax County

1651. Hanover County

1652. Henrico County (part) (excluding the city of Richmond)

1653. City of Richmond: Clay and Jefferson wards

1654. City of Richmond: Madison, Marshall, and Monroe wards

1655. Henrico County (part) (excluding the city of Richmond)

1656. Henry and Highland Counties

1657. Isle of Wight, James City, and King and Queen Counties

1658. King George, King William, Lancaster, and Lee Counties

1659. Loudoun County

1660. Louisa County

1661. Lunenburg County

1662. Madison and Mathews Counties

1663. Mecklenburg and Middlesex Counties

1664. Montgomery and Nansemond Counties

1665. Nelson and New Kent Counties
1666. Norfolk County (part)
1667. Norfolk County (part)
1668. Northampton County
1669. Northumberland, Nottoway, and Orange Counties
1670. Page and Patrick Counties
1671. Pittsylvania County
1672. Powhatan County
1673. Prince Edward, Prince George, Princess Anne, and Prince William Counties
1674. Pulaski, Rappahannock, and Richmond Counties
1675. Roanoke and Rockbridge Counties
1676. Rockingham County
1677. Russell and Scott Counties
1678. Shenandoah County
1679. Smyth, Southampton, and Spotsylvania Counties
1680. Stafford, Surry, Sussex, Tazewell, Warren, and Warwick Counties
1681. Washington and Westmoreland Counties
1682. Wise, Wythe, and York Counties

Washington.
1683. Chehalis, Clallam, Clark, Cowlitz, Island, Jefferson, King, Kitsap, Klickitat, Lewis, Mason, Pacific, Pierce, Skamania, Stevens, Thurston, Wahkiakum, Walla Walla, Whitcom, Snohomish, and Yakima Counties

West Virginia.
1684. Barbour and Berkeley Counties
1685. Boone, Braxton, Brooke, Cabell, Calhoun, and Clay Counties
1686. Doddridge, Fayette, Gilmer, and Grant Counties
1687. Greenbrier, Hampshire, and Hancock Counties
1688. Hardy and Harrison Counties
1689. Jackson and Jefferson Counties
1690. Kanawha County
1691. Lewis, Lincoln, and Logan Counties
1692. Mason County
1693. Marshall and Marion Counties
1694. McDowell, Mercer, Mineral, and Monongalia Counties
1695. Monroe, Morgan, and Nicholas Counties
1696. Ohio County
1697. Pendleton, Pleasants, Pocahontas, and Preston Counties
1698. Putnam, Raleigh, Randolph, and Ritchie Counties
1699. Roane and Taylor Counties
1700. Tucker, Tyler, and Upshur Counties
1701. Wayne, Webster, Wetzel, and Wirt Counties
1702. Wood and Wyoming Counties

Wisconsin.
1703. Adams, Ashland, Barron, Bayfield, and Brown Counties

1704. Buffalo, Burnett, and Calumet Counties
1705. Chippewa and Clark Counties
1706. Columbia County
1707. Crawford County
1708. Dane County (part)
1709. Dane County (part)
1710. Dodge County (part)
1711. Dodge County (part)
1712. Door, Douglas, Dunn, and Eau Claire Counties
1713. Fond du Lac County (part)
1714. Fond du Lac County (part)
1715. Green and Green Lake Counties
1716. Grant County (part)
1717. Grant County (part)
1718. Iowa and Jackson Counties
1719. Jefferson County
1720. Juneau, Kenosha, and Kewaunee Counties
1721. La Crosse County
1722. Lafayette County
1723. Manitowoc County
1724. Marathon and Marquette Counties
1725. Milwaukee County (excluding the city of Milwaukee)
1726. City of Milwaukee, wards 1 and 2
1727. City of Milwaukee, wards 3-5
1728. City of Milwaukee, wards 6-9
1729. Monroe County
1730. Oconto and Outagamie Counties
1731. Ozaukee, Pepin, and Pierce Counties
1732. Polk and Portage Counties
1733. Racine County
1734. Richland County
1735. Rock County (part)
1736. Rock County (part)
1737. St. Croix and Trempealeau Counties
1738. Vernon County
1739. Sauk and Shawano Counties
1740. Sheboygan County
1741. Walworth County
1742. Washington County
1743. Waukesha County
1744. Waupaca and Waushara Counties
1745. Winnebago County (excluding the city of Oshkosh)
1746. City of Oshkosh
1747. Wood County

Wyoming.
1748. Entire territory

Ninth Census of Minnesota, 1870. T132. 13 rolls
1. Aitkin, Anoka, Becker, Beltrami, Benton, Big Stone, Blue Earth, Brown, Carlton, Carver (part), and Cass (1 page) Counties

2. Carter (part), Cass (part), Chippewa, Chisago, Clay, Cottonwood, Crow Wing, and Dakota (part) Counties

3. Dakota (part), Dodge, Douglas, Faribault, and Fullmore (part) Counties

4. Fullmore (part), Freeborn, and Goodhue (part) Counties

5. Goodhue (part), Grant, and Hannepin (part) Counties

6. Hannepin (part), Houston, Isanti, Itasca, Jackson, Kanabee, Pine (2 pages), Kandiyohi, Lake, Lac Qui Parle, and Le Sueur (part) Counties

7. Le Sueur (part), McLeod, Martin, Masker, Mille Lac, Monogolia, Morrison, and Mower Counties

8. Mower (part), Murray, Nicollet, Nobles, Rock, and Olmstead (part) Counties

9. Olmstead (part), Otter Tail, Pine (part), Kanabec (1 page), Pope, Redwood, Renville, Rice, and Ramsey (part) Counties

10. Ramsey (part), Saint Louis, Scott, Sherbourne, and Sibley (part) Counties

11. Sibley (part), Stearns, Steel, Stevens, Traverse (1 page), Todd-Morrison-Todd-Morrison-Traverse, and Wabasha (part) Counties

12. Wabasha (part), Wadena, Waseca, Washington, Watonwan, Wilkin, Clay (1 page), Polk, Pembina-Wilkin-Clay-Polk-Pembina, and Winona (part) Counties

13. Winona (part) and Wright Counties

SOUNDEX

SOUNDEX (PHONETIC INDEX) TO THE 1880 POPULATION SCHEDULES. 2,367 ROLLS. 16-MM.

For guidance on the use of Soundex, see the Introduction to this catalog.
In the lists below the roll number is followed by the soundex code range for that roll.

Alabama. T734.

1. A-123 — A-423
2. A-425 — A-652 (K)
3. A-652 (L) — B-253
4. B-254 — B-366
5. B-400 — B-423
6. B-424 — B-526
7. B-530 — B-622
8. B-623 — B-635 (N)
9. B-635 (N) — B-652 (F)
10. B-652 (G) — C-156
11. C-160 — C-350
12. C-352 — C-452 (K)
13. C-452 (L) — C-514
14. C-515 — C-616 (K)
15. C-616 (L) — C-641
16. C-642 — D-120 (R)
17. D-120 (S) — D-330
18. D-340 — D-540
19. D-541 — E-265
20. E-300 — F-236 (I)
21. F-236 (J) — F-526
22. F-530 — F-663
23. G-000 — G-416
24. G-420 — G-600
25. G-610 — G-650 (I)
26. G-650 (J) — H-200 (I)
27. H-200 (J) — H-33 (M)
28. H-300 (N) — H-400 (M)
29. H-400 (N) — H-520(I)
30. H-520 (J) — H-555
31. H-560 — H-626
32. H-630 — I-163
33. I-200 — J-500
34. J-520 (A) — J-520 (R)
35. J-520 (S) — J-525 (O)
36. J-525 (P) — K-400 (I)
37. K-400 (J) — K-615
38. K-620 — L-200 (I)
39. L-200 (J) — L-365
40. L-400 — L-565
41. L-600 — M-216
42. M-220 — M-245 (L)
43. M-245 (M) — M-260 (K)
44. M-260 (L) — M-326
45. M-340 — M-520 (I)
46. M-520 (J) — M-610
47. M-612 — M-635
48. M-636 — N-540
49. N-550 — P-116
50. P-120 — P-362 (K)
51. P-362(L) — P-500
52. P-510 — P-625
53. P-626 — R-100
54. R-120 — R-200 (C)
55. R-200 (D) — R-300 (G)
56. R-300 (H) — R-533
57. R-534 — S-220
58. S-230 — S-340 (I)
59. S-340 (J) — S-366
60. S-400 — S-516
61. S-520 — S-530 (L)
62. S-530 (M) — S-552 (I)
63. S-552 (J) — T-263
64. T-300 — T-500
65. T-512 — T-525
66. T-526 — T-656
67. T-660 — W-251
68. W-252 — W-316
69. W-320 — W-365
70. W-400 — W-426 (D)
71. W-426 (E) — W-452 (I)
72. W-452 (J) — W-526
73. W-530 — Y-520
74. Y-521 — Institutions

Arizona. T735.

1. A-000 — G-560
2. G-610 — Institutions

Arkansas. T736.

1. A-000 — A-362
2. A-400 — B-226
3. B-230 — B-424
4. B-425 — B-600
5. B-610 — B-635
6. B-636 — B-653
7. B-654 — C-256
8. C-260 — C-461
9. C-462 — C-615
10. C-616 — C-665
11. D-000 — D-265
12. D-300 — D-645
13. D-650 — E-663
14. F-000 — F-625
15. F-626 — G-365
16. G-400 — G-620
17. G-621 — H-165
18. H-200 — H-323
19. H-325 — H-452
20. H-453 — H-556
21. H-560 — H-646
22. H-650 — J-520 (I)
23. J-520 (J) — J-525 (S)
24. J-525 (T) — K-556
25. K-560 — L-265
26. L-300 — M-000
27. M-100 — M-244
28. M-245 — M-300
29. M-320 — M-526
30. M-530 — M-634
31. M-635 — N-631
32. N-632 — P-326
33. P-330 — P-616
34. P-620 — R-100 (W)
35. R-100 (W) — R-240
36. R-242 — R-506
37. R-510 — S-300 (J)
38. S-300 (L) — S-363 (I)
39. S-363 (J) — S-530 (B)
40. S-530 (C) — S-556
41. S-560 — T-460 (L)
42. T-460 (M) — T-626

43. T-630 — W-230
44. W-231 — W-325
45. W-326 — W-424
46. W-425 — W-452 (K)
47. W-452 (L) — Y-500
48. Y-520 — Institutions

California. T737.

1. A-000 — B-164
2. B-200 — B-426
3. B-430 — B-625
4. B-626 — C-000
5. C-100 — C-451
6. C-452 — C-616
7. C-620 — D-250
8. D-251 — D-626
9. D-630 — F-325
10. F-326 — F-656
11. F-660 — G-600
12. G-610 — H-166
13. H-200 — H-400 (L)
14. H-400 (M) — H-620 (I)
15. H-620 (J) — J-520 (L)
16. J-520 (M) — K-520 (I)
17. K-520 (J) — L-216
18. L-200 (M) — L-565
19. L-600 — M-246
20. M-250 — M-420
21. M-421 — M-600
22. M-610 — N-265
23. N-300 — P-165
24. P-200 — P-620
25. P-621 — R-200 (L)
26. R-200 (M) — R-536
27. R-540 — S-326
28. S-330 — S-500 (K)
29. S-500 (L) — S-600
30. S-610 — T-616
31. T-620 — W-300 (A)
32. W-300 (A) — W-435
33. W-436 — Z-655
34. Not Reported —
    Institutions

Colorado. T738.

1. A-160 — C-145
2. C-420 — G-416
3. G-420 — K-460
4. K-500 — M-620
5. M-622 — S-146
6. S-150 — W-265

7. W-300 — Institutions

Connecticut. T739.

1. A-100 — B-246
2. B-250 — B-466
3. B-500 — B-650 (I)
4. B-650 (J) — C-335
5. C-340 — C-524
6. C-525 — D-146
7. D-150 — D-555
8. D-560 — F-565
9. F-600 — G-563
10. G-600 — H-165
11. H-200 — G-465
12. H-500 — J-520
13. J-521 — K-656
14. L-000 — L-540
15. L-550 — M-263
16. M-264 — M-610
17. M-613 — O-265
18. O-300 — P-624
19. P-625 — R-311
20. R-312 — S-314
21. S-315 — S-530 (D)
22. S-530 (E) — T-463
23. T-500 — W-346
24. W-355 — W-655
25. W-656 — Institutions

Dakota. T740.

1. A-100 — B-651
2. B-652 — G-463
3. G-500 — K-465
4. K-500 — O-423
5. O-425 — S-530
6. S-531 — Institutions

Delaware. T741.

1. A-130 — B-263
2. B-300 — C-616
3. C-620 — G-362
4. G-400 — H-526
5. H-530 — L-526
6. L-530 — P-412
7. P-415 — S-365
8. S-400 — W-423
9. W-425 — Institutions

District of Columbia. T742.

1. A-000 — B-650
2. B-652 — D-465

3. D-500 — G-663
4. H-000 — J-655
5. K-000 — M-426
6. M-430 — P-626
7. P-630 — S-526
8. S-530 — W-420
9. W-421 — Institutions

Florida. T743.

1. A-100 — B-400
2. B-412 — B-663
3. C-000 — C-626
4. C-630 — E-363
5. E-400 — G-564
6. G-600 — H-400
7. H-412 — J-510
8. J-520 — L-000
9. L-100 — M-250
10. M-251 — M-660
11. N-000 — P-626
12. P-630 — R-660
13. S-000 — S-531
14. S-532 — V-656
15. W-000 — W-452 (I)
16. W-452 (J) — Institutions

Georgia. T744.

1. A-000 — A-352 (D)
2. A-352 (F) — A-526
3. A-530 — A-663
4. B-000 — B-256
5. B-260 — B-356
6. B-360 — B-425
7. B-426 — B-520
8. B-521 — B-620 (C)
9. B-620 (D) — B-625
10. B-626 — B-650 (A)
11. B-650 (B) — B-650 (S)
12. B-650 (T) — B-655 (I)
13. B-655 (J) — C-200 (I)
14. C-200 (J) — C-400 (I)
15. C-400 (J) — C-452
16. C-453 — C-510
17. C-512 — C-600 (P)
18. C-600 (R) — C-636 (E)
19. C-636 (F) — D-120 (D)
20. D-120 (E) — D-216
21. D-220 — D-424
22. D-430 — D-541
23. D-542 — E-152
24. E-162 — E-456

25. E-460 — F-432 (K)
26. F-432 (L) — F-625
27. F-626 — G-120
28. G-125 — G-420 (K)
29. G-420 (L) — G-600
30. G-610 — G-645
31. G-650 — G-666
32. H-000 — H-234
33. H-235 — H-325 (G)
34. H-325 (H) — H-400 (R)
35. H-400 (S) — H-465
36. H-500 — H-536 (J)
37. H-536 (J) — H-620 (E)
38. H-620 (F) — H-630 (S)
39. H-630 (T) — I-560
40. I-600 — J-250
41. J-252 — J-520 (M)
42. J-520 (N) — J-525 (I)
43. J-525 (J) — J-635 (G)
44. J-635 (H) — K-520 (D)
45. K-520 (E) — L-000 (J)
46. L-000 (J) — L-200
47. L-210 — L-500 (I)
48. L-500 (J) — L-612
49. L-620 — M-215
50. M-216 — M-245 (L)
51. M-245 (M) — M-260
52. M-261 — M-324 (J)
53. M-324 (J) — M-460 (I)
54. M-460 (J) — M-600 (C)
55. M-600 (D) — M-624 (K)
56. M-624 (L) — N-166
57. N-200 — N-645
58. N-650 — P-165
59. P-200 — P-362 (P)
60. P-362 (R) — P-523
61. P-524 — P-625 (K)
62. P-625 (L) — R-000 (J)
63. R-000 (L) — R-163 (R)
64. R-163 (S) — R-260
65. R-261 — R-400 (G)
66. R-400 (H) — S-000
67. S-100 — S-265
68. S-300 — S-332
69. S-334 — S-363 (K)
70. S-363 (L) — S-500
71. S-510 — S-530 (G)
72. S-530 (H) — S-530 (Z)
73. S-531 — S-616
74. S-620 — T-413
75. T-416 — T-516

76. T-520 — T-610
77. T-611 — U-516
78. U-520 — W-230
79. W-231 — W-300 (V)
80. W-300 (W) — W-361
81. W-362 — W-423
82. W-424 — W-426
83. W-430 — W-452 (J)
84. W-452 (J) — W-516
85. W-520 — W-635
86. W-640 — Institutions

Idaho. T745.
1. A-000 — M-655
2. N-000 — Institutions

Illinois. T746.
1. A-000 — A-234
2. A-235 — A-416 (I)
3. A-416 (J) — A-526
4. A-530 — A-634
5. A-635 — B-200 (I)
6. B-200 (J) — B-246
7. B-250 — B-262
8. B-263 — B-355
9. B-356 — B-420 (J)
10. B-420 (K) — B-452 (L)
11. B-452 (M) — B-525
12. B-526 — B-600 (I)
13. B-600 (J) — B-620 (J)
14. B-620 (J) — B-626 (D)
15. B-626 (E) — B-634 (I)
16. B-634 (J) — B-646
17. B-650 — B-651
18. B-652 — B-654
19. B-655 — C-155 (I)
20. C-155 (J) — C-226
21. C-230 — C-400 (C)
22. C-400 (D) — C-435
23. C-436 — C-462 (D)
24. C-462 (E) — C-514 (L)
25. C-514 (M) — C-552 (L)
26. C-552 (M) — C-616 (I)
27. C-616 (J) — C-632 (I)
28. C-632 (J) — C-650
29. C-651 — D-120 (I)
30. D-120 (J) — D-200 (J)
31. D-200 (K) — D-260
32. D-261 — D-400
33. D-410 — D-514
34. D-515 — D-552

35. D-553 — D-650
36. D-651 — E-246
37. E-250 — E-425
38. E-426 — E-625
39. E-630 — F-260 (D)
40. F-260 (E) — F-426
41. F-430 — F-520 (I)
42. F-520 (J) — F-620 (F)
43. F-620 (G) — F-640 (I)
44. F-640 (J) — G-100
45. G-110 — G-316
46. G-320 — G-421
47. G-422 — G-520
48. G-521 — G-615 (I)
49. G-615 (J) — G-634
50. G-635 — G-652
51. G-653 — H-146
52. H-150 — H-200 (I)
53. H-200 (J) — H-236
54. H-240 — H-263
55. H-264 — H-356
56. H-360 — H-400
57. H-410 — H-452
58. H-453 — H-520 (L)
59. H-520 (M) — H-536 (I)
60. H-536 (J) — H-566
61. H-600 — H-626
62. H-630 — H-646
63. H-650 — I-645
64. I-650 — J-516
65. J-520 — J-524
66. J-525 — J-525 (P)
67. J-525 (R) — K-166
68. K-200 — K-400 (I)
69. K-400 (J) — K-452
70. K-453 — K-520 (I)
71. K-520 (J) — K-550
72. K-551 — K-650
73. K-651 — L-140
74. L-141 — L-216
75. L-220 — L-300 (I)
76. L-300 (J) — L-500 (O)
77. L-500 (P) — L-523
78. L-524 — L-562
79. L-563 — M-200 (A)
80. M-200 (B) — M-216
81. M-220 — M-242 (F)
82. M-242 (G) — M-250 (R)
83. M-250 (S) — M-266 (L)
84. M-256 (M) — M-300 (I)
85. M-300 (J) — M-366

86. M-400 — M-460 (A)
87. M-460 (B) — M-460 (Z)
88. M-461 — M-535
89. M-536 — M-600 (J)
90. M-600 (J) — M-620 (G)
91. M-620 (H) — M-625 (L)
92. M-625 (M) — M-646
93. M-650 — N-246
94. N-250 — N-516
95. N-620 — O-215
96. O-240 — O-500
97. O-510 — P-200 (L)
98. P-200 (M) — P-361
99. P-362 — P-412 (F)
100. P-412 (G) — P-516
101. P-520 — P-620 (Q)
102. P-620 (R) — P-635
103. P-636 — R-100
104. R-113 — R-166
105. R-200 — R-226
106. R-230 — R-262
107. R-263 — R-320 (F)
108. R-320 (G) — R-400 (L)
109. R-400 (M) — R-500 (L)
110. R-500 (M) — R-550
111. R-551 — S-136
112. S-140 — S-162 (L)
113. S-162 (M) — S-256
114. S-260 — S-315 (L)
115. S-315 (M) — S-340 (F)
116. S-340 (G) — S-363
117. S-364 — S-363
118. S-364 — S-420 (I)
119. S-420 (J) — S-466
120. S-460 — S-620 (L)
121. S-620 (M) — S-630 (F)
122. S-630 (G) — S-630 (M)
123. S-630 (M) — S-636 (I)
124. S-636 (J) — S-662
126. S-663 — S-626
126. S-630 — T-146
127. T-160 — T-416
128. T-420 — T-612 (O)
129. T-612 (P) — T-610
130. T-612 — T-666 (G)
131. T-666 (H) — V-426
132. V-430 — W-100
133. W-116 — W-236
134. W-240 — W-300 (J)
136. W-300 (J) — W-332
136. W-340 — W-416

137. W-416 — W-420 (V)
138. W-420 (W) — W-426 (E)
139. W-426 (F) — W-462 (F)
140. W-462 (G) — W-616
141. W-620 — W-623 (P)
142. W-623 (R) — Y-320
143. Y-326 — Institutions

Indiana. T747.

1. A-000 — A-364
2. A-366 — A-636 (I)
3. A-636 (J) — B-200 (F)
4. B-200 (G) — B-266
6. B-266 — B-346
6. B-346 — B-420
7. B-421 — B-600
8. B-610 — B-666
9. B-600 — B-622
10. B-623 — B-634 (I)
11. B-634 (J) — B-660 (K)
12. B-660 (L) — B-666 (I)
13. B-666 (J) — C-200 (B)
14. C-200 (C) — C-330
16. C-340 — C-446
16. C-460 — C-466
17. C-600 — C-661
18. C-662 — C-620 (G)
19. C-620 (H) — C-640 (I)
20. C-640 (J) — D-120 (J)
21. D-120 (J) — D-246
22. D-260 — D-400
23. D-410 — D-641
24. D-542 — E-154
25. E-155 — E-420
26. E-421 — F-200 (G)
27. F-200 (H) — F-420 (K)
28. F-420 (L) — F-536
29. F-540 — F-641
30. F-642 — G-200
31. G-210 — G-426
32. G-430 — G-600
33. G-610 — G-634
34. G-635 — H-000
35. H-100 — H-200 (F)
36. H-200 (G) — H-246
37. H-250 — H-325 (I)
38. H-325 (J) — H-400 (S)
39. H-400 (T) — H-500 (G)
40. H-500 (H) — H-636
41. H-536 — H-616
42. H-620 — H-635 (F)

43. H-635 (G) — I-666
44. J-000 — J-520 (J)
45. J-520 (J) — J-525 (V)
46. J-525 (W) — K-265
47. K-300 — K-466
48. K-500 — K-533
49. K-534 — L-000 (G)
50. L-000 (H) — L-200 (R)
51. L-200 (S) — L-340
52. L-341 — L-520
53. L-521 — L-643
54. L-650 — M-216 (K)
56. M-216 (L) — M-245 (J)
56. M-245 (K) — M 255
57. M-266 — M-324
68. M-326 — M-460 (A)
59. M-460 (B) — M-500
60. M-510 — M-600 (I)
61. M-600 (J) — M-620 (M)
62. M-620 (N) — M-635 (P)
63. M-635 (R) — N-252
64. N-253 — O-155
65. O-160 — O-666
66. P-000 — P-350
67. P-351 — P-451
68. P-462 — P-620 (K)
69. P-620 (L) — P-653
70. P-664 — R-162
71. R-153 — R-200
72. R-210 — R-263
73. R-265 — R-360
74. R-361 — R-543 (I)
75. R-543 (J) — S-151
76. S-152 — S-200
77. S-210 — S-315
78. S-316 — S-345
79. S-346 — S-362
80. S-363 — S-416
81. S-420 — S-511
82. S-612 — S-530 (F)
83. S-530 (G) — S-532
84. S-533 — S-661
86. S-662 — S-666
86. S-660 — T-460 (D)
87. T-460 (E) — T-624
88. T-525 — T-651
89. T-652 — V-523
90. V-524 — W-226
91. W-230 — W-300 (J)
92. W-300 (J) — W-366
93. W-360 — W-420

94. W-421 — W-435
95. W-436 — W-616
96. W-620 — W-630
97. W-631 — Z-462
98. Z-600 — Institutions

Iowa. T748.

1. A-000 — A-436
2. A-436 — A-661
3. A-652 — B-236
4. B-240 — B-345
5. B-346 — B-434
6. B-435 — B-530
7. B-531 — B-620 (R)
8. B-620 (S) — B-634 (I)
9. B-634 (J) — B-652 (E)
10. B-652 (F) — C-154
11. C-155 — C-346
12. C-350 — C-454
13. C-455 — C-523
14. C-524 — C-620 (I)
15. C-620 (J) — C-646
16. C-650 — D-146
17. D-150 — D-366
18. D-400 — D-536
19. D-540 — E-152 (I)
20. E-152 (J) — E-426
21. E-430 — F-235
22. F-236 — F-456
23. F-460 — F-635
24. F-636 — G-320
25. G-321 — G-514
26. G-500 — G-626
27. G-630 — H-100 (I)
28. H-100 (J) — H-200 (R)
29. H-200 (S) — H-300 (I)
30. H-300 (J) — H-400 (R)
31. H-400 (S) — H-500
32. H-510 — H-536
33. H-540 — H-626
34. H-630 — I-460
35. I-500 — J-520 (J)
36. J-520 (J) — J-525 (S)
37. J-525 (T) — K-365
38. K-400 — K-520 (G)
39. K-520 (H) — K-624
40. K-625 — L-200 (I)
41. L-200 (J) — L-356
42. L-360 — L-531
43. L-532 — M-166
44. M-200 — M-240 (I)

45. M-240 (J) — M-253 (I)
46. M-253 (J) — M-320 (I)
47. M-320 (J) — M-460 (B)
48. M-460 (C) — M-534
49. M-535 — M-620 (D)
50. M-620 (E) — M-635
51. M-636 — N-366
52. N-400 — O-235
53. O-236 — O-615
54. O-620 — P-361
55. P-362 — P-452
56. P-463 — P-626 (G)
57. P-626 (H) — R-100
58. R-110 — R-200 (Q)
59. R-200 (R) — R-266
60. R-300 — R-500 (L)
61. R-500 (M) — S-116
62. S-120 — S-200
63. S-210 — S-320 (O)
64. S-320 (P) — S-361
65. S-362 — S-423
66. S-424 — S-624
67. S-526 — S-630 (R)
68. S-630 (S) — S-600
69. S-610 — T-266
70. T-260 — T-620 (D)
71. T-620 (E) — T-663
72. T-664 — V-616
73. V-620 — W-266
74. W-260 — W-361
76. W-362 — W-426 (D)
76. W-426 (E) — W-462 (L)
77. W-462 (M) — W-623
78. W-624 — Institutions

Kansas. T749.

1. A-000 — A-636 (I)
2. A-636 (J) — B-264
3. B-266 — B-420
4. B-421 — B-634
5. B-535 — B-630 (L)
6. B-630 (M) — B-652 (O)
7. B-652 (P) — C-234
8. C-236 — C-462
9. C-463 — C-666
10. C-600 — C-640 (I)
11. C-640 (J) — D-246
12. D-250 — D-524
13. D-525 — E-265
14. E-300 — F-266
15. F-260 — F-622

16. F-623 — G-316
17. G-320 — G-616
18. G-620 — H-100
19. H-120 — H-252 (I)
20. H-252 (J) — H-400 (R)
21. H-400 (S) — H-531
22. H-532 — H-630 (K)
23. H-630 (L) — J-520 (C)
24. J-520 (D) — J-656
26. K-000 — K-520 (L)
26. K-520 (M) — L-156
27. L-160 — L-510
28. L-512 — M-165
29. M-200 — M-245
30. M-246 — M-323
31. M-324 — M-460
32. M-462 — M-620 (K)
33. M-620 (L) — N-240
34. N-242 — O-126
35. O-430 — P-362
36. P-363 — P-624
37. P-625 — R-163 (I)
38. R-163 (J) — R-300 (L)
39. R-300 (M) — R-546
40. R-550 — S-265
41. S-300 — S-350
42. S-351 — S-435
43. S-436 — S-530 (J)
44. S-530 (J) — S-616
45. S-620 — T-460 (I)
46. T-460 (J) — T-655
47. T-656 — W-200
48. W-210 — W-350
49. w-351 — W-425
50. W-426 — W-622
51. W-623 — Institutions

Kentucky. T750.

1. A-000 — A400
2. A-410 — A-626
3. A-630 — B-230
4. B-231 — B-325
5. B-326 — B-420
6. B-421 — B-520
7. B-521 — B-620 (I)
8. B-620 (J) — B-632
9. B-633 — B-650 (J)
10. B-650 (J) — B-654
11. B-655 — C-156
12. C-160 — C-256
13. C-260 — C-435

14. C-436 — C-462
16. C-463 — C-536
16. C-540 — C-620 (I)
17. C-620 (J) — C-640 (M)
18. C-640 (N) — D-120 (S)
19. D-120 (T) — D-262
20. D-263 — D-524
21. D-525 — D-650
22. D-651 — E-336
23. E-340 — E-646
24. E-650 — F-432 (K)
25. F-432 (L) — F-616
26. F-620 — F-666
27. G-000 — G-355
28. G-360 — G-600 (G)
29. G-600 (H) — G-630 (K)
30. G-630 (L) — H-000
31. H-100 — H-200 (V)
32. H-200 (W) — H-252 (R)
33. H-252 (S) — H-365
34. H-400 — H-435
35. H-436 — H-524
36. H-525 — H-615
37. H-616 — H-634
38. H-635 — I-666
39. J-000 — J-520 (I)
40. J-620 (J) — J-625 (K)
41. J-525 (L) — K-260
42. K-300 — K-614
43. K-515 — K-646
44. K-650 — L-200 (S)
45. L-200 (T) — L-463
46. L-500 — L-666
47. M-000 — M-216 (I)
48. M-216 (J) — M-250 (P)
49. M-250 (R) — M-264
50. M-300 — M-446
51. M-450 — M-531
52. M-532 — M-620 (C)
53. M-620 (D) — M-635 (L)
54. M-635 (M) — N-351
55. N-352 — O-236
56. O-240 — P-200 (L)
57. P-200 (M) — P-400 (R)
58. P-400 (S) — P-600 (K)
59. P-600 (L) — P-626
60. P-630 — R-151
61. R-152 — R-200 (M)
62. R-200 (N) — R-300 (I)
63. R-300 (J) — R-463
64. R-500 — S-124

65. S-125 — S-236
66. S-240 — S-325
67. S-326 — S-361
68. S-362 — S-434
69. S-435 — S-530 (A)
70. S-530 (B) — S-530 (W)
71. S-530 (W) — S-620
72. S-621 — T-346
73. T-350 — T-512 (I)
74. T-512 (J) — T-614
75. T-615 — V-220
76. V-230 — W-226
77. W-230 — W-311
78. W-312 — W-362
79. W-363 — W-425 (J)
80. W-425 (J) — W-452 (A)
81. W-452 (B) — W-536
82. W-540 — Y-520 (G)
83. Y-520 (H) — Institutions

Louisiana. T751.

1. A-000 — A-450
2. A-451 — B-145
3. B-150 — B-345
4. B-346 — B-450
5. B-451 — B-616
6. B-620 — B-630 (I)
7. B-630 (J) — B-650 (M)
8. B-650 (N) — C-156
9. C-160 — C-415
10. C-416 — C-513
11. C-514 — C-626
12. C-630 — D-120 (I)
13. D-120 (J) — D-250 (I)
14. D-250 (J) — D-520
15. D-521 — E-246
16. E-250 — F-366
17. F-400 — F-636
18. F-640 — G-356
19. G-360 — G-600
20. G-610 — G-650 (D)
21. G-650 (E) — H-200 (I)
22. H-200 (J) — H-400 (L)
23. H-400 (M) — H-536
24. H-400 (M) — H-536
25. H-630 (H) — J-250 (E)
26. J-250 (F) — J-520 (M)
27. J-520 (N) — J-525 (M)
28. J-526 (N) — K-516
29. K-520 — L-144
30. L-145 — L-246

31. L-250 — L-536 (G)
32. L-536 (H) — M-220
33. M-221 — M-316
34. M-320 — M-460 (L)
35. M-460 (M) — M-620 (C)
36. M-620 (D) — N-163
37. N-200 — O-365
38. O-400 — P-366
39. P-400 — P-620 (L)
40. P-620 (M) — R-146
41. R-150 — R-240
42. R-241 — R-400
43. R-410 — S-166
44. S-200 — S-362
45. S-363 — S-520
46. S-621 — S-635
47. S-536 — T-246
48. T-250 — T-516
49. T-520 — T-656 (I)
50. T-656 (J) — W-230
51. W-231 — W-324
52. W-325 — W-425 (O)
53. W-425 (P) — W-452 (J)
54. W-462 (J) — Y-500
55. Y-520 — Institutions

Maine. T752.

1. A-000 — B-242
2. B-243 — D-500
3. B-510 — B-646
4. B-650 — C-265
5. C-300 — C-516
6. C-520 — C-651
7. C-652 — D-500
8. D-510 — E-463
9. E-500 — F-626
10. F-630 — G-455
11. G-456 — H-100
12. H-120 — H-400 (I)
13. H-400 (J) — H-630
14. H-631 — K-366
15. K-400 — L-166
16. L-200 — L-625
17. L-630 — M-266
18. M-300 — M-620 (G)
19. M-620 (H) — M-666
20. N-000 — P-456
21. P-460 — R-000
22. R-100 — R-463
23. R-500 — S-315
24. S-316 — S-626

25. S-530 — T-131
26. T-132 — T-646
27. T-650 — W-346
28. W-350 — W-425
29. W-426 — Institutions

Maryland. T753.

1. A-000 — A-536
2. A-540 — B-260 (F)
3. B-260 (G) — B-425
4. B-426 — B-600 (I)
5. B-600 (J) — B-634
6. B-635 — B-654
7. B-655 — C-326
8. C-340 — C-500
9. C-510 — C-632
10. C-633 — D-166
11. D-200 — D-500
12. D-510 — E-256
13. E-260 — F-262
14. F-263 — F-641
15. F-642 — G-426
16. G-430 — G-634
17. G-635 — H-160
18. H-161 — H-325
19. H-326 — H-516
20. H-520 — H-620
21. H-621 — J-245
22. J-250 — J-525 (I)
23. J-525 (J) — K-424
24. K-425 — K-666
25. L-000 — L-332
26. L-340 — M-164
27. M-200 — M-252
28. M-253 — M-445
29. M-450 — M-600 (R)
30. M-600 (S) — N-200
31. N-210 — O-525
32. O-530 — P-536
33. P-540 — P-666
34. Q-000 — R-240
35. R-241 — R-436
36. R-450 — S-161
37. S-162 — S-326
38. S-330 — S-414
39. S-415 — S-530 (F)
40. S-530 (G) — S-562
41. S-563 — T-460 (I)
42. T-460 (J) — T-626
43. T-630 — W-251
44. W-252 — W-400

45. W-410 — W-444
46. W-445 — W-630
47. W-631 — Institutions

Massachusetts. T754.

1. A-000 — A-450
2. A-452 — B-226
3. B-230 — B-345
4. B-346 — B-434
5. B-435 — B-600 (D)
6. B-600 (E) — B-624
7. B-625 — B-650 (B)
8. B-650 (C) — B-655 (I)
9. B-655 (J) — C-200 (K)
10. C-200 (L) — C-365
11. C-400 — C-452 (I)
12. C-452 (J) — C-513
13. C-514 — C-562
14. C-563 — C-631
15. C-632 — C-665
16. D-000 — D-246
17. D-250 — D-450 (K)
18. D-450 (L) — D-536
19. D-540 — D-650
20. D-651 — E-523
21. E-524 — F-326
22. F-330 — F-466
23. F-500 — F-652 (I)
24. F-652 (J) — G-350
25, G-351 — G-430
26. G-431 — G-620
27. G-621 — G-666
28. H-000 — H-240
29. H-241 — H-365
30. H-400 — H-453 (I)
31. H-453 (J) — H-545
32. H-550 — H-635
33. H-636 — J-516
34. J-520 — K-346
35. K-350 — K-513
36. K-514 — L-000 (G)
37. L-000 (H) — L-226
38. L-230 — L-516
39. L-520 — L-600 (I)
40. L-600 (J) — M-235 (I)
41. M-235 (J) — M-250 (L)
42. M-250 (M) — M-263 (H)
43. M-263 (I) — M-420
44. M-421 — M-524
45. M-525 — M-610 (I)
46. M-610 (J) — M-625

47. M-626 — N-242
48. N-243 — O-165 (H)
49. O-165 (I) — O-540 (L)
50. O-540 (M) — P-360
51. P-362 — P-600 (F)
52. P-600 (G) — P-630 (F)
53. P-630 (G) — R-152 (L)
54. R-152 (M) — R-250
55. R-251 — R-300 (L)
56. R-300 (M) — R-536
57. R-540 — S-162
58. S-163 — S-336
59. S-340 — S-415 (D)
60. S-415 (D) — S-500 (L)
61. S-500 (M) — S-530 (V)
62. S-530 (W) — S-630
63. S-631 — T-460 (E)
64. T-460 (F) — T611
65. T-612 — W-123
66. W-140 — W-316
67. W-320 — W-420 (I)
68. W-420 (J) — W-452 (D)
69. W-452 (E) — W-651
70. W-652 — Institutions

Michigan. T755.

1. A-000 — A-450 (E)
2. A-450 (F) — A666
3. B-000 — B-250
4. B-251 — B-356
5. B-360 — B-452 (I)
6. B-452 (J) — B546
7. B-550 — B-622
8. B-623 — B-635
9. B-636 — B-653 (I)
10. B-653 (J) — C-200 (G)
11. C-200 (H) — C-400 (L)
12. C-400 (M) — C-462 (O)
13. C-462 (P) — C-561
14. C-562 — C-630
15. C-632 — D-116
16. D-120 — D-251
17. D-252 — D-500 (L)
18. D-500 (M) — D-616
19. D-620 — E-366
20. E-400 — F-200
21. F-210 — F-461
22. F-462 — F-636
23. F-640 — G-316
24. G-320 — G-466
25. G-500 — G-635 (I)

26. G-635 (J) — H-136
27. H-140 — H-236
28. H-240 — H-346
29. H-350 — H-451
30. H-452 — H-536 (I)
31. H-536 (J) — H-630 (M)
32. H-630 (N) — I-566
33. I-600 — J-525 (F)
34. J-525 (G) — K-336
35. K-340 — K-520 (G)
36. K-520 (H) — K-666
37. L-000 — L-206
38. L-210 — L-506
39. L-510 — L-606
40. L-610 — M-234
41. M-235 — M-252
42. M-253 — M-320
43. M-321 — M-460 (K)
44. M-460 (L) — M-600 (C)
45. M-600 (D) — M-624
46. M-625 — N-153
47. N-160 — N-635
48. N-636 — O-566
49. O-600 — P-356
50. P-360 — P-456 (I)
51. P-456 (J) — P-625 (I)
52. P-625 (J) — R-136
53. R-140 — R-236
54. R-240   R-316
55. R-320 — R-534
56. R-535 — S-152
57. S-153 — S-306
58. S-310 — S-350 (F)
59. S-350 (G) — S-400 (I)
60. S-400 (J) — S-500 (I)
61. S-500 (J) — S-530 (J)
62. S-530 (J) — S-546
63. S-550 — S-666
64. T-000 — T-466
65. T-500 — T-626
66. T-630 — V-516
67. V-520 — W-166
68. W-200 — W-300 (S)
69. W-300 (T) — W-416
70. W-420 — W-431
71. W-432 — W-566
72. W-600 — Y-520
73. Y-521 — Institutions

Minnesota. T756.

1. A-000 — A-536 (O)

2. A-536 (P) — B-316
3. B-320 — B-546
4. B-550 — B-646
5. B-650 — C-365
6. C-400 — C-606
7. C-610 — D-226
8. D-230 — D-546
9. D-550 — E-526
10. E-530 — F-466
11. F-500 — G-356
12. G-360 — G-633
13. G-634 — H-251
14. H-252 — H-452
15. H-453 — H-620
16. H-621 — J524
17. J-525 — K-166
18. K-200 — K-520
19. K-521 — L-156
20. L-160 — L-524
21. L-525 — M-234
22. M-235 — M-324
23. M-325 — M-600 (I)
24. M-600 (J) — N-266
25. N-300 — O-424
26. O-425 — P-246
27. P-250 — P-526
28. P-530 — R-200 (I)
29. R-200 (J) — R-520
30. R-521 — S-256
31. S-260 — S-366
32. S-400 — S-530 (D)
33. S-530 (E) — S-654
34. S-655 — T-616
35. T-620 — W-224
36. W-230 — W-425
37. W-426 — Institutions

Mississippi. T757.

1. A-000 — A-450 (G)
2. A-450 (H) — A-666
3. B-000 — B-260 (M)
4. B-260 (N) — B-400 (M)
5. B-400 (N) — B-500 (K)
6. B-500 (L) — B-620 (D)
7. B-620 (E) — B-632
8. B-633 — B-650 (L)
9. B-650 (M) — B-656
10. B-660 — C-236
11. C-240 — C-446
12. C-450 — C-500 (K)
13. C-500 (L) — C-614

14. C-615 — C-636
15. C-640 — D-120
16. D-123 — D-406
17. D-410 — D-621
18. D-622 — E-363
19. E-364 — F-426
20. F-430 — F-626
21. F-630 — G-246
22. G-250 — G-506
23. G-510 — G-635 (F)
24. G-635 (G) — H-124
25. H-125 — H-252 (G)
26. H-252 (H) — H-400 (I)
27. H-400 (J) — H-513
28. H-514 — H-544
29. H-545 — H-625 (K)
30. H-625 (L) — I-116
31. I-120 — J-460
32. J-500 — J-520 (R)
33. J-520 (S) — J-525 (J)
34. J-525 (K) — K-266
35. K-300 — K-623
36. K-624 — L-200 (J)
37. L-200 (J) — L-466
38. L-500 — L-666
39. M-000 — M-226
40. M-230 — M-246
41. M-250 — M-266
42. M-300 — M-451
43. M-452 — M-600 (I)
44. M-600 (J) — M-625 (M)
45. M-625 (N) — N-400 (K)
46. N-400 (L) — O-466
47. O-500 — P-361
48. P-362 — P-525
49. P-530 — P-630
50. P-631 — R-152 (K)
51. R-152 (L) — R-241
52. R-242 — R-341
53. R-342 — S-144
54. S-145 — S-300 (L)
55. S-300 (M) — S-361
56. S-362 — S-434
57. S-435 — S-530 (G)
58. S-530 (H) — S-536 (M)
59. S-536 (N) — T-256
60. T-260 — T-511
61. T-512 — T-564
62. T-600 — V-246
63. V-250 — W-252
64. W-253 — W-325 (F)

65. W-325 (G) — W-420 (K)
66. W-420 (L) — W-426
67. W-430 — W-452 (M)
68. W-452 (M) — W-623 (I)
69. W-623 (J) — Institutions

Missouri. T758.

1. A-000 — A-352 (K)
2. A-352 (L) — A-450 (S)
3. A-450 (T) — A-653
4. A-654 — B-226
5. B-230 — B-260 (R)
6. B-260 (S) — B-366
7. B-400 — B-425
8. B-426 — B-500 (S)
9. B-500 (T) — B-566
10. B-600 — B-620 (M)
11. B-620 (N) — B-625
12. B-626 — B-635 (I)
13. B-635 (J) — B-650 (M)
14. B-650 (N) — B-653 (R)
15. B-653 (S) — C-155
16. C-156 — C-236
17. C-240 — C-414
18. C-415 — C-454
19. C-455 — C-514 (I)
20. C-514 (J) — C-560
21. C-561 — C-622
22. C-623 — C-640 (I)
23. C-640 (J) — D-120 (B)
24. D-120 (C) — D-166
25. D-200 — D-324
26. D-325 — D-500 (R)
27. D-500 (S) — D-600 (I)
28. D-600 (J) — E-152
29. E-153 — E-366
30. E-400 — E-566
31. E-600 — F-266
32. F-300 — F-456
33. F-460 — F-622
34. F-623 — F-652 (R)
35. F-652 (S) — G-246
36. G-250 — G-420
37. G-421 — G-546
38. G-550 — G-620
39. G-621 — G-650 (L)
40. G-650 (M) — H-136
41. H-140 — H-200 (L)
42. H-200 (M) — H-251
43. H-252 — H-324
44. H-325 — H-400 (K)

45. H-400 (L) — H-451
46. H-452 — H-250 (S)
47. H-520 (T) — H-542
48. H-543 — H-620 (I)
49. H-620 (J) — H-632
50. H-633 — 1-466
51. I-500 — J-366
52. J-400 — J-522
53. J-523 — J-546
54. J-550 — K-324
55. K-325 — K-456
56. K-460 — K-524
57. K-525 — K-626
58. K-630 — L-146
59. L-150 — L-235
60. L-236 — L-416
61. L-420 — L-522
62. L-523 — L-651
63. L-652 — M-206
64. M-210 — M-240 (L)
65. M-240 (M) — M-250 (V)
66. M-250 (W) — M-262
67. M-263 — M-324
68. M-325 — M-456
69. M-460 — M-500 (L)
70. M-500 (M) — M-600 (C)
71. M-600 (D) — M-611
72. M-612 — M-625
73. M-626 — N-000
74. N-100 — N-400 (Q)
75. N-410 — O-164 (mixed
    codes)
76. O-165 — O-520
77. O-521 — P-230
78. P-231 — P-400 (G)
79. P-400 (H) — P-466
80. P-500 — P-620 (L)
81. P-620 (M) — P-636 (I)
82. P-636 (J) — R-151
83. R-152 — R-200 (I)
84. R-200 (J) — R-254
85. R-255 — R-320 (G)
86. R-320 (H) — R-452
87. R-453 — R-543
88. R-544 — S-150 (O)
89. S-152 (P) — S-234
90. S-235 — S-315 (I)
91. S-315 (J) — S-340 (L)
92. S-340 (M) — S-360
93. S-361 — S-406
94. S-410 — S-452

95. S-453 — S-525
96. S-526 — S-530 (J)
97. S-530 (J) — S-536 (I)
98. S-536 (J) — S-606
99. S-610 — S-666
100. T-000 — T-416
101. T-420 — T-516
102. T-520 — T-620
103. T-621 — U-466
104. U-500 — V-536
105. V-540 — W-235
106. W-236 — W-300 (M)
107. W-300 (N) — W-346
108. W-350 — W-420 (I)
109. W-420 (J) — W-425 (R)
110. W-425 (S) — W-452 (E)
111. W-452 (F) — W-516
112. W-520 — W-630
113. W-631 — Y-526
114. Y-530 — Institutions

Montana. T759.

1. A-000 — N-666
2. O-100 — Institutions

Nebraska. T760.

1. A-000 — B-260
2. B-262 — B-616
3. B-620 — C-166
4. C-200 — C-614
5. C-615 — D-465
6. D-500 — F-256
7. F-260 — G-446
8. G-450 — H-236
9. H-240 — H-536
10. H-540 — J-525 (E)
11. J-525 (F) — K-626
12. K-630 — L-636
13. L-640 — M-426
14. M-430 — M-634
15. M-635 — P-265
16. P-300 — R-146
17. R-150 — S-126
18. S-130 — S-363
19. S-364 — S-546
20. S-550 — T-644
21. T-650 — W-416
22. W-420 — Institutions

Nevada. T761.

1. A-000 — L-261

2. L-300 — W-666
3. Y-000 — Institutions

New Hampshire. T762.
1. A-100 — B-452
2. B-453 — C-206
3. C-210 — C-666
4. D-000 — E-556
5. E-560 — G-600
6. G-610 — H-516
7. H-520 — K-666
8. L-000 — M-266
9. M-300 — P-166
10. P-200 — R-236
11. R-240 — S-516
12. S-520 — W-166
13. W-200 — Institutions

New Jersey. T763.
1. A-100 — A-536 (I)
2. A-536 (J) — B-260 (I)
3. B-260 (J) — B-435
4. B-436 — B-616
5. B-620 — B-646
6. B-650 — C-106
7. C-11O — C-415
8. C-416 — C-514 (I)
9. C-514 (J) — C-620
10. C-621 — D-000 (I)
11. D-000 (J) — D-316
12. D-320 — D-546
13. D-550 — E-363
14. E-364 — F-366
15. F-400 — F-636
16. F-640 — G-266
17. G-300 — G-616
18. G-620 — H-154
19. H-155 — H-256
20. H-260 — H-430
21. H-431 — H-541
22. H-542 — H-651
23. H-652 — I-525 (I)
24. I-525 (J) — K-446
25. K-450 — K-650
26. K-651 — L-336
27. L-340 — L-646
28. L-650 — M-246
29. M-250 — M-320
30. M-321 — M 500
31. M-510 — M-620 (I)
32. M-620 (J) — N-346

33. N-350 — O-566
34. O-600 — P-450
35. P-451 — P-662
36. Q-000 — R-240
37. R-241 — R-466
38. R-500 — S-160
39. S-161 — S-340
40. S-341 — S-400
41. S-410 — S-530 (C)
42. S-530 (D) — S-540
43. S-541 — T-346
44. T-350 — T-616
45. T-620 — V-530
46. V-531 — W-255
47. W-256 — W-420
48. W-421 — W-460
49. W-461 — Institutions

New Mexico. T764.
1. A-000 — C-120
2. C-122 — G-620 (F)
3. G-620 (G) — M-231
4. M-232 — O-632
5. O-633 — S-522 (I)
6. S-522 (J) — Institutions

New York. T765.
1. A-000 — A-256
2. A-260 — A-416
3. A-420 — A-520
4. A-521 — A-646
5. A-650 — B-200 (A)
6. B-200 (A) — B-226
7. B-230 — B-255 (L)
8. B-255 (M) — B-266
9. B-300 — B-346
10. B-350 — B-400 (V)
11. B-400 (W) — B-432
12. B-433 — B-462
13. B-463 — B-526 (I)
14. B-5 26 (J) — B-556
15. B-560 — B-620 (A)
16. B-620 (B) — B-620 (V)
17. B-620 (W) — B-626 (I)
18. B-626 (J) — B-632 (C)
19. B-632 (D) — B-636
20. B-640 — B-650 (J)
21. B-650 (J) — B-652 (G)
22. B-652 (H) — B-653 (S)
23. B-653 (T) — C-100 (I)
24. C-100 (J) — C-200 (B)

25. C-200 (C) — C-230
26. C-231 — C-320
27. C-321 — C-414
28. C-415 — C-450 (J)
29. C-450 (J) — C-460
30. C-461 — C-500 (G)
31. C-500 (H) — C-515
32. C-516 — C-540 (K)
33. C-540 (L) — C-563
34. C-564 — C-615 (M)
35. C-615 (N) — C-625 (L)
36. C-625 (M) — C-640 (J)
37. C-640 (J) — C-652
38. C-653 — D-100 (I)
39. D-100 (J) — D-136
40. D-140 — D-230
41. D-231 — D-260 (V)
42. D-260 (W) — D-400 (B)
43. D-400 (C) — D-450 (J)
44. D-450 (J) — D-500 (L)
45. D-500 (M) — D-525 (F)
46. D-525 (G) — D-556
47. D-560 — D-624 (I)
48. D-624 (J) — E-152 (L)
49. E-152 (M) — E-266
50. E-300 — E-435
51. E-436 — E-640
52. E-641 — F-236 (D)
53. F-236 (E) — F-324
54. F-325 — F-430 (E)
55. F-430 (F) — F-460 (D)
56. F-460 (E) — F-540
57. F-541 — F-625
58. F-626 — F-640
59. F-641 — F-655
60. F-656 — G-200
61. G-210 — G-361
62. G-362 — G-425
63. G-426 — G-460
64. G-461 — G-600 (M)
65. G-600 (N) — G-620 (L)
66. G-620 (M) — G-635 (Q)
67. G-635 (R) — G-652 (G)
68. G-652 (H) — H-100 (F)
69. H-100 (G) — H-160
70. H-161 — H-200 (K)
71. H-200 (L) — H-234
72. H-235 — H-252 (Q)
73. H-252 (R) — H-320
74. H-321 — H-400 (D)
75. H-400 (E) — H-415

76. H-416 — H-446	127. O-235 — O-353	178. W-300 (J) — W-340
77. H-450 — H-500 (Q)	128. O-354 — O-541	179. W-341 — W-400 (D)
78. H-500 (R) — H-525	129. O-542 — P-200 (K)	180. W-400 (E) — W-420 (J)
79. H-526 — H-543 (Q)	130. P-200 (L) — P-330	181. W-420 (J) — W-425 (G)
80. H-543 (R) — H-610	131. P-332 — P-400 (K)	182. W-425 (H) — W-436 (K)
81. H-611 — H-625 (L)	132. P-400 (L) — P-450 (I)	183. W-436 (L) — W-455
82. H-625 (M) — H-635 (I)	133. P-450 (J) — P-536	184. W-456 — W-536 (L)
83. H-635 (J) — H-655 (L)	134. P-540 — P-620 (Q)	185. W-536 (M) — W-630 (Q)
84. H-655 (M) — J-212 (F)	135. P-620 (R) — P-630 (I)	186. W-630 (R) —Y-520 (I)
85. J-212 (G) — J-520 (C)	136. P-630 (J) — Q-251	187. Y-520 (J) — Institutions
86. J-520 (D) — J-525 (E)	137. Q-252 — R-140	
87. J-525 (F) — J-666	138. R-141 — R-163 (R)	*North Carolina. T766.*
88. K-000 — K-250 (J)	139. R-163 (S) — R-200 (R)	1. A-000 — A-423 (I)
89. K-250 (K) — K-400 (J)	140. R-200 (S) — R-250	2. A-423 (J) — A-536 (L)
90. K-400 (J) — K-450 (I)	141. R-251 — R-266	3. A-536 (M) — B-230 (K)
91. K-450 (J) — K-500 (O)	142. R-300 — R-325	4. B-230 (L) — B-316
92. K-500 (P) — K-520 (P)	143. R-326 — R-400 (L)	5. B-320 — B-420 (I)
93. K-520 (R) — K-550 (I)	144. R-400 (M) — R-500 (P)	6. B-420 (J) — B-466
94. K-550 (J) — K-626	145. R-500 (P) — R-543 (L)	7. B-500 — B-566
95. K-630 — L-000 (S)	146. R-543 (M) — S-000 (O)	8. B-600 — B-626
96. L-000 (T) — L-152 (I)	147. S-000 (P) — S-146	9. B-630 — B-650 (A)
97. L-152 (J) — L-200 (L)	148. S-150 — S-163 (D)	10. B-650 (B) — B-652 (I)
98. L-200 (M) — L-255	149. S-163 (E) — S-251	11. B-652 (J) — C-116
99. L-256 — L-350	150. S-252 — S-315 (D)	12. C-120 — C-200 (V)
100. L-351 — L-516 (G)	151. S-315 (E) — S-326	13. C-200 (W) — C-416
101. L-516 (H) — L-523	152. S-330 — S-350	14. C-420 — C-500 (I)
102. L-524 — L-550	153. S-351 — S-362 (B)	16. C-600 (M) — C-633
103. L-551 — L-652 (L)	154. S-362 (C) — S-365 (E)	17. C-634 — D-120 (B)
104. L-652 (M) — M-200 (S)	155. S-365 (F) — S-415 (L)	18. D-120 (C) — D-213
105. M-200 (T) — M-230	156. S-415 (M) — S-431	19. D-214 — D-466
106. M-231 — M-240 (K)	157. S-432 — S-466	20. D-500 — D-650
107. M-240 (L) — N-246 (L)	158. S-500 — S-516 (L)	21. D-651 — E-363
108. M-246 (M) — M-252 (I)	159. S-516 (M) — S-530 (C)	22. E-364 — F-236
109. M-252 (J) — M-255 (Q)	160. S-530 (C) — S-530 (J)	23. F-240 — F-466
110. M-255 (R) — M-263 (B)	161. S-530 (J) — S-530 (S)	24. F-500 — F-654
111. M-263 (C) — M-300 (I)	162. S-530 (S) — S-536 (A)	25. F-655 — G-356
112. M-300 (J) — M-346	163. S-536 (B) — S-55O (I)	26. G-360 — G-566
113. M-350 — M-426	164. S-550 (J) — S-600 (L)	27. G-600 — G-635
114. M-430 — M-460 (D)	165. S-600 (M) — S-635	28. G-636 — H-116
115. M-460 (E) — M-500 (A)	166. S-636 —T-150 (L)	29. H-120 — H-231
116. M-500 (B) — M-525 (I)	167. T-150 (M) —T-400 (L)	30. H-232 — H-324
117. M-525 (J) — M-566	168. T-400 (M) —T-511	31. H-325 — H-400 (S)
118. M-600 (A) — M-600 (L)	169. T-512 —T-525 (L)	32. H-400 (T) — H-513
119. M-600 (M) — M-610 (S)	170. T-525 (M) —T-620 (L)	33. H-514 — H-536 (O)
120. M-610 (T) — M-620 (O)	171. T-620 (M) —T-656 (L)	34. H-536 (P) — H-620 (Q)
121. M-620 (P) — M-630 (L)	172. T-656 (M) —V-400 (I)	35. H-620 (R) — H-635
122. M-630 (M) — M-650 (I)	173. V-400 (J) —V-525 (F)	36. H-636 — J-206
123. M-650 (J) — N-242 (E)	174. V-525 (G) —V-565	37. J-210 — J-520 (K)
124. N-242 (F) — N-425 (L)	175. V-566 — W-200 (I)	38. J-520 (L) — J-525 (J)
125. N-245 (M) — N-636	176. W-200 (J) — W-256 (C)	39. J-525 (J) — J-666
126. N-640 — O-234	177. W-256 (D) — W-300 (J)	40. K-000 — K-523

41. K-5 24 — L-152
42. L-15 3 — L-266
43. L-300 — L-520 (L)
44. L-520 (M) — M-000
45. M-100 — M-234
46. M-235 — M-250 (I)
47. M-250 (J) — M-263
48. M-264 — M-420 (L)
49. M-420 (M) — M-536
50. M-540 — M-600 (S)
51. M-600 (T) — M-630
52. M-631 — N-366
53. N-400 — O-366
54. O-400 — P-306
55. P-310 — P-412 (I)
56. P-412 (J) — P-600 (O)
57. P-600 (P) — P-626 (C)
58. P-626 (D) — R-120 (I)
59. R-120 (J) — R-200 (K)
60. R-200 (L) — R-300 (J)
61. R-300 (L) — R-526
62. R-530 — S-161
63. S-162 — S-315 (I)
64. S-315 (J) — S-353
65. S-354 — S-426
66. S-430 — S-530 (A)
67. S-530 (B) — S-530 (W)
68. S-530 (W) — S-611
69. S-612 — T-366
70. T-400 — T-512
71. T-514 — T-655
72. T-656 — W-166
73. W-200 — W-300 (M)
74. W-300 (N) — W-340 (K)
75. W-340 (L) — W-420 (R)
76. W-420 (S) — W-451
77. W-452 — W-452 (S)
78. W-452 (T) — W-631
79. W-632 — Institutions

Ohio. T767.

1. A-000 — A-351
2. A-352 — A-450 (I)
3. A-450 (J) — A-626
4. A-630 — B-200 (B)
5. B-200 (C) — B-236
6. B-240 — B-260 (I)
7. B-260 (J) — B-320
8. B-321 — B-400 (K)
9. B-400 (L) — B-434
10. B-435 — B-500

11. B-510 — B-546
12. B-550 — B-612
13. B-613 — B-621
14. B-622 — B-630 (I)
15. B-630 (J) — B-635
16. B-636 — B-650 (N)
17. B-650 (O) — B-653 (D)
18. B-653 (E) — C-116
19. C-120 — C-200 (J)
20. C-200 (J) — C-330
21. C-340 — C-420 (I)
22. C-420 (J) — C-455 (I)
23. C-455 (J) — C-506
24. C-510 — C-546
25. C-550 — C-613
26. C-614 — C-624
27. C-625 — C-642
28. C-643 — D-100 (O)
29. D-100 (P) — D-136
30. D-140 — D-250 (N)
31. D-250 (O) — D-361
32. D-362 — D-500 (I)
33. D-500 (J) — D-541
34. D-542 — D-625
35. D-626 — E-226
36. E-230 — E-420 (I)
37. E-420 (J) — E-561
38. E-562 — F-236 (I)
39. F-236 (J) — F-366
40. F-400 — F-460 (I)
41. F-460 (J) — F-600 (I)
42. F-600 (J) — F-631
43. F-632 — F-655 (I)
44. F-655 (J) — G-246
45. G-250 — G-416 (I)
46. G-416 (J) — G-506
47. G-510 — G-612
48. G-613 — G-634
49. G-635 — G-652 (G)
50. G-652 (H) — H-140
51. H-141 — H-200 (B)
52. H-200 (C) — H-230
53. H-231 — H-252
54. H-253 — H-325 (I)
55. H-325 (J) — H-400 (J)
56. H-400 (J) — H-436
57. H-440 — H-515
58. H-516 — H-535
59. H-536 — H-556
60. H-560 — H-622
61. H-623 — H-635 (K)

62. H-635 (L) — I-524
63. I-525 — J-366
64. J-400 — J-522
65. J-523 — J-525 (V)
66. J-525 (W) — K-236
67. K-240 — K-400 (J)
68. K-400 (J) — K460 (K)
69. K-460 (L) — K-520 (K)
70. K-520 (L) — K-556
71. K-560 — K-633
72. K-634 — L-142
73. L-143 — L-200 (V)
74. L-200 (W) — L-316
75. L-320 — L-500
76. L-510 — L-524
77. L-525 — L-600 (E)
78. L-600 (F) — M-200 (J)
79. M-200 (J) — M-220
80. M-221 — M-242 (I)
81. M-242 (J) — M-250 (O)
82. M-250 (J) — M-256 (K)
83. M-256 (L) — M-316
84. M-320 — M-416
85. M-420 — M-460 (C)
86. M-460 (D) — M-460 (V)
87. M-460 (W) — M-532 (I)
88. M-532 (J) — M-600 (J)
89. M-600 (J) — M-620 (F)
90. M-620 (G) — M-625 (E)
91. M-625 (F) — M-636
92. M-640 — N-240 (I)
93. N-240 (J) — N-452
94. N-453 — O-216
95. O-220 — O-566
96. O-600 — P-256
97. P-260 — P-362 (S)
98. P-362 (T) — P-450
99. P-451 — P-616
100. P-620 — P-626 (L)
101. P-626 (M) — R-000 (M)
102. R-000 (N) — R-163 (D)
103. R-163 (E) — R-200 (K)
104. R-200 (L) — R-250
105. R-251 — R-300 (J)
106. R-300 (J) — R-356
107. R-360 — R-500 (L)
108. R-500 (M) — R-560 (I)
109. R-560 (J) — S-133
110. S-134 — S-160 (K)
111. S-160 (L) — S-234
112. S-235 — S-310

113. S-311 — S-322	9. B-360 — B-420 (G)	60. H-200 (A) — H-200 (S)
114. S-323 — S-342	10. B-420 (H) — B-450 (I)	61. H-200 (T) — H-244
115. S-343 — S-356	11. B-450 (J) — B-513	62. H-245 — H-263 (I)
116. S-360 — S-363 (V)	12. B-514 — B-536	63. H-263 (J) — H-361
117. S-363 (W) — S-420 (I)	13. B-540 — B-600 (J)	64. H-362 — H-416
118. S-420 (J) — S-460 (I)	14. B-600 — B-620 (J)	65. H-420 — H-454
119. S-460 (J) — S-520	15. B-620 (J) — B-624	66. H-455 — H-520 (D)
120. S-521 — S-530 (G)	16. B-625 — B-630	67. H-520 (E) — H-535
121. S-530 (H) — S-530 (V)	17. B-631 — B-640 (F)	68. H-536 — H-552
122. S-530 (W) — S-536 (S)	18. B-640 (G) — B-650 (Q)	69. H-553 — H-616 (J)
123. S-536 (T) — S-566	19. B-650 (R) — B-652	70. H-616 (J) — H-630 (S)
124. S-600 — S-632 (K)	20. B-653 — B-666	71. H-630 (T) — H-650
125. S-632 (L) — T-246	21. C-000 — C-200 (I)	72. H-651 — I-656
126. T-250 — T-460 (J)	22. C-200 (J) — C-316	73. J-000 — J-520 (C)
127. T-460 (J) — T-520 (I)	23. C-320 — C-416	74. J-520 (D) — J-523 (L)
128. T-520 (J) — T-623	24. C-420 — C-452 (I)	75. J-523 (M) — J-635 (I)
129. T-624 — U-465	25. C-452 (J) — C-466	76. J-635 (J) — K-226
130. U-512 — V-525	26. C-500 — C-516 (K)	77. K-230 — K-400 (B)
131. V-526 — W-160 (K)	27. C-516 (L) — C-560 (P)	78. K-400 (C) — K-426
132. W-160 (L) — W-251	28. C-560 (R) — C-616 (I)	79. K-430 — K-466
133. W-252 — W-300 (N)	29. C-616 (J) — C-625	80. K-500 — K-520 (I)
134. W-300 (O) — W-354	30. C-626 — C-646	81. K-520 (J) — K-530
135. W-355 — W-410 (L)	31. C-650 — D-116	82. K-531 — K-620 (E)
136. W-410 (M) — W-424	32. D-120 — D-143	83. K-620 (F) — K-652 (I)
137. W-425 — W-430	33. D-145 — D-250 (I)	84. K-652 (J) — L-140
138. W-431 — W-452 (M)	34. D-250 (J) — D-320	85. L-141 — L-200 (K)
139. W-452 (N) — W-535	35. D-321 — D-420	86. L-200 (L) — L-252
140. W-536 — W-630 (L)	36. D-421 — D-514	87. L-253 — L-340
141. W-630 (M) — Y-516	37. D-515 — D-546	88. L-341 — L-520 (C)
142. Y-520 — Z-564	38. D-550 — D-625	89. L-520 (D) — L-525
143. Z-565 — Institutions	39. D-626 — E-152	90. L-526 — L-566
	40. E-153 — E-262	91. L-600 — M-200 (C)
Oregon. T768.	41. E-263 — E-440	92. M-200 (D) — M-213
1. A-000 — C-166	42. E-450 — E-640	93. M-214 — M-230
2. C-200 — D-660	43. E-641 — F-236	94. M-231 — M-240 (L)
3. E-000 — H-366	44. F-240 — F-356	95. M-240 (M) — M-245 (B)
4. H-400 — L-166	45. F-360 — F-451	96. M-245 (C) — M-250 (K)
5. L-200 — M-666	46. F-452 — F-523	97. M-250 (L) — M-254 (B)
6. N-000 — R-526	47. F-524 — F-622	98. M-254 (C) — M-260 (F)
7. R-530 — T-626	48. F-623 — F-646	99. M-260 (G) — M-263 (S)
8. T-630 — Institutions	49. F-650 — F-666	100. M-263 (T) — M-320 (R)
	50. G-000 — G-255	101. M-320 (S) — M-400 (G)
Pennsylvania. T769.	51. G-256 — G-400	102. M-400 (H) — M-450
1. A-000 — A-351	52. G-410 — G-430	103. M-451 — M-560 (J)
2. A-352 — A-450 (K)	53. G-431 — G-535	104. M-460 (J) — M-500 (C)
3. A-450 (L) — A-536 (V)	54. G-536 — G-613 (I)	105. M-500 (D) — M-532 (I)
4. A-536 (W) — B-151	55. G-613 (J) — G-625	106. M-532 (J) — M-600 (H)
5. B-152 — B-233	56. G-626 — G-650 (J)	107. M-600 (H) — M-60 (W)
6. B-234 — B-256	57. G-650 (J) — G-655	108. M-600 (W) — M-620 (J)
7. B-260 — B-300 (I)	58. G-660 — H-155 (C)	109. M-620 (J) — M-625 (O)
8. B-300 (J) — B-356	59. H-155 (D) — H-200 (A)	110. M-625 (P) — M-640

111. M-641 — N-240 (K)	162. W-425 (J) — W-435 (K)	30. L-200 — L-620 (I)
112. N-240 (L) — N-424	163. W-435 (L) — W-452 (L)	31. L-620 (J) — M-200 (R)
113. N-425 — O-164	164. W-452 (M) — W-531	32. M-200 (S) — M-242
114. O-165 — O-416	165. W-532 — W-623	33. M-243 — M-262
115. O-420 — P-156	166. W-624 — Y-236	34. M-263 — M-446
116. P-160 — P-350 (K)	167. Y-240 — Y-626	35. M-460 — M-600 (R)
117. P-350 (L) — P-406	168. Y-630 — Institutions	36. M-600 (S) — M-626
118. P-410 — P-516		37. M-626 — N-666
119. P-520 — P-620 (R)	*Rhode Island. T770.*	38. O-000 — P-361
120. P-620 (S) — P-636	1. A-000 — B-566	39. P-362 — P-616
121. P-640 — R-100 (R)	2. B-600 — C-445	40. P-620 — R-100
122. R-100 (S) — R-163 (I)	3. C-450 — D-400	41. R-120 — R-200 (L)
123. R-163 (J) — R-200 (N)	4. D-410 — G-366	42. R-200 (M) — R-263 (I)
124. R-200 (O) — R-250 (K)	5. G-400 — H-526	43. R-263 (J) — R-636
125. R-250 (L) — R-266	6. H-530 — L-256	44. R-636 — S-300
126. R-300 — R-320 (K)	7. L-260 — M-366	45. S-310 — S-366
127. R-320 (L) — R-360	8. M-400 — P-242	46. S-366 — S-626
128. R-361 — R-500 (S)	9. P-250 — S-135	47. S-626 — S-636
129. R-500 (T) — R-544	10. S-140 — T-466	48. S-640 — T-226
130. R-545 — S-100 (I)	11. T-500 — Institutions	49. T-230 — T-620 (L)
131. S-100 (J) — S-152 (D)		50. T-620 (M) — V-620
132. S-152 (E) — S-160	*South Carolina. T771.*	51. V-522 — W-252 (I)
133. S-161 — S-236	1. A-000 — A-451	52. W-252 (J) — W-326 (F)
134. S-240 — S-300	2. A-452 — B-246	53. W-326 (G) — W-426 (D)
135. S-310 — S-320 (L)	3. B-250 — B-400	54. W-426 (E) — W-462 (E)
136. S-320 (M) — S-340 (J)	4. B-410 — B-524	55. W-462 (F) — W-623 (C)
137. S-340 (K) — S-352	5. B-525 — B-623 (I)	56. W-623 (D) — Institutions
138. S-353 — S-362 (R)	6. B-623 (J) — B-650 (D)	
139. S-362 (S) — S-365 (R)	7. B-650 (F) — B-653 (L)	*Tennessee. T772.*
140. S-365 (S) — S-420	8. B-653 (M) — C-234	1. A-000 — A-416
141. S-421 — S-452	9. C-235 — C-452	2. A-420 — A-536 (L)
142. S-453 — S-513	10. C-453 — C-545	3. A-536 (M) — B-200 (O)
143. S-514 — S-630 (A)	11. C-550 — C-636 (K)	4. B-200 (P) — B-266
144. S-530 (A) — S-530 (J)	12. C-636 (L) — D-120 (V)	5. B-300 — B-400 (L)
145. S-530 (J) — S-530 (Z)	13. D-120 (W) — D-500	6. B-400 (M) — B-452
146. S-531 — S-536 (S)	14. D-510 — E-152 (I)	7. B-453 — B-536
147. S-536 (T) — S-660 (K)	15. E-152 (J) — F-236	8. B-550 — B-622
148. S-660 (L) — S-620	16. F-240 — F-600	9. B-623 — B-634 (I)
149. S-621 — S-661	17. F-610 — G-226	10. B-634 (L) — B-650 I)
160. S-662 — T-436	18. G-230 — G-434	11. B-650 (M) — B-653 (R)
161. T-440 — T-612	19. G-435 — G-616	12. B-653 (S) — C-200 (D)
162. T-613 — T-600	20. G-616 — G-660 (S)	13. C-200 (E) — C-322
163. T-610 — T-662	21. G-660 (T) — H-236	14. C-323 — C-435
164. T-653 — V-366	22. H-240 — H-400 (R)	15. C-436 — C-500 (I)
165. V-400 — W-136	23. H-400 (S) — H-630	16. C-500 J) — C-552 (L)
156. W-140 — W-230	24. H-631 — H-626	17. C-552 (M) — C-622
167. W-231 — W-266	25. H-626 — J-246	18. C-623 — C-640 (L)
168. W-300 — W-324	26. J-260 — J-620 (L)	19. C-640 (M) — D-120 (L)
169. W-326 — W-362 (I)	27. J-620 (M) — J-625 (M)	20. D-120 (M) — D-250 (L)
160. W-362 (J) — W-420 (F)	28. J-526 (N) — K-616	21. D-250 (M) — D-516
161. W-420 (G) — W-426 (I)	29. K-620 — L-166	22. D-520 — D-646

23. D-650 — E-363 (J)
24. E-363 (L) — F-235
25. F-236 — F-455
26. F-456 — F-636
27. F-640 — G-236
28. G-240 — G-450 (I)
29. G-450 (J) — F-615
30. G-616 — G-650 (S)
31. G-650 (T) — H-200 (C)
32. H-200 (D) — H-250
33. H-252 — H-346
34. H-350 — H-400
35. H-410 — H-520 (I)
36. H-520 (J) — H-542
37. H-543 — H-624
38. H-625 — H-651
39. H-652 — J-366
40. J-400 — J-520 (V)
41. J-520 (W) — J-525 (R)
42. J-525 (S) — K-400 (L)
43. K-400 (M) — K-600
44. K-610 — L-200 (C)
45. L-200 (D) — L-340
46. L-341 — L-521
47. L-522 — M-200 (F)
48. M-200 (G) — M-235
49. M-236 — M-250 (K)
50. M-250 (L) — M-265
51. M-266 — M-425
52. M-426 — M-520
53. M-521 — M-600
54. M-610 — M-635 (D)
55. M-636 (E) — N-260
56. N-251 — O-162
57. O-163 — P-116
58. P-120 — P-360
59. P-361 — P-500
60. P-510 — P-622
61. P-623 — P-651
62. P-652 — R-163 (D)
63. R-163 (E) — R-240
64. R-241 — R-316
65. R-320 — R-520
66. R-521 — S-156
67. S-160 — S-315 (I)
68. S-316 (J) — S-362
69. S-353 — S-431
70. S-432 — S-530 (A)
71. S-530 (A) — S-530 (R)
72. S-530 (S) — S-552 (I)
73. S-552 (J) — T-211

74. T-212 — T-460 (J)
75. T-460 (J) — T-516
76. T-520 — T-636
77. T-640 — V-516
78. V-520 — W-251
79. W-252 — W-300
80. W-310 — W-361
81. W-362 — W-420 (D)
82. W-420 (E) — W-426 (I)
83. W-426 (J) — W-452 (K)
84. W-452 (L) — W-622
85. W-623 — Y-520
86. Y-521 — Institutions

Texas. T773.
1. A-000 — A-416
2. A-420 — A-536 (R)
3. A-536 (S) — B-226
4. B-230 — B-336
5. B-340 — B-425
6. B-426 — B-525
7. B-526 — B-620 (Q)
8. B-620 (R) — B-635 (F)
9. B-635 (G) — B-650 (V)
10. B-650 (W) — C-136
11. C-140 — C-236
12. C-240 — C-436
13. C-440 — C-500 (G)
14. C-500 (H) — C-600 (L)
15. C-600 (M) — C-631
16. C-632 — D-116
17. D-120 — D-166
18. D-200 — D-450
19. D-451 — D-566
20. D-600 — E-336
21. E-340 — E-663
22. F-000 — F-454
23. F-455 — F-631
24. F-632 — G-246
25. G-250 — G-456
26. G-460 — G-620 (B)
27. G-620 (C) — G-650 (L)
28. G-650 (M) — H-200 (I)
29. H-200 (J) — H-300 (F)
30. H-300 (G) — H-400 (L)
31. H-400 (M) — H-513
32. H-514 — H-543
33. H-545 — H-625
34. H-626 — I-136
35. I-140 — J-446
36. J-450 — J-523

37. J-524 — J-525 (W)
38. J-525 (W) — K450
39. K-451 — K-623
40. K-624 — L-200 (J)
41. L-200 (J) — L-365
42. L-400 — L-565
43. L-563 — M-211
44. M-212 — M-245 (Q)
45. M-245 (R) — M-260
46. M-261 — M-420 (I)
47. M-420 (J) — M-520
48. M-521 — M-600
49. M-610 — M-635 (I)
50. M-635 (J) — N-366
51. N-400 — O-416
52. O-420 — P-346
53. P-350 — P-456
54. P-460 — P-622
55. P-623 — R-000 (D)
56. R-000 (E) — R-163 (S)
57. R-163 (T) — R-240
58. R-241 — R-326
59. R-330 — R-533
60. R-534 — S-162 (I)
61. S-162 (J) — S-315 (L)
62. S-315 (M) — S-362 (L)
63. S-362 (M) — S-434
64. S-435 — S-530 (B)
65. S-530 (C) — S-530
66. S-531 — S-626
67. S-630 — T-456
68. T-460 — T-520 (J)
69. T-520 (J) — T-653
70. T-654 — W-000
71. W-100 — W-300 (F)
72. W-300 (G) — W-340
73. W-341 — W-420
74. W-421 — W-452 (A)
75. W-452 (B) — W-452 (V)
76. W-452 (W) — W-636
77. W-640 — Institutions

Utah. T774.
1. A-000 — C-400
2. C-410 — F-426
3. F-430 — H-624
4. H-625 — M-216
5. M-220 — P-446
6. P-450 — S-530 (I)
7. S-530 (J) — Institutions

Vermont. T775.

1. A-000 — B451
2. B-452 — C-145
3. C-150 — C-626
4. C-630 — D-666
5. E-000 — G-416
6. G-420 — H-336
7. H-400 — J-666
8. K-000 — L-566
9. L-600 — M-620
10. M-621 — P-466
11. P-500 — R-266
12. R-300 — S-462
13. S-500 — T-666
14. U-000 — W-566
15. W-600 — Institutions

Virginia. T776.

1. A-000 — A-446
2. A-450 — A-536 (I)
3. A-536 (J) — A-651
4. A-652 — B-246
5. B-250 — B-346
6. B-350 — B-420 (L)
7. B-420 (M) — B-500
8. B-510 — B-615
9. B-616 — B-623 (F)
10. B-623 (G) — B-634
11. B-635 — B-650 (M)
12. B-650 (N) — B-654
13. B-655 — C-200 (K)
14. C-200 (L) — C-400
15. C-410 — C-455 (L)
16. C-455 (M) — C-516
17. C-520 — C-616
18. C-620 — C-635
19. C-636 — C-652
20. C-653 — D-150
21. D-151 — D-340
22. D-342 — D-534
23. D-535 — E-166
24. E-200 — E-516
25. E-520 — F-426
26. F-430 — F-600
27. F-610 — F-666
28. G-000 — G-400
29. G-410 — G-600 (L)
30. G-600 (M) — G-635 (L)
31. G-635 (M) — H-125 (I)
32. H-125 (J) — H-246
33. H-250 — H-400 (V)

34. H-400 (W) — H-520 (Q)
35. H-520 (R) — H-611
36. H-612 — H-624
37. H-625 — I-550
38. I-610 — J-250 (V)
39. J-250 (W) — J-520 (L)
40. J-520 (M) — J-525 (G)
41. J-525 (H) — J-556
42. J-560 — K-500
43. K-510 — L-000 (R)
44. L-000 (S) — L-200 (V)
45. L-200 (W) — L-500
46. L-510 — M-000 (I)
47. M-000 (J) — M-241
48. M-242 — M-300 (I)
49. M-300 (J) — M-451
50. M-452 — M-560 (I)
51. M-560 (J) — M-620 (V)
52. M-620 (W) — M-663
53. N-000 — N-626
54. N-630 — P-200 (F)
55. P-200 (G) — P-400 (L)
56. P-400 (M) — P-531
57. P-532 — P-625 (I)
58. P-625 (J) — P-666
59. R-000 — R-163 (I)
60. R-163 (J) — R-256
61. R-260 — R-326
62. R-330 — R-543 (I)
63. R-543 (J) — S-163 (I)
64. S-163 (J) — S-315 (M)
65. S-315 (N) — S-362
66. S-363 — S-435
67. S-436 — S-530 (F)
68. S-530 (G) — S-530
69. S-531 — S-636
70. S-640 — T-460 (B)
71. T-460 (C) — T-512 (L)
72. T-512 (M) — T-600 (I)
73. T-600 (J) — T-656
74. T-660 — W-166
75. W-200 — W-300 (G)
76. W-300 (H) — W-325 (C)
77. W-325 D) — W-356
78. W-360 — W-425 (J)
79. W-425 (J) — W-451
80. W-452 — W-466
81. W-500 — W-630 (L)
82. W-630 (M) — Institutions

Washington. T777.

1. A-000 — G-466
2. G-500 — M-465
3. M-500 — V-666
4. W-000 — Institutions

West Virginia. T778.

1. A-000 — B-233
2. B-234 — B-526
3. B-530 — B-650
4. B-651 — C-346
5. C-350 — C-536
6. C-540 — C-646
7. C-650 — D-446
8. D-450 — E-424
9. E-425 — F-622
10. F-623 — G-436
11. G-440 — H-166
12. H-200 — H-400 (I)
13. H-400 (J) — H-556
14. H-560 — J-466
15. J-500 — K-400
16. K-410 — L-200 (O)
17. L-200 (P) — L-566
18. L-600 — M-250
19. M-251 — M-460 (I)
20. M-460 (J) — M-625 (I)
21. M-625 (J) — O-265
22. O-300 — P-566
23. P-600 — R-162
24. R-163 — R-466
25. R-500 — S-266
26. S-300 — S-366
27. S-400 — S-530
28. S-531 — T-366
29. T-400 — V-466
30. V-500 — W-326
31. W-330 — W-452 (R)
32. W-452 (S) — Institutions

Wisconsin. T779.

1. A-000 — A-536 (N)
2. A-536 (O) — B-253
3. B-254 — B-426
4. B-430 — B-600 (G)
5. B-600 (H) — B-632 (I)
6. B-632 (J) — B-655
7. B-656 — C-426
8. C-430 — C-614
9. C-615 — D-120
10. D-121 — D-451

11. D-452 — D-650
12. D-651 — E-625
13. E-630 — F-456
14. F-460 — G-136
15. G-140 — G-466
16. G-500 — G-650 (I)
17. G-650 (J) — H-216
18. H-220 — H-415
19. H-416 — H-525 (N)
20. H-525 (O) — H-634
21. H-635 — J-520 (L)
22. J-520 (M) — K-146
23. K-150 — K-451
24. K-452 — K-566
25. K-600 — L-136
26. L-140 — L-500
27. L-510 — L-625 (L)
28. L-625 (M) — M-250 (K)
29. M-250 (L) — M-416
30. M-420 — M-556
31. M-560 — M-625
32. M-626 — N-425 (M)
33. N-425 (N) — O-425 (A)
34. O-425 (B) — P-316
35. P-320 — P-416
36. P-420 — P-641
37. P-642 — R-216
38. R-220 — R-366
39. R-400 — S-136
40. S-140 — S-315 (K)
41. S-315 (L) — S-362 (I)
42. S-362 (J) — S-460
43. S-461 — S-530 (S)
44. S-530 (T) — S-636 (I)
45. S-636 (J) —T-434
46. T-435 —T-655
47. T-656 — W-156
48. W-160 —W-351
49. W-352 —W-446
50. W-450 —Y-466
51. Y-500 — Institutions

Wyoming. T780.
1. A-000 — Institutions

**TENTH CENSUS OF THE UNITED STATES, 1880. T9.
1,454 ROLLS.**

Alabama.

1. Autauga, Baldwin, and Bibb (part: EDs 1-3, sheet 50) Counties
2. Bibb (cont'd: ED 3, sheet 51-end) Blount, and Barbour (part: EDs 1-15, sheet 8) Counties
3. Barbour (cont'd: ED 15, sheet 9-end) and Bullock (part: EDs 1-33, sheet 20) Counties
4. Bullock (cont'd ED 33, sheet 21-end), Butler, and Calhoun (part: EDs 1-10, sheet 2) Counties
5. Calhoun (cont'd: ED 10, sheet 3-end) and Chambers (part: EDs 1-175, sheet 12) Counties
6. Chambers (cont'd: ED 179, sheet 1-end), Cherokee, Chilton, and Choctaw (part: EDs 1-16, sheet 22) Counties
7. Choctaw (cont'd: ED 16, sheet 23-end), Clarke, and Clay (part: EDs 1-38, sheet 37) Counties
8. Clay (cont'd: ED 39, sheet 1-end), Cleburne, Coffee, and Colbert Counties
9. Conecuh, Coosa, Covington, and Crenshaw (part: EDs 1-57, sheet 12) Counties
10. Crenshaw (cont'd: ED 57, sheet 13-end), Cullman, Dale, and Dallas (part: EDs 1-48, sheet 14) Counties
11. Dallas County (cont'd: ED 48, sheet 15-ED 75, sheet 16)
12. Dallas (cont'd: ED 75, sheet 17-end), De Kalb, Elmore, and Escambia Counties
13. Etowah, Fayette, Franklin, and Geneva Counties
14. Greene and Hale (part: EDs 1-55, sheet 22) Counties
15. Hale (cont'd: ED 55, sheet 23-end) and Henry (part: EDs 1-84, sheet 40) Counties
16. Henry (cont'd: ED 84, sheet 41-end), Jackson, and Jefferson (part: EDs 1-68, sheet 24) Counties
17. Jefferson (cont'd: ED 68, sheet 25-end), Lamar, and Lauderdale (part: EDs 1-145, sheet 38) Counties
18. Lauderdale (cont'd: ED 145, sheet 39-end) and Lawrence Counties
19. Lee and Limestone (part: EDs 1-182, sheet 12) Counties
20. Limestone (cont'd: ED 182, sheet 13-end) and Lowndes (part: EDs 1-111, sheet 6) Counties
21. Lowndes (cont'd: ED 111, sheet 7-end), Macon, and Madison (part: EDs 1-207, sheet 18) Counties
22. Madison (cont'd: ED 207, sheet 19-end) and Marengo (part: EDs 1-94, sheet 36) Counties
23. Marengo (cont'd: ED 94, sheet 37-end), Marion, and Marshall (part: EDs 1-252, sheet 20) Counties
24. Marshall (cont'd: ED 252, sheet 21-end), Monroe, and Mobile (part: EDs 1-119, sheet 20) Counties
25. Mobile County (cont'd: ED 119, sheet 210-ED 144, sheet 72)
26. Montgomery County (part: ED 124, sheet 1-ED 138, sheet 6)
27. Montgomery (cont'd: ED 138, sheet 7-end), Morgan, and

Perry (part: EDs 1-279, sheet 40) Counties
28. Perry (cont'd: ED 279, sheet 41-end) and Pickens (part: EDs 1-102, sheet 17) Counties
29. Pickens (cont'd: ED 102, sheet 18-end) Pike, and Randolph (part: EDs 1-110, sheet 22) Counties
30. Randolph (cont'd: ED 110, sheet 23-end) and Russell Counties
31. St. Clair, Shelby, and Sumter (part: EDs 1-165, sheet 28) Counties
32. Sumter (cont'd: ED 165, sheet 29-end) and Talladega (part: EDs 1-138, sheet 2) Counties
33. Talladega (cont'd: ED 138, sheet 3-end), Tallapoosa, and Tuscaloosa (part: EDs 1-155, sheet 35) Counties
34. Tuscaloosa (cont'd: ED 155, sheet 36-end), Walker, Washington, and Wilcox (part: EDs 1-184, sheet 18) Counties
35. Wilcox (cont'd: ED 184, sheet 19-end) and Winston Counties

Arizona.

36. Apache, Maricopa, Mohave, Pima, and Pinal (part: EDs 1-11, sheet 7) Counties
37. Pinal (cont'd: ED 11, sheet 8-end), Yavapai, and Yuma Counties

Arkansas.

38. Arkansas, Ashley, Baxter, and Benton (part: EDs 1-15, sheet 20) Counties
39. Benton (cont'd: ED 15, sheet 21 end), Boone, Bradley, Calhoun, and Carroll (part: EDs 1-28, sheet 20) Counties
40. Carroll (cont'd: ED 28, sheet 21-end), Chicot, Clark, Clay, and Columbia (part: EDs 1-36, sheet 13) Counties
41. Columbia (cont'd: ED 36, sheet 14-end), Conway, Craighead, and Crawford (part: EDs 1-48, sheet 12) Counties
42. Crawford (cont'd: ED 48, sheet 13-end), Crittenden, Cross, Dallas, and Desha (part: EDs 1-72, sheet 3) Counties
43. Desha (cont'd: ED 72, sheet 4-end), Dorsey, Drew, and Faulkner (part: EDs 1-55, sheet 24) Counties
44. Faulkner (cont'd: ED 55, sheet 25-end) and Franklin Counties
45. Fulton, Garland, Grant, and Greene Counties
46. Hempstead, Hot Spring, Howard, and Independence (part: EDs 1-118, sheet 13) Counties
47. Independence (cont'd : EDs 1-18, sheet 14-end), Izard, and Jackson Counties
48. Jefferson, Johnson, and Lafayette (part: EDs 1-154, sheet 59) Counties
49. Lafayette (cont'd: ED 154, sheet 60-end), Lawrence, Lee, Lincoln, and Little River (part: EDs 1-183, sheet 16) Counties

50. Little River (cont'd: ED 183, sheet 17-end), Logan, Lonoke, and Madison Counties

51. Marion, Miller, Mississippi, and Monroe (part: EDs 1-209, sheet 18) Counties

52. Monroe (cont'd: ED 209, sheet 19-end), Montgomery, Nevada, Newton, and Ouchita (part: EDs 1-227, sheet 26) Counties

53. Ouachita (cont'd: ED 227, sheet 27-end), Perry, Phillips, Pike, Poinsett, and Polk (part: EDs 1-127, sheet 10) Counties

54. Polk (cont'd: ED 127, sheet 11-end), Pope, Prairie, and Pulaski (part: EDs 1-145, sheet 26) Counties

55. Pulaski (cont'd: ED 145, sheet 27-end), Randolph, and St. Francis (part: EDs 1-261, sheet 26) Counties

56. St. Francis (cont'd: ED 261, sheet 27-end), Saline, Scott, Searey, and Sebastian (part: EDs 1-179, sheet 24) Counties

57. Sebastian (cont'd: ED 179, sheet 25-end), Sevier, Sharp, Stone, and Union (part: EDs 1-271, sheet 16) Counties

58. Union (cont'd: ED 271, sheet 17-end) Van Buren, and Washington (part: EDs 1-213, sheet 18) Counties

59. Washington (cont'd: ED 213, sheet 19-end), White, and Woodruff (part: EDs 1-298, sheet 10) Counties

60. Woodruff (cont'd: ED 298, sheet 11-end) and Yell Counties

California.

61. Alameda County (part: EDs 1-11, sheet 24)

62. Alameda (cont'd: ED 12, sheet 1-end) and Alpine Counties

63. Amador, Butte, and Calaveras (part: EDs 1-42, sheet 16) Counties

64. Calaveras (cont'd: ED 42, sheet 17-end), Colusa, and Contra Costa Counties

65. Del Norte, El Dorado, Fresno, and Humboldt (part: EDs 1-30, sheet 36) Counties

66. Humboldt (cont'd: ED 30, sheet 37-end), Inyo, Kera, Lake, Lassen, and Los Angeles (part: EDs 1-218, sheet 40) Counties

67. Los Angeles County (cont'd: ED 218, sheet 41-end)

68. Marin, Mariposa, Mendocino, and Merced Counties

69. Modoc, Mono, Monterey, and Napa Counties

70. Nevada, Placer, and Plumas Counties

71. Sacramento and San Benito (part: EDs 1-60, sheet 52) Counties

72. San Benito (cont'd: ED 60, sheet 53-end), San Bernardino, and San Diego Counties and city of San Francisco, wards 1 and 2 (part: ED 11, sheet 31)

73. City of San Francisco, wards 2, 3, and 4 (cont'd: ED 12, sheet 1-ED 41, sheet 14)

74. City of San Francisco, wards 4-8 (cont'd: ED 41, sheet 15-ED 75, sheet 12)

75. City of San Francisco, wards 8 and 9 (cont'd: ED 75, sheet 13-ED 110, sheet 31; ED 104B; ED 104C; EDs 259-260)

76. City of San Francisco, ward 10 (cont'd: ED 111, sheet 1-ED 145, sheet 80)

77. City of San Francisco, ward 11 (cont'd: ED 146, sheet 1-ED 173, sheet 40)

78. City of San Francisco, wards 11 and 12 (cont'd: ED 174, sheet 1-ED 205, sheet 6)

79. City of San Francisco, ward 12 (cont'd: ED 205, sheet 7-end), and San Joaquin County (part: EDs 1-97, sheet 26)

80. San Joaquin (cont'd: ED 97, sheet 27-end), San Luis Obispo, and San Mateo Counties

81. Santa Barbara and Santa Clara (part: EDs 1-252, sheet 36) Counties

82. Santa Clara (cont'd: ED 252, sheet 37-end), Santa Cruz, Shasta, and Sierra (part: EDs 1-97, sheet 4) Counties

83. Sierra (cont'd: ED 97, sheet 5-end) Siskiyou, and Solano Counties

84. Sonoma, Stanislaus, and Sutter (part: EDs 1-138, sheet 26) Counties

85. Sutter (cont'd: ED 138, sheet 27-end), Tehama, Trinity, Tullare, and Tulolumne Counties

86. Ventura, Yolo, and Yuba Counties

Colorado.

87. Arapahoe County (part: ED 4, sheet 24)

88. Arapoahoe (cont'd: ED 4, sheet 25-end), Bent, and Boulder (part: EDs 1-24, sheet 14) Counties

89. Boulder (cont'd: ED 24, sheet 15-end) Chaffee, Clear Creek, Conejos, Costilla, and Custer Counties

90. Douglas, Elbert, El Paso, Fremont, Gilpin, Grand, Gunnis, Hinsdale, and Huerfano (part: EDs 1-60 sheet 44) Counties

91. Huerfano (cont'd: ED 60, sheet 45-end), Jefferson, La Plata, and Lake Counties

92. Larimer, Las Animas, Ouray, Park, Pueblo, Rio Grande, Routt, Saguache, San Juan, and Summit (part: EDs 1-105, sheet 30) Counties

93. Summit (cont'd: ED 105, sheet 31-end) and Weld Counties

Connecticut.

94. Fairfield County (part: ED 108, sheet 1-ED 120, sheet 12)

95. Fairfield County (cont'd: ED 120, sheet 13-ED 138, sheet 35)

96. Fairfield County (cont'd: ED 139, sheet 1-ED 155, sheet 52)

97. Fairfield County (cont'd: ED 155, sheet 53-end) and city of Hartford (part: ED 1, sheet 1-ED 13, sheet 26)

98. City of Hartford and Hartford County (cont'd: ED 13, sheet 27-ED 26, sheet 31)

99. Hartford County (excluding the city of Hartford) (cont'd: ED 27, sheet 1-ED 49, sheet 12)

100. Hartford (excluding the city of Hartford) (cont'd: ED 49, sheet 13-end) and Litchfield (part: EDs 1-8, sheet 24) Counties

101. Litchfield County (cont'd: ED 8, sheet 25-end)

102. Middlesex County

103. New Haven County (excluding the city of New Haven) (part: ED 33, sheet 1-ED 52, sheet 16)

104. New Haven County (excluding the city of New Haven) (cont'd: ED 52, sheet 17-ED 69, sheet 20)

105. New Haven County (cont'd: ED 69, sheet 21-ED 82 sheet 56) and city of New Haven, wards 1-5

106. City of New Haven, wards 6-13, and New Haven County (excluding the city of New Haven) (cont'd: ED 83, sheet 1-ED 102, sheet 12)

107. New Haven County (excluding the city of New Haven) (cont'd: ED 102, sheet 13-end) and New London (part: EDs 1-96, sheet 44) Counties

108. New London County (cont'd: ED 96, sheet 45-ED 117, sheet 22)

109. New London (cont'd: ED 117, sheet 23-end), Tolland, and Windham (part: EDs 1-124, sheet 34) Counties

110. Windham County (cont'd: ED 124, sheet 35-end)

Dakota.

111. Aurora, Barnes, Borman, Rusk, Walworth, Campbell, Beadle, Billings, Bon Homme, Brookings, Brown, Brule, Burleigh, Cass, and Clark Counties

112. Clay, Codington, Custer, Davison, Day, Deuel, Emmons, Forsyth, Shannon, Foster, Faulk, Grand Forks, Grant, Hamlin, Hand, Hanson, Hughes (part: ED 99 sheet 11-ED 99, sheet 13), Stanley (part: ED 90, sheet 13 [1 page only]), Hughes (cont'd: ED 90, sheet 14-ED 90, sheet 19), Stanley (cont'd: ED 90, sheet 20 [1 page only]), Hutchinson, Armstrong, and Kidder Counties

113. Kingsbury, Lake, Lawrence, Mandan, Lincoln, Lyman, Buffalo, McCook, Meyer, Miner, and Minnehaha Counties

114. Moody, Morton, Pembina, Pennington, Ramsey, Ransom (part: ED 57, sheet 1-ED 57, sheet 14) La Moure, Ransom (part: ED 57, sheet 16-ED 57, sheet 18), Richland, Spink, Stanley (cont'd: ED 90, sheet 1-ED 90, sheet 29), Stevens, Stutsman, Sully, Todd, Carles Mix, Couglas, Traill, Turner, and Union (part: EDs 1-4, sheet 18) Counties

115. Union (cont'd: ED 4, sheet 19-end), Wallette, Mountrail, Williams, Howard, and Yankton Counties, the Sisseton and Wahpeton Indian Reservations, and Fort Sisseton

Delaware.

116. Kent County (part: EDs 1-37, sheet 14)

117. Kent (cont'd: ED 37, sheet 15-end) and Sussex (part: EDs 1-50, sheet 30) Counties

118. Sussex (cont'd: ED 50, sheet 31-end) and New Castle (part: EDs 1-11, sheet 24) Counties

119. New Castle County (cont'd: ED 11, sheet 25-ED 26, sheet 18)

120. New Castle County (cont'd: ED 26, sheet 19-end)

District of Columbia.

121. District of Columbia and city of Washington (part: ED 1, sheet 1-ED 22, sheet 26)

122. City of Washington (cont'd: ED 23, sheet 1-ED 27, sheet 45; ED 94, sheet 1-ED 95, sheet 13; ED 28, sheet 1-ED 29, sheet 44; ED 96, sheet 1-ED 96, sheet 17; ED 30, sheet 1-ED 37, sheet 55; ED 97, sheet 1-ED 98, sheet 18; ED 38, sheet 1-ED 38, sheet 46; ED 99, sheet 1-ED 99, sheet 8; ED 39, sheet 1-ED 41, sheet 54; ED 100, sheet 1-ED 100, sheet 19; ED 42, sheet 1-ED 42, sheet 55)

123. City of Washington (cont'd: ED 43, sheet 9-ED 54, sheet 38; ED 101 sheet 1-ED 101, sheet 7; ED 55, sheet 1-ED 70, sheet 32)

124. City of Washington (cont'd: ED 70, sheet 33-ED 72, sheet 52; ED 102, sheet 1-ED 107, sheet 26; ED 73, sheet 1-ED 79, sheet 55; ED 104, sheet 1-ED 104, sheet 13; ED 106, sheet 1-ED 106, sheet 6; ED 108, sheet 1; ED 79, sheet 2-ED 90, sheet 35)

Florida.

125. Alachua and Baker Counties

126. Bradford, Brevard, Calhoun, Clay, Columbia, Dade, and Duval Counties

127. Escambia, Franklin, and Gadsden (part: EDs 1-53, sheet 16) Counties

128. Gadsden (cont'd: ED 53, sheet 17-end), Hamilton, Hernando, Hillsborough, Holmes, and Jackson Counties

129. Jefferson, Lafayette, and Leon (part: EDs 1-91, sheet 30) Counties

130. Leon (cont'd: ED 91, sheet 31-end), Levy, Liberty, Madison, Manatee, and Marion Counties

131. Monroe, Nassau, Orange, Polk, Putnam, and St. Johns (part: EDs 1-140, sheet 5) Counties

132. St. Johns (cont'd: ED 140, sheet 6-end), Santa Rosa, Sumter, Suwannee, Taylor, Volusia, Wakulla, Walton, and Washington Counties

Georgia.

133. Appling, Baker, Baldwin, Banks, and Bartow (part: EDs 1-2, sheet 52) Counties

134. Bartow (cont'd: ED 2, sheet 53-end), Berrien, and Bibb (part: EDs 1-13, sheet 56) Counties

135. Bibb (cont'd: ED 14, sheet 1-end), Brooks, Bryan, and Bulloch Counties

136. Burke, Butts, and Calhoun (part: EDs 1-8, sheet 75) Counties

137. Calhoun (cont'd: ED 9, sheet 76-end), Camden, Campbell, Carroll, and Catoosa (part: EDs 1-12, sheet 8) Counties

138. Catoosa (cont'd: ED 12, sheet 9-end), Charlton, and Chatham (part: EDs 1-32, sheet 26) Counties

139. Chatham (cont'd: ED 32, sheet 27-end), Chattahoochee, Chattooga, and Cherokee (part: EDs 1-24, sheet 34) Counties

140. Cherokee (cont'd: ED 24, sheet 35-end) Clarke, Clay, Clayton, and Clinch Counties

141. Cobb, Coffee, Colquitt, Columbia, and Coweta (part: EDs 1-38, sheet 26) Counties

142. Coweta (cont'd: ED 38, sheet 27-end), Crawford, Dade, and Dawson Counties

143. Decatur, De Kalb, Dodge, and Dooly (part: EDs 1-20, sheet 2, and ED 20, sheet 4) Counties

144. Dooly (cont'd: ED 20, sheet 3; ED 20 sheet 1; ED 20, sheet 5-end) Dougherty, Douglas, and Early (part: EDs 1-27, sheet 58) Counties

145. Early (cont'd: ED 27 sheet 59-end), Echols, Effingham, Elbert, Emanuel, and Fannin Counties

146. Fayette, Floyd, and Forsyth (part: ED 73, sheet 1-12) Counties

147. Forsyth (cont'd: ED 73, sheet 13-end), Franklin, and Fulton (part: EDs 1-90, sheet 32) Counties

148. Fulton (cont'd: ED 90, sheet 33-end), Gilmer, and Glascock Counties

149. Glynn, Gordon, Greene, and Gwinnett (part: EDs 1-123, sheet 20) Counties

150. Gwinnett (cont'd: ED 123, sheet 21-end), Habersham, Hall, and Hancock (part: EDs 1-48, sheet 26) Counties

151. Hancock (cont'd: ED 48, sheet 27-end), Haralson, Harris, and Hart Counties

152. Heard, Henry, and Houston (part: EDs 1-31, sheet 53) Counties

153. Houston (cont'd: ED 31, sheet 54-end), Irwin, Jackson, and Jasper (part: EDs 1-75, sheet 19) Counties

154. Jasper (cont'd: ED 75, sheet 20-end), Jefferson, Johnson, Jones, and Laurens (part: EDs 1-63, sheet 28) Counties

155. Laurens (cont'd: ED 63, sheet 29-end), Lee, Liberty, Lincoln, and Lowndes (part: EDs 1-73, sheet 10) Counties

156. Lowndes (cont'd: ED 73, sheet 11-end) Lumpkin, McDuffie, McIntosh, and Macon Counties

157. Madison, Marion, and Meriwether Counties

158. Miller, Milton, Mitchell, and Monroe Counties

159. Montgomery, Morgan, Murray, and Muscogee Counties

160. Newton, Oconee, Oglethorpe, Paulding, and Pickens (part: EDs 1-162, sheet 16) Counties

161. Pickens (cont'd: ED 162, sheet 17-end) Pierce, Pike, and Polk Counties

162. Pulaskis, Putnam, Quitman, Rabun, and Randolph (part: EDs 1- 59, sheet 28) Counties

163. Randolph (cont'd: ED 59, sheet 29-end) and Richmond (part: EDs 1-103, sheet 58) Counties

164. Richmond (cont'd: ED 103, sheet 59-end), Rockdale, Schley, Screven, and Spalding (part: EDs 1-116, sheet 30)

Counties

165. Spalding (cont'd: ED 116, sheet 1-end) Stewart, and Sumter (part: EDs 1-74, sheet 60) Counties

166. Sumter (cont'd: ED 74, sheet 61-end), Talbot, Taliaferro, Tattnall, Taylor, Telfair, and Telrell (part: EDs 1-79, sheet 59) Counties

167. Terrell (cont'd: ED 79, sheet 60-end), Thoomas, Towns, and Troup (part: EDs 1-130, sheet 22) Counties

168. Troup (cont'd: ED 130, sheet 23-end) and Twiggs Counties

169. Union, Upson, Walker, and Walton (part: ED 116, sheet 20, 23-24) Counties

170. Walton (cont'd: ED 116, sheet 21, 22, 25-end) Ware, Warren, and Washington (part: EDs 1-127, sheet 22) Counties

171. Washington (cont'd: ED 127, sheet 23-end), Wayne, Webster, White, and Whitfield Counties

172. Wilcox, Wilkes, Wilkinson, and Worth Counties

Idaho.

173. Entire territory

Illinois.

174. Adams County (part: EDs 1-25, sheet 4)

175. Adams (cont'd: ED 25, sheet 5-end), Alexander, and Bond (part: EDs 1-66, sheet 16) Counties

176. Bond (cont'd: ED 66, sheet 17-end), Boone, and Brown Counties

177. Bureau and Calhoun (part: EDs 1-44, sheet 12) Counties

178. Calhoun (cont'd: ED 44, sheet 13-end) Carroll, and Cass Counties

179. Champaign County (part: EDs 1-18, sheet 4)

180. Champaign (cont'd: ED 18, Sheet 5-end) and Christian (part: EDs 1-69, sheet 26) Counties

181. Christian (cont'd: ED 69, sheet 27-end), Clark, and Clay (part: EDs 1-148, sheet 16) Counties

182. Clay (cont'd: ED 148, sheet 17-end), Clinton, and Coles (part: EDs 1-49, sheet 38) Counties

183. Coles (cont'd: ED 49, sheet 39-end), Crawford, and Cumberland (part: EDs 1-63, sheet 2) Counties

184. Cumberland (cont'd: ED 63, sheet 3-end) and city of Chicago, wards 1 and 2 (part: ED 1, sheet 1-ED 12, sheet 8)

185. City of Chicago, wards 2 and 3 (cont'd: ED 12, sheet 9-ED 20, sheet 37)

186. City of Chicago, ward 4 (cont'd: ED 21, sheet 1-ED 30, sheet 52)

187. City of Chicago, wards 4 and 5 (cont'd: ED 30, sheet 49-ED 39, sheet 46)

188. City of Chicago, wards 5 and 6 (cont'd: ED 40, sheet 1-ED 53, sheet 20)

189. City of Chicago, ward 6 (cont'd: ED 53, sheet 21-ED 62,

sheet 41)

190. City of Chicago, ward 7 (cont'd: ED 63, sheet 1-ED 77, sheet 42)

191. City of Chicago, ward 7 (cont'd: ED 77, sheet 43-ED 90, sheet 34)

192. City of Chicago, wards 8-11 (cont'd: ED 90, sheet 35-ED 105, sheet 16)

193. City of Chicago, wards 11 and 12 (cont'd: ED 105, sheet 17- ED 115, sheet 8)

194. City of Chicago, wards 12 and 13 (cont'd: ED 115, sheet 9-ED 130, sheet 24)

195. City of Chicago, wards 13 and 14 (cont'd: ED 130, sheet 25- ED 111, sheet 36)

196. City of Chicago, ward 14 (cont'd: ED 111, sheet 37-ED 155, sheet 49)

197. City of Chicago, wards 15 and 16 (cont'd: ED 156, sheet 1-ED 170, sheet 52)

198. City of Chicago, wards 16-18 (cont'd: ED 170, sheet 53-ED 184, sheet 2)

199. City of Chicago, ward 18 (cont'd: ED 184, sheet 3-ED 195, sheet 32)

200. Cook County (excluding the city of Chicago) (cont'd: ED 195, sheet 33-ED 208, sheet 61)

201. Cook County (excluding the city of Chicago) (cont'd: ED 209, sheet 1-ED 223, sheet 14)

202. Cook County (excluding the city of Chicago) (cont'd: ED 223, sheet 15-end) and De Kalb (part: EDs 1-45, sheet 26) Counties

203. De Kalb (cont'd: ED 45, sheet 27-end) De Witt, Douglas, and Du Page (part: EDs 1-247, sheet 12) Counties

204. Du Page (cont'd: ED 247, sheet 13-end), Edwards, and Edgar (part: EDs 1-97, sheet 18) Counties

205. Edgar (cont'd: ED 97, sheet 19-end) and Effingham Counties

206. Fayette and Ford Counties

207. Franklin and Fulton (part: EDs 1-46, sheet 4) Counties

208. Fulton (cont'd: ED 46, sheet 5-end) and Gallatin Counties

209. Greene and Grundy (part: EDs 1-12, sheet 12) Counties

210. Grundy (cont'd: ED 12, sheet 13-end) and Hamilton Counties

211. Hancock and Hardin Counties

212. Henderson and Henry (part: EDs 1-104, sheet 32) Counties

213. Henry (cont'd: ED 104, sheet 33-end) and Iroquois (part: EDs 1-125, sheet 40) Counties

214. Iroquois (cont'd: ED 125, sheet 41-end) and Jackson (part: EDs 1-39, sheet 21) Counties

215. Jackson (cont'd: ED 39, sheet 25-end), Jasper, and Jefferson (part: EDs 1-19, sheet 26) Counties

216. Jefferson (cont'd: ED 49, sheet 27-end), Jersey, and Jo Daviess (part: EDs 1-55, sheet 16) Counties

217. Jo Daviess (cont'd: ED 55, sheet 17-end), Johnson and Kane

(part: EDs 1-74, sheet 22) Counties

218. Kane County (cont'd: ED 74, sheet 23-end)

219. Kankakee and Kendall Counties

220. Knox County (part: EDs 1-152, sheet 23)

221. Knox (cont'd: ED 152, sheet 24-end) and Lake Counties

222. La Salle County (part: EDs 1-669, sheet 14)

223. La Salle County (cont'd: ED 66, sheet 15-ED 86, sheet 24)

224. La Salle (cont'd: ED 86, sheet 25-end) and Lawrence (part: EDs 1-197, sheet 4) Counties

225. Lawrence (cont'd: ED 197, sheet 5-end), Leon, and Livingston (part: EDs 1-102, sheet 4) Counties

226. Livingston County (cont'd: ED 102, sheet 5-end)

227. Logan and McDonough (part: EDs 1-164, sheet 6) Counties

228. McDonough (cont'd: ED 164, sheet 7-end) and McHenry Counties

229. Macon and McLean (part: ED 161, sheet 10) Counties

230. McLean County (cont'd: ED 161, sheet 11-ED 179, sheet 22)

231. McLean County (cont'd: ED 179, sheet 23-end)

232. Macoupin County

233. Madison County (part: EDs 1-28, sheet 4)

234. Madison (cont'd: ED 28, sheet 5-end), Marion, and Marshall (part: ED 1-144, sheet 23) Counties

235. Marshall (cont'd: ED 144, sheet 24-end), Mason, and Massac (part: ED 63, sheet 34) Counties

236. Massac (cont'd: ED 63, sheet 35-end), Menard, and Mercer Counties

237. Monroe and Montgomery Counties

238. Morgan and Moultrie (part: EDs 1-167, sheet 25) Counties

239. Moultrie (cont'd: ED 168, sheet 1-end) and Ogle (part: EDs 1-165, sheet 10) Counties

240. Ogle (cont'd: ED 165, sheet 11-end) and Peoria (part: EDs 1-211, sheet 16) Counties

241. Peoria (cont'd: ED 211, sheet 17-end) and Perry (part: EDs 1-75, sheet 58) Counties

242. Perry (cont'd: ED 75, sheet 59-end), Piatt, and Pike (part: EDs 1-188, sheet 44) Counties

243. Pike (cont'd: ED 188, sheet 45-end), Pope, and Pulaski (part: EDs 1-90, sheet 19) Counties

244. Pulaski (cont'd: ED 90, sheet 20-end), Putnam, and Randolph Counties

245. Richland and Rock Island (part: EDs 1-246, sheet 35) Counties

246. Rock Island (cont'd: ED 246, sheet 36-end) and St. Clair (part: EDs 1-38, sheet 61) Counties

247. St. Clair County (cont'd: ED 39, sheet 1-ED 57, sheet 8)

248. St. Clair (cont'd: ED 57, sheet 9-end), Saline, and Sangamon (part: EDs 1-206, sheet 10) Counties

249. Sangamon County (cont'd: ED 206, sheet 11-ED 230, sheet 33)

250. Sangamon (cont'd: ED 230, sheet 34-end), Schuyler, and

Scott Counties

251. Shelby County (part: EDs 1-200, sheet 54)

252. Shelby (cont'd: ED 200, sheet 55-end), Stark, and Stephenson (part: EDs 1-180, sheet 34) Counties

253. Stephenson (cont'd: ED 180, sheet 35-end) and Tazewell (part: EDs 1-253, sheet 2) Counties

254. Tazewell (cont'd: ED 253, sheet 3-end), Union, and Vermilion (part: EDs 1-207, sheet 4) Counties

255. Vermilion County (cont'd: ED 207, sheet 5-ED 223, sheet 32)

256. Wabash, Warren, and Washington (part: EDs 1-129, sheet 12) Counties

257. Washington (cont'd: ED 129, sheet 13-end), Wayne, and White (part: EDs 1-148, sheet 2) Counties

258. White (cont'd: ED 148, sheet 3-end) and Whiteside (part: EDs 1-206, sheet 28) Counties

254. Whiteside (cont'd: ED 206, sheet 29-end) and Williamson Counties

260. Will County (part: ED 188, sheet 1-ED 211, sheet 68)

261. Will (cont'd: ED 211, sheet 69-end) and Winnebago (part: EDs 1-231, sheet 4) Counties

262. Winnebago (cont'd: ED 231, sheet 5-end) and Woodford Counties

Indiana.

263. Adams County (part: EDs 1-135, sheet 10)

264. Adams (cont'd: ED 135, sheet 11-end) and Allen (part: EDs 1-118, sheet 38) Counties

265. Allen (cont'd: ED 118, sheet 39-end) and Bartholomew (part: EDs 1-6, sheet 6) Counties

266. Bartholomew (cont'd: ED 6, sheet 7-end), Benton, Blackford, and Boone (part: EDs 1-121, sheet 12) Counties

267. Boone (cont'd: ED 121, sheet 13-end), Brown, and Carroll (part: EDs 1-21, sheet 10) Counties

268. Carroll (cont'd: ED 21, sheet 11-end) and Cass Counties

269. Clark and Clay (part: EDs 1-233, sheet 32) Counties

270. Clay (cont'd: ED 234, sheet 1-end), Clinton, and Crawford (part: EDs 1-25, sheet 27) Counties

271. Crawford (cont'd: ED 25, sheet 28-end) and Daviess Counties

272. Dearborn County (part: EDs 1-3, sheet 4)

273. Dearborn (cont'd: ED 3, sheet 5-end), Decatur, and De Kalb (part: EDs 1-88, sheet 16) Counties

274. De Kalb (cont'd: ED 88, sheet 17-end), Delaware, and Dubois (part: ED 163, sheet 20) Counties

275. Dubois (cont'd: ED 163, sheet 21-end) and Elkhart Counties

276. Fayette and Floyd (part: EDs 1-67, sheet 16) Counties

277. Floyd (cont'd: ED 67, sheet 17-end) and Fountain (part: EDs 1-82, sheet 10) Counties

278. Fountain (cont'd: ED 82, sheet 11-end), Franklin, and

Fulton (part: EDs 1-43, sheet 14) Counties

279. Fulton (cont'd: ED 43, sheet 15-end), Gibson, and Grant (part: EDs 1-172, sheet 36) Counties

280. Grant (cont'd: ED 172, sheet 37-end) and Greene (part: EDs 1-306, sheet 24) Counties

281. Greene (cont'd: ED 307, sheet 1-end) and Hamilton Counties

282. Hancock and Harrison (part: EDs 1-92, sheet 34) Counties

283. Harrison (cont'd: ED 92, sheet 35-end) and Hendricks Counties

284. Henry and Howard (part: EDs 1-47, sheet 16) Counties

285. Howard (cont'd: ED 47, sheet 17-end) and Huntington Counties

286. Jackson, Jasper, and Jay (part: EDs 1-150, sheet 35) Counties

287. Jay (cont'd: ED 151, sheet 1-end) and Jefferson (part: EDs 1-127, sheet 20) Counties

288. Jefferson (cont'd: ED 127, sheet 21-end), Jennings, and Johnson (part: EDs 1-154, sheet 14) Counties

289. Johnson (cont'd: ED 154, sheet 15-end) and Knox Counties

290. Kosciusko and Lagrange (part: EDs 1-15, sheet 8) Counties

291. Lagrange (cont'd: ED 18, sheet 4-end), Lake, and La Porte (part: EDs 1-79, sheet 78) Counties

292. La Porte (cont'd: ED 79, sheet 79-end) and Lawrence Counties

293. Madison and Marion (part: EDs 1-96, sheet 31) Counties

294. Marion County (cont'd: ED 96, sheet 32 -ED 111, sheet 32)

295. Marion County (cont'd: ED 111, sheet 33-ED 124, sheet 5)

296. Marion County (cont'd: ED 124, sheet 9-ED 131, sheet 77)

297. Marshall County (part: EDs 1-109, sheet 2)

298. Marshall (cont'd: ED 109, sheet 3-end), Martin, and Miami (part: EDs 1-123, sheet 2) Counties

299. Miami (cont'd: ED 123, sheet 3-end) and Monroe (part: EDs 1-291, sheet 10) Counties

300. Monroe (cont'd: ED 291, sheet 11-end) and Montgomery Counties

301. Morgan, Newton, and Noble (part: EDs 1-70, sheet 11) Counties

302. Noble (cont'd: ED 70, sheet 11-end), Ohio, Orange, and Owen (part: EDs 1-249, sheet 6) Counties

303. Owen (cont'd: ED 249, sheet 7-end) and Parke Counties

304. Perry, Pike, and Porter (part: EDs 1-139, sheet 14) Counties

305. Porter (cont'd: ED 139, sheet 15-end), Posey, and Pulaski (part: EDs 1-150, sheet 12) Counties

306. Pulaski (cont'd: ED 150, sheet 13-end), Putnam, and Randolph (part: EDs 1-164, sheet 17) Counties

307. Randolph (cont'd: ED 164, sheet 18-end) and Ripley (part: EDs 1-158, sheet 28) Counties

308. Ripley (cont'd: ED 158, sheet 29-end), Rush, and St. Joseph (part: EDs 1-160, sheet 6) Counties

309. St. Joseph (cont'd: ED 160, sheet 7-end), Scott, and Shelby

(part: EDs 1-201, sheet 24) Counties

310. Shelby (cont'd: ED 201, sheet 25-end) and Starke Counties

311. Spencer County (part: ED 41, sheet 1-ED 47, sheet 41)

312. Spencer (cont'd: ED 48, sheet 1-end), Steuben, and Sullivan (part: EDs 1-322, sheet 4) Counties

313. Sullivan (cont'd: ED 322, sheet 5-end), Switzerland, and Tippecanoe (part: EDs 1-26, sheet 26; ED 332, sheet 1-ED 332, sheet 15; ED 36, sheet 16; ED 27, sheet 1-2) Counties

314. Tippecanoe County (cont'd: ED 27, sheet 3-end)

315. Tipton and Wabash Counties

316. Union and Vanderburgh (part: EDs 1-72, sheet 14) Counties

317. Vanderburgh County (cont'd: ED 72, sheet 15-end)

318. Vermillion and Vigo (excluding the city of Terre Haute) Counties

319. City of Terre Haute

320. Warren and Warwick (part: EDs 1-63, sheet 1) Counties

321. Warrick (cont'd: ED 63, sheet 5-end), Washington, and Wayne (part: EDs 1-61, sheet 3) Counties

322. Wayne County (cont'd: ED 61, sheet 1-end)

323. Wells and White (part: EDs 1-177, sheet 28) Counties

324. White (cont'd: ED 177, sheet 29-end) and Whitley Counties

Iowa.

325. Adair, Adams, and Allamakee (part: EDs 1-17, sheet 12) Counties

326. Allamakee (cont'd: ED 17, sheet 13-end), Appanoose, Audubon, and Benton (part: EDs 1-29, sheet 10) Counties

327. Benton (cont'd: ED 29, sheet 11-end) and Black Hawk (part: EDs 1-63, sheet 26) Counties

328. Black Hawk (cont'd: ED 64, sheet 1-end), Boone, and Bremer (part: EDs 1-78, sheet 6) Counties

329. Bremer (cont'd: ED 78, sheet 7-end), Buchanan, Buena Vista, and Butler (part: EDs 1-101, sheet 14) Counties

330. Butler (cont'd: ED 101, sheet 15-end), Calhoun, Carroll, and Cass (part: EDs 1-33, sheet 16) Counties

331. Cass (cont'd: ED 33, sheet 17-end), Cedar, and Cerro Gordo (part: EDs 1-44, sheet 5)) Counties

332. Cerro Gordo (cont'd: ED 44, sheet 51-end), Chickasaw, Cherokee, and Clark (part: EDs 1-43, sheet 21) Counties

333. Clarke (cont'd: ED 43, sheet 22-end), Clay, and Clayton Counties

334. Clinton County

335. Crawford, Dallas, and Davis (part: EDs 1-49, sheet 4) Counties

336. Davis (cont'd: ED 49, sheet 5-end) Decatur, and Delaware Counties

337. Des Moines, Dickinson, and Dubuque (part: EDs 1-170, sheet 14) Counties

338. Dubuque (cont'd: ED 170, sheet 15-end) and Emmet Counties

339. Fayette County (part: EDs 191-208, sheet 18)

340. Fayette (cont'd: ED 209, sheet 1-end), Floyd, Franklin, and Fremont (part: EDs 1-65, sheet 6) Counties

341. Fremont (cont'd: ED 65, sheet 7-end), Greene, and Grundy Counties

342. Guthrie, Hamilton, Hancock, and Hardin (part: EDs 1-115, sheet 31) Counties

343. Hardin (cont'd: ED 116, sheet 1-end), Harrison, and Henry (part: EDs 1-89, sheet 10) Counties

344. Henry (cont'd: ED 89, sheet 11-end), Howard, Humboldt, and Ida (part: EDs 1-135, sheet 12) Counties

345. Ida (cont'd: ED 135, sheet 13-end), Iowa, and Jackson (part: EDs 1-317, sheet 26) Counties

346. Jackson (cont'd: ED 317, sheet 27-end), Jasper, and Jefferson (part: EDs 1-74, sheet 25) Counties

347. Jefferson (cont'd: ED 75, sheet 1-end) and Johnson (part: EDs 1-229, sheet 8) Counties

348. Johnson (cont'd: ED 229, sheet 9-end), Jones, and Keokuk (part: EDs 1-152, sheet 32) Counties

349. Keokuk (cont'd: ED 152, sheet 33-end), Kossuth, and Lee (part: ED 13, sheet 8) Counties

350. Lee (cont'd: ED 13, sheet 9-end) and Louisa Counties

351. Linn and Lucas (part: EDs 1-102, sheet 4) Counties

352. Lucas (cont'd: ED 102, sheet 5-end) and Lyon Counties

353. Madison and Mahaska (part: ED 175, sheet 16) Counties

354. Mahaska (cont'd: ED 175, sheet 17-end) and Marion Counties

355. Marshall County (part: EDs 1-298, sheet 10) Counties

356. Marshall (cont'd: ED 298, sheet 11-end), Mills, and Mitchell Counties

357. Monona, Monroe, and Montgomery Counties

358. Muscatine, O,Brien, Osceola, and Page (part: EDs 1-153, sheet 12) Counties

359. Page (cont'd: ED 153, sheet 13-end), Palo Alto, Plymouth, Pocahontas, and Polk (part: EDs 1-161, sheet 22) Counties

360. Polk County (cont'd: ED 161, sheet 23-end)

361. Pottawattamie County (part: EDs 1-248, sheet 25) Counties

362. Pottawattamie (cont'd: ED 248, sheet 26-end), Poweshiek, Ringgold, and Sac (part: EDs 1-186, sheet 5) Counties

363. Sac (cont'd: ED 186, sheet 5-end) and Scott (part: EDs 1-274, sheet 22) Counties

364. Scott (cont'd: ED 274, sheet 23-end), Shelby, Sioux, and Story (part: EDs 1-203, sheet 2) Counties

365. Story (cont'd: ED 203, sheet 3-end) and Tama Counties

366. Taylor and Union Counties

367. Van Buren and Wapello (part: EDs 1-67, sheet 2) Counties

368. Wapello (cont'd: ED 67, sheet 3-end), Warren, and Washington (part: EDs 1-140, sheet 64) Counties

369. Washington (cont'd: ED 140, sheet 65-end), Wayne, and

Webster (part: ED 226, sheet 10) Counties

370. Webster (cont'd: ED 226, sheet 11-end), Winnebago, Winneshiek, and Woodbury (part: EDs 1-240, sheet 4) Counties

371. Woodbury (cont'd: ED 240, sheet 5-end), Worth, and Wright Counties

Kansas.

372. Allen, Anderson, Arapahoe, and Atchison Counties

373. Barber, Barton, and Bourbon (part: EDs 1-31, sheet 14) Counties

374. Bourbon (cont'd: ED 31, sheet 15-end), Brown, Buffalo, and Butler (part: EDs 1-154, sheet 12) Counties

375. Butler (cont'd: ED 154, sheet 13-end), Chase, Chautauqua, and Cherokee (part: EDs 1-40, sheet 28) Counties

376. Cherokee (cont'd: ED 41, sheet 1-end), Cheyenne, Clark, Clay, and Cloud (part: EDs 1-41, sheet 8) Counties

377. Cloud (cont'd: ED 41, sheet 9-end), Coffey, Comanche, and Cowley (part: EDs 1-185, sheet 6) Counties

378. Cowley (cont'd: ED 185, sheet 7-end), Crawford, and Davis (part: ED s1-52, sheet 8) Counties

379. Davis (cont'd: ED 52, sheet 9-end), Decatur, Dickinson, and Doniphan Counties

380. Douglas, Edwards, and Elk Counties

381. Ellis, Ellsworth, Foote, Ford, and Franklin (part: EDs 1-92, sheet 17) Counties

382. Franklin (cont'd: ED 92, sheet 17-end), Gove, Graham, Grant, Greeley, Greenwood, Hamilton, Harper, and Harvey Counties

383. Hodgeman, Jackson, Jefferson, and Jewell (part: EDs 1-127, sheet 14) Counties

384. Jewell (cont'd: ED 127, sheet 15-end), Johnson, Kansas, Kearny Kingman, and Labette (part: EDs 1-108, sheet 29) Counties

385. Labette (cont'd: ED 109, sheet 1-end), Lane, and Leavenworth (part: EDs 1-153, sheet 10) Counties

386. Leavenworth (cont'd: ED 153, sheet 11-end), Lincoln, and Linn (part: ED 131, sheet 14) Counties

387. Linn (cont'd: ED 131, sheet 15-end), Lyon, and McPherson Counties

388. Marion, Marshall, Meade, and Miami (part: EDs 1-138, sheet 6) Counties

389. Miami (cont'd: ED 138, sheet 7-end), Mitchell, and Montgomery (part EDs 1-154, sheet 46) Counties

390. Montgomery (cont'd: ED 154, sheet 47-end), Morris, Nemaha, and Neosho (part: EDs 1-165, sheet 14) Counties

391. Neosho (cont'd: ED 165, sheet 15-end), Ness, Norton, and Osage (part: EDs 1-36, sheet 19) Counties

392. Osage (cont'd: ED 36, sheet 19-end), Osborne, Ottawa, Pawnee, and Phillips (part: EDs 1-227, sheet 16) Counties

393. Phillips (cont'd: ED 227, sheet 17-end) Pottawatomie, Pratt,

Rawlins, and Reno (part: EDs 1-287, sheet 14) Counties

394. Reno (cont'd: ED 287, sheet 15-end), Republic, Rice, and Riley (part: EDs 1-254, sheet 28) Counties

395. Riley (cont'd: ED 254, sheet 29-end), Rooks, Rush, Russell, and Saline (part: EDs 1-293, sheet 26) Counties

396. Saline (cont'd: ED 294, sheet 1-end), Scott, Sedgwick, Sequoyah, Seward, and Shawnee (part: EDs 1-3, sheet 34) Counties

397. Shawnee (cont'd: ED 3, sheet 35-end), Sheridan, Sherman, and Smith Counties

398. Stafford, Stanton, Stevens, Sumner, Thomas, Trego, and Wabaunsee (part: EDs 1-120, sheet 10) Counties

399. Wabaunsee (cont'd: ED 120, sheet 11-end), Wallace, Washington, Wichita, Wilson, and Woodson (part: EDs 1-56, sheet 10) Counties

400. Woodson (cont'd: ED 56, sheet 11-end) and Wyandotte Counties

Kentucky.

401. Adair, Allen, Anderson, and Ballard Counties

402. Barren, Bath, and Bell (part: EDs 1-7, sheet 27) Counties

403. Bell (cont'd: ED 7, sheet 27-end), Boone, Bourbon, and Boyd (part: EDs 1-122, sheet 2) Counties

404. Boyd (cont'd: ED 122, sheet 3-end), Boyle, Bracken, and Breathitt (part: EDs 1-14, sheet 58) Counties

405. Breathitt (cont'd: ED 14, sheet 59-end), Breckinridge, and Bullitt (part: EDs 1-34, sheet 16) Counties

406. Bullitt (cont'd: ED 34, sheet 17-end) Butler, Caldwell, and Calloway (part: ED 102, sheet 36) Counties

407. Calloway (cont'd: ED 102, sheet 37-end) and Campbell (part: ED 48, sheet 10) Counties

408. Campbell (cont'd: ED 48, sheet 11-end), Carroll, Carter, and Casey Counties

409. Christian and Clark (part: EDs 1-54, sheet 12) Counties

410. Ciark (cont'd: ED 54, sheet 13-end), Clay, Clinton, Crittenden, and Cumberland (part: EDs 1-34, sheet 3) Counties

411. Cumberland (cont'd: ED 34, sheet 3-end), Daviess, and Edmonson (part: EDs 1-11, sheet 28) Counties

412. Edmonson (cont'd: ED 11, sheet 29-end), Elliott, Estill, and Fayette (part: EDs 1-65, sheet 20) Counties

413. Fayette (cont'd: ED 65, sheet 21-end), Fleming, and Floyd (part: EDs 1-36, sheet 8) Counties

414. Floyd (cont'd: ED 36, sheet 9-end), Franklin, Fulton, Gallatin, and Garrard (part: EDs 1-41, sheet 40) Counties

415. Garrard (cont'd: ED 41, sheet 41-end), Grant, and Graves (part: EDs 1-92, sheet 28) Counties

416. Graves (cont'd: ED 92, sheet 29-end), Grayson, and Green Counties

417. Greenup, Hancock, and Hardin (part: EDs 1-70, sheet 28) Counties

418. Hardin (cont'd: ED 71, sheet 1-end), Harlan, Harrison, and Hart (part: EDs 1-80, sheet 14) Counties

419. Hart (cont'd: ED 80, sheet 13-end) and Henderson Counties

420. Henry, Hickman, and Hopkins (part: EDs 1-198, sheet 32) Counties

421. Hopkins (cont'd: ED 198, sheet 33-end), Jackson, and Jefferson (excluding the city of Louisville) Counties and city of Louisville, ward 1 (part: EDs 1-101, sheet 64) Counties

422. City of Louisville, wards 1-5 (cont'd: ED 101, sheet 65-ED 117, sheet 34)

423. City of Louisville, wards 5-10 (cont'd: ED 117, sheet 35-ED 140, sheet 22)

424. City of Louisville, ward 10 (cont'd: ED 140, sheet 23-end)

425. Jessamine, Johnson, and Kenton (part: EDs 1-120, sheet 40) Counties

426. Kenton (cont'd: ED 120, sheet 41-end) and Knox (part: EDs 1-54, sheet 44) Counties

427. Knox (cont'd: ED 54, sheet 43-end), Larue, Laurel, Lawrence, and Lee (part: EDs 1-60, sheet 20) Counties

428. Lee (cont'd: ED 60, sheet 21-end), Leslie, Letcher, Lewis, and Lincoln (part: EDs 1-70, sheet 53) Counties

429. Lincoln (cont'd: ED 70, sheet 54-end), Livingston, and Logan Counties

430. Lyon, McCracken, and McLean Counties

431. Madison and Magoffin Counties

432. Marion, Marshall, Martin, and Mason (part: EDs 1-68, sheet 18) Counties

433. Mason (cont'd: ED 68, sheet 19-end), Meade, and Menifee Counties

434. Mercer, Metcalfe, Monroe, and Montgomery (part: EDs 1-128, sheet 4) Counties

435. Montgomery (cont'd: ED 128, sheet 5-end), Morgan, Muhlenberg, and Nelson (part: EDs 1-210, sheet 29) Counties

436. Nelson (cont'd: ED 210, sheet 29-end), Nicholas, and Ohio Counties

437. Oldham and Owen (part: EDs 1-142, sheet 18) Counties

438. Owen (cont'd: ED 142, sheet 19-end), Owsley, Pendleton, and Perry Counties

439. Pike County

440. Powell, Pulaski, Robertson, and Rockcastle (part: EDs 1-97, sheet 12) Counties

441. Rockcastle (cont'd: ED 97, sheet 13-end), Rowan, Russell, Scott, and Shelby (part: EDs 1-186, sheet 14) Counties

442. Shelby (cont'd: ED 186, sheet 15-end), Simpson, Spencer, Taylor, and Todd (part: EDs 1-69, sheet 10) Counties

443. Todd (cont'd: ED 69, sheet 11-end), Trigg, and Trimble Counties

444. Union and Warren (part: EDs 1-235, sheet 49) Counties

445. Warren (cont'd: ED 236, sheet 1-end), Washington, and Wayne Counties

446. Webster, Whitley, Wolfe, and Woodford Counties

Louisiana.

447. Ascension and Assumption (part: EDs 1-101, sheet 36) Parishes

448. Assumption (cont'd: ED 101, sheet 37-end), Avoyelles, Bienville, and Bossier (part: EDs 1-11, sheet 109) Parishes

449. Bossier (cont'd: ED 11, sheet 110-end), Caddo, and Calcasieu (part: EDs 1-8, sheet 50) Parishes

450. Calcasieu (cont'd: ED 8, sheet 51-end), Caldwell, and Cameron (part: EDs 1-5, sheet 16) Parishes

451. Cameron (cont'd: ED 5, sheet 17-end), Catahoula, Claiborne, and Concordia (part: EDs 1-21, sheet 28) Parishes

452. Concordia (cont'd: ED 21, sheet 29-end), De Soto, East Baton Rouge, and East Carroll (part: EDs 1-27, sheet 49) Parishes

453. East Carroll (cont'd: ED 28, sheet 1-end), East Feliciana, Franklin, Grant, and Iberia (part: EDs 1-26, sheet 32) Parishes

454. Iberia (cont'd: ED 26, sheet 33-end), Iberville, Jackson, and Jefferson (part: EDs 1-117, sheet 38) Parishes

455. Jefferson (cont'd: ED 117, sheet 39-end), Lafayette, and Lafourche Parishes

456. Lincoln, Livingston, Madison, and Morehouse (part: EDs 1-53, sheet 44) Parishes

457. Morehouse (cont'd: ED 54, sheet 1-end) and Natchitoches Parishes

458. City of New Orleans, wards 1 and 2 (part: ED 1, sheet 1-ED 8, sheet 20)

459. City of New Orleans, wards 2 and 3 (cont'd: ED 8, sheet 21-ED 26, sheet 10)

460. City of New Orleans, ward 4 (cont'd: ED 27, sheet 1-ED 31, sheet 40)

461. City of New Orleans, wards 4-7 (cont'd: ED 31, sheet 41-ED 49, sheet 28)

462. City of New Orleans, wards 7-9 (cont'd: ED 49, sheet 29-ED 64, sheet 88)

463. City of New Orleans, wards 9-11 (cont'd: ED 64, sheet 89-ED 81, sheet 24)

464. City of New Orleans, wards 11-17 (cont'd: ED 81, sheet 25-end) and Ouachita (part: EDs 1-62, sheet 26) Parishes

465. Ouachita (cont'd: ED 62, sheet 27-end), Plaquemines, Pointe Coupee, and Rapides (part: EDs 1-37, sheet 46) Parishes

466. Rapides Parish (cont'd: ED 37, sheet 47-end)

467. Red River, Richland, Sabine, St. Bernard, and St. Charles (part: EDs 1-150, sheet 100) Parishes

468. St. Charles (cont'd: ED 150, sheet 101-end), St. Helena, and St. James Parishes

469. St. John the Baptist and St. Landry (part: EDs 1-2, sheet 46) Parishes

470. St. Landry (cont'd: ED 2, sheet 47-end) and St. Martin (part: EDs 1-37 sheet 8) Parishes

471. St. Martin (cont'd: ED 37, sheet 9-end), St. Mary, St. Tammany, and Tagipahoa Parishes

472. Tensas and Terrebonne (part: EDs 1-192, sheet 4) Parishes

473. Terrebonne (cont'd: ED 192, sheet 5-end), Union, Vermilion, Vernon, Washington, and Webster (part: EDs 1-30, sheet 20) Parishes

474. Webster (cont'd: ED 30, sheet 21-end), West Baton Rouge, West Carroll, West Feliciana, and Winn Parishes

Maine.

475. Androscoggin County

476. Aroostook County (part: EDs 1-216, sheet 2)

477. Aroostook (cont'd: ED 216, sheet 3-end) and Cumberland (part: EDs 1-34, sheet 32) Counties

478. Cumberland County (cont'd: ED 35, sheet 1-ED 49, sheet 30)

479. Cumberland (cont'd: ED 49, sheet 31-end) and Franklin Counties

480. Hancock County

481. Kennebec County (part: ED 1-100, sheet 7)

482. Kennebec (cont'd: ED 100, sheet 7-end) and Knox (part: EDs 1-111, sheet 7) Counties

483. Knox (cont'd: ED 111, sheet 8-end) and Lincoln (part: EDs 1-130, sheet 44) Counties

484. Lincoln (cont'd: ED 130, sheet 45-end) and Oxford (part: EDs 1-141, sheet 9) Counties

485. Oxford (cont'd: ED 141, sheet 9-end) and Penobscot (part: EDs 1-29, sheet 6) Counties

486. Penobscot County (cont'd: ED 29, sheet 7-end)

487. Piscataquis and Somerset (part: EDs 1-171, sheet 48) Counties

488. Somerset (cont'd: ED 171, sheet 49-end), Sagadahoc, and Waldo (part: EDs 1-83, sheet 10) Counties

489. Waldo (cont'd: ED 83, sheet 11-end) and Washington (part: EDs 1-176, sheet 30) Counties

490. Washington (cont'd: ED 176, sheet 31-end) and York (part: EDs 1-185, sheet 4) Counties

491. York County (cont'd: ED 185, sheet 5-ED 206, sheet 24)

492. York County (cont'd: ED 206, sheet 25-end)

Maryland.

493. Allegany County (part: EDs 1-12, sheet 46)

494. Allegany (cont'd: ED 12, sheet 47-end) and Anne Arundel Counties

495. Baltimore County (excluding the city of Baltimore) (part: EDs 1-240, sheet 14)

496. Baltimore County (excluding the city of Baltimore) (cont'd: ED 240, sheet 15-end)

497. City of Baltimore, wards 1 and 2 (part: EDs 1-21, sheet 8)

498. City of Baltimore, wards 2-5 (cont'd: ED 21, sheet 9-ED 48, sheet 26)

499. City of Baltimore, wards 5-7 (cont'd: ED 48, sheet 27-ED 62, sheet 32; ED 261, sheet 1-sheet 23; ED 63, sheet 1-ED 75, sheet 44; ED 267, sheet 1-ED 267, sheet 10)

500. City of Baltimore, wards 8-11 (cont'd: ED 76 sheet 1-ED 98, sheet 2)

501. City of Baltimore, wards 11-14 (cont'd: ED 98, sheet 3-ED 125, sheet 6)

502. City of Baltimore, wards 14 and 15 (cont'd: ED 125, sheet 7-ED 139, sheet 25)

503. City of Baltimore, wards 16-18 (cont'd: ED 140, sheet 1-ED 171, sheet 18)

504. City of Baltimore, wards 18 and 19 (cont'd: ED 171, sheet 19-ED 199, sheet 30)

505. City of Baltimore, wards 19 and 20 (cont'd: ED 264, sheet 1-11; ED 200, sheet 1-ED 218, sheet 28), Calvert, and Caroline (part: ED 1, sheet 10) Counties

506. Caroline (cont'd: ED 1, sheet 11-end) and Carroll (part: EDs 1-60, sheet 25) Counties

507. Carroll (cont'd: ED 60, sheet 26-end) and Cecil Counties

508. Charles and Dorchester (part: EDs 1-29, sheet 25) Counties

509. Dorchester (cont'd: ED 29, sheet 26-end), Garrett, and Frederick (part: EDs 1-74, sheet 16) Counties

510. Frederick (cont'd: ED 74, sheet 17-end) and Harford (part: EDs 1-36, sheet 10) Counties

511. Harford (cont'd: ED 36, sheet 11-end) and Howard Counties

512. Kent and Montgomery Counties

513. Prince Georges County (part: EDs 1-9, sheet 10)

514. Prince Georges (cont'd: ED 9, sheet 11-end), Queen Annes, and St. Mary's (part: EDs 1-140, sheet 2) Counties

515. St. Mary's (cont'd: ED 140, sheet 3-end), Somerset, and Talbot (part: EDs 1-80, sheet 12) Counties

516. Talbot (cont'd: ED 80, sheet 13-end) and Washington (part: EDs 1-159, sheet 17) Counties

517. Washington (cont'd: ED 160, sheet 1-end), Wicomico and Worcester (part: EDs 1-98, sheet 12) Counties

518. Worcester County (cont'd: ED 98, sheet 13-end)

Massachusetts.

519. Barnstable County (part: EDs 1-15, sheet 2)

520. Barnstable (cont'd: ED 15, sheet 3-end) and Berkshire (part: EDs 1-40, sheet 46) Counties

521. Berkshire County (cont'd: ED 41, sheet 1-ED 57, sheet 58)

522. Berkshire (cont'd: ED 57, sheet 59-end) and Bristol (excluding cities of Fall River, New Bedford, and Taunton) (part: EDs 1-68, sheet 35) Counties

523. Bristol County (excluding cities of Fall River, New Bedford,

and Taunton) (cont'd: ED 68, sheet 35-ED 82, sheet 22)

524. City of Fall River (cont'd: ED 83, sheet 1-ED 90, sheet 28)

525. City of Fall River (cont'd: ED 90, sheet 29-end), city of New Bedford, and city of Taunton (part: ED 118, sheet 116)

526. City of Taunton (cont'd: ED 118, sheet 117-end) and Dukes and Essex (excluding cities of Gloucester, Haverhill, Lawrence, Lynn, Newburyport, and Salem) (part: EDs 1-139, sheet 18) Counties

527. Essex County (excluding the cities of Gloucester, Haverhill, Lawrence, Lynn, Newburyport, and Salem) (cont'd: ED 139, sheet 19-ED 157, sheet 36)

528. Essex County (excluding the cities of Gloucester, Haverhill, Lawrence, Lynn, Newburyport, and Salem) (cont'd: ED 158, sheet 1-ED 173, sheet 26)

529. Essex County (excluding the cities of Gloucester, Haverhill, Lawrence, Lynn, Newburyport, and Salem) (cont'd: ED 173, sheet 27-end), city of Gloucester and City of Haverhill, wards 1-5 (part: EDs 1-187, sheet 70)

530. City of Haverhill, ward 6, and city of Lawrence (cont'd: ED 187, sheet 71-ED 204, sheet 41)

531. City of Lynn and city of Newburyport, wards 1 and 2 (cont'd: ED 205, sheet 1-ED 224, sheet 24)

532. City of Newburyport, wards 2-6, and city of Salem (cont'd: ED 224, sheet 25-ED 241, sheet 37)

533. Franklin County

534. Hampden County (excluding the cities of Holyoke and Springfield) (part: EDs 1-293, sheet 64)

535. Hampden County (excluding the cities of Holyoke and Springfield) (cont'd: ED 294, sheet 1 end) and city of Holyoke (part: EDs 1-307, sheet 34)

536. City of Springfield (cont'd: ED 308, sheet 1-ED 321, sheet 59)

537. Hampshire County (part: EDs 1-346, sheet 27)

538. Hampshire (cont'd: ED 347, sheet 1-end) and Middlesex (excluding the cities of Cambridge, Lowell, Newton, and Somerville) (part: EDs 1-366, sheet 10)

539. Middlesex County (excluding the cities of Cambridge, Lowell, Newton, and Somerville) (cont'd: ED 366, sheet 11-ED 385, sheet 77)

540. Middlesex County (excluding the cities of Cambridge, Lowell, Newton, and Somerville) (cont'd: ED 386, sheet 1-ED 401, sheet 26)

541. Middlesex County (excluding the cities of Cambridge, Lowell, Newton, and Somerville) (cont'd: ED 401, sheet 27-ED 412, sheet 22)

542. Middlesex County (excluding the cities of Cambridge, Lowell, Newton, and Somerville) (cont'd: ED 412, sheet 23-ED 426, sheet 10)

543. Middlesex County (excluding the cities of Cambridge, Lowell, Newton, and Somerville) (cont'd: ED 426, sheet 11-ED 441, sheet 38)

544. City of Cambridge and city of Lowell (part: ED 441, sheet 39-ED 457, sheet 3)

545. City of Lowell (cont'd: ED 457, sheet 3-ED 472, sheet 48)

546. Cities of Newton and Somerville (cont'd: ED 473, sheet 1-ED 491, sheet 34)

547. Nantucket and Norfolk (part: EDs 1-508, sheet 60) Counties

548. Norfolk County (cont'd: ED 509, sheet 1-ED 523, sheet 40)

549. Norfolk (cont'd: ED 523, sheet 41-end) and Plymouth (part: EDs 1-540, sheet 2) Counties

550. Plymouth County (cont'd: ED 540, sheet 3-ED 560, sheet 72)

551. Plymouth County (cont'd: ED 560, sheet 73-end)

552. Suffolk County (excluding the city of Boston) and city of Boston, wards 1-3 (part: ED 574, sheet 1-ED 598, sheet 26)

553. City of Boston, wards 3-6 (cont'd: ED 598, sheet 27-ED 621, sheet 53)

554. City of Boston, wards 6-9 (cont'd: ED 622, sheet 4-ED 642, sheet 26)

555. City of Boston, wards 9-11 (cont'd: ED 642, sheet 27-ED 666, sheet 7)

556. City of Boston, wards 11-17 (cont'd: ED 666, sheet 7-ED 684 sheet 36)

557. City of Boston, wards 14-16 (cont'd: ED 685, sheet 1-ED 704, sheet 8)

558. City of Boston, wards 16-18 (cont'd: ED 704, sheet 9-ED 725, sheet 16)

559. City of Boston, wards 18-20 (cont'd: ED 725, sheet 17-ED 745, sheet 30)

560. City of Boston, wards 20-22 (cont'd: ED 745, sheet 31-ED 765, sheet 3)

561. City of Boston, wards 22-25 (cont'd: ED 765, sheet 3-ED 786, sheet 18)

562. City of Boston, ward 25 (cont'd: ED 786, sheet 19-end) and Worcester County (excluding cities of Fitchburg and Worcester) (part: EDs 1-805, sheet 43)

563. Worcester County (excluding cities of Fitchburg and Worcester) (cont'd: ED 805, sheet 44-ED 830, sheet 42)

564. Worcester County (excluding cities of Fitchburg and Worcester) (cont'd: ED 831, sheet 1-ED 843, sheet 8)

565. Worcester County (excluding cities of Fitchburg and Worcester) (cont'd: ED 843, sheet 9-ED 858, sheet 26)

566. Worcester County (excluding cities of Fitchburg and Worcester) (cont'd: ED 858, sheet 27-ED 873, sheet 43)

567. City of Fitchburg and city of Worcester, wards 1-4 (part: ED 874, sheet 1-ED 889, sheet 12)

568. City of Worcester, wards 4-8 (cont'd: ED 889, sheet 13-end)

Michigan.

569. Alcona (part: ED 1, sheet 1-ED 3, sheet 20) and Allegan (part: EDs 1-25, sheet 45) Counties

570. Allegan (cont'd: ED 25, sheet 46-end), Alpena, Antrim, Baraga, and Barry (part: EDs 1-46 sheet 10) Counties

571. Barry (cont'd: ED 46, sheet 11-end) and Bay (part: EDs 1-25, sheet 29) Counties

572. Bay (cont'd: ED 25, sheet 30-end), Benzie, and Berrien (part: ED 1-17, sheet 10) Counties

573. Berrien (cont'd: ED 17, sheet 11-end) and Branch Counties

574. Calhoun County (part: EDs 1-48, sheet 14)

575. Calhoun (cont'd: ED 48, sheet 13-end) and Cass Counties

576. Charlevoix, Cheboygan, Chippewa, Alcona (part: ED 5, sheet 1-ED 5, sheet 15) Calre, and Clinton (part: EDs 1-66, sheet 2)

577. Clinton (cont'd: ED 50, sheet 1-end), Delta, and Eaton (part: EDs 1-66, sheet 2)

578. Eaton (cont'd: ED 66, sheet 3-end), Emmet, Gladwin, and Grand Traverse Counties

579. Genesee and Gratiot (part: EDs 1-91, sheet 10) Counties

580. Gratiot (cont'd: ED 91, sheet 11-end) and Hillsdale (part: EDs 1-87, sheet 14) Counties

581. Hillsdale (cont'd: ED 87, sheet 15-end) and Houghton Counties

582. Huron and Ingham (part: EDs 1-127, sheet 19) Counties

583. Ingham (cont'd: ED 128, sheet 1-end) and Ionia (part: EDs 1-95, sheet 22) Counties

584. Ionia (cont'd: ED 95, sheet 23-end), Iosco, Isabella, and Isle Royal Counties

585. Jackson County

586. Kalamazoo County (part: EDs 1-144, sheet 14)

587. Kalamazoo (cont'd: ED 144, sheet 15-end), Kalkaska, and Kent (part: EDs 1-130, sheet 12) Counties

588. Kent County (cont'd: ED 130, sheet 13-end)

589. Keweenaw Lake, Lapeer, and Leelanau Counties

590. Lenawee County (part: EDs 1-153, sheet 16)

591. Lenawee County (cont'd: ED 153, sheet 17-end)

592. Livingston, Mackinac, and Macomb (part: EDs 1-209, sheet 20) Counties

593. Macomb (cont'd: ED 209, sheet 21-end), Manistee, Manitou, and Marquette (part: ED 23, sheet 2) Counties

594. Marquette (cont'd: ED 23, sheet 3-end), Mason, and Mecosta (part: ED 172, sheet 87; ED 172, sheet 2-ED 180, sheet 76) Counties

595. Menominee, Midland, Missaukee, and Monroe (part: ED 178, sheet 18) Counties

596. Monroe (cont'd: ED 178, sheet 19-end) and Montcalm (part: EDs 1-236, sheet 21) Counties

597. Montcalm (cont'd: ED 236, sheet 22-end) and Muskegon (part: EDs 1-193, sheet 46) Counties

598. Muskegon (cont'd: ED 193, sheet 47-end), Newaygo, and Oakland (part: EDs 1-256, sheet 28) Counties

599. Oakland (cont'd: ED 256, sheet 29-end) and Oceana Counties

600. Ogemaw, Ontonagon, Osceola, Oscoda, Otsego, and Ottawa (part: EDs 1-239, sheet 28) Counties

601. Ottawa (cont'd: ED 239, sheet 29-end), Presque Isle, Roscommon, and Saginaw (part: EDs 1-298, sheet 42) Counties

602. Saginaw County (cont'd: ED 299, sheet 1-ED 320, sheet 23)

603. Saginaw (cont'd: ED 320, sheet 23-end) and St. Joseph Counties

604. St. Clair County (part: EDs 1-379, sheet 14)

605. St. Clair (cont'd: ED 379, sheet 15-end) and Sanilac (part: EDs 1-342, sheet 6) Counties

606. Sanilac (cont'd: ED 342, sheet 7-end), Schoolcraft, and Shiawassee Counties

607. Tuscola and Van Buren (part: EDs 1-214, sheet 10) Counties

608. Van Buren (cont'd: ED 214, sheet 11-end) and Washtenaw (part: EDs 1-236 sheet 10)

609. Washtenaw (cont'd: ED 237, sheet 11-end), Mecosta (cont'd: ED 253, sheet 1-ED 253, sheet 19), Wexford, and Wayne (excluding the city of Detroit) (part: EDs 1-252, sheet 40) Counties

610. Wayne County (excluding the city of Detroit) (cont'd: ED 252, sheet 41-end) and city of Detroit, ward 1 (part: EDs 1-270, sheet 41)

611. City of Detroit, wards 2-5 (cont'd: ED 271, sheet 1-ED 277, sheet 2)

612. City of Detroit, wards 5-8 (cont'd: ED 277, sheet 3-ED 293, sheet 37)

613. City of Detroit, wards 8-11 (cont'd: ED 294, sheet 1-ED 308, sheet 24)

614. City of Detroit, wards 11-13 (cont'd: ED 308, sheet 25-ED 316, sheet 19)

Minnesota.

615. Aitkin, Anoka, Becker, Polk (part: ED 219, sheet 20-ED 219, sheet 24), Beltrami, Benton, Big Stone, and Blue Earth Counties

616. Brown, Carlton, and Carver (part: EDs 1-93, sheet 25) Counties

617. Carver (cont'd: ED 94, sheet 1-end), Cass, Chippewa, Chisago, Clay, Cook, Cottonwood, Crow Wing, and Dakota (part: EDs 1-195, sheet 32) Counties

618. Dakota (cont'd: ED 195, sheet 33-end), Dodge, Douglas, and Faribault (part: EDs 1-16, sheet 16) Counties

619. Faribault (cont'd: ED 56, sheet 13-end) and Fillmore Counties

620. Freeborn and Goodhue (part: EDs 1-153, sheet 8) Counties

621. Goodhue (cont'd: ED 153, sheet 9-end), Grant, and Hennepin (part: ED 227, sheet 1-ED 231, sheet 35) Counties

622. Hennepin County (cont'd: ED 232, sheet 1-ED 254, sheet 51)

623. Hennepin (cont'd: ED 207, sheet 1-ED 226, sheet 10) and Houston (part: EDs 1-114, sheet 22) Counties

624. Houston (cont'd: ED 115, sheet 1-end), Isanti, Itasca, Jackson, Kanabec, Kandiyohi, Kittson, Lac qui Parle, Lake, and Le Sueur (part: EDs 1-120, sheet 16) Counties

625. Le Sueur (cont'd: ED 120, sheet 17-end), Lincoln, Lyon, and McLeod Counties

626. Marshall, Martin, Meeker, Mille Lacs, Morrison, and Mower Counties

627. Murray, Nicollet, Nobles, and Olmsted (part: EDs 1-200, sheet 18) Counties

628. Olmsted (cont'd: ED 200, sheet 19-end) and Otter Tail (part: EDs 1-175, sheet 4) Counties

629. Otter Tail (cont'd: ED 176, sheet 1-end), Pine, Pipestone, Polk (part: ED 194 sheet 1-ED 212 sheet 7), and Pope Counties

630. Ramsey County (part: EDs 1-16, sheet 10)

631. Ramsey (cont'd: ED 16, sheet 11-end), Redwood, and Renville (part: EDs 1-41, sheet 26) Counties

632. Renville (cont'd: ED 41, sheet 27-end), Rice, Rock, and St. Louis Counties

633. Scott and Sherburne (part: ED 67, sheet 7) Counties

634. Sherburne (cont'd: ED 67, sheet 8-end), Sibley, and Stearns Counties

635. Steele, Stevens, Swift, Todd, Traverse, and Wabasha (part: EDs 1-177, sheet 23) Counties

636. Wabasha (cont'd: ED 178, sheet 1-end), Wadena, Waseca, and Washington (part: EDs 1-30, sheet 10) Counties

637. Washington (cont'd: ED 30, sheet 11-end), Watonwan, Wilkin, and Winona (part: EDs 1-289, sheet 26) Counties

638. Winona (cont'd: ED 289, sheet 27-end), Wright, and Yellow Medicine Counties

Mississippi.

639. Adams County (part: EDs 1-55, sheet 53)

640. Adams (cont'd: ED 56, sheet 1-end), Alcorn, and Amite Counties

641. Attala, Benton, and Bolivar (part: EDs 1-141, sheet 54) Counties

642. Bolivar (cont'd: ED 141, sheet 55-end), Calhoun, and Carroll (part: EDs 1-24, sheet 55) Counties

643. Carroll (cont'd: ED 24, sheet 56-end), Chickasaw, Choctaw, and Claiborne (part: EDs 1-65, sheet 54) Counties

644. Claiborne (cont'd: ED 65, sheet 55-end), Clarke, and Clay (part: EDs 1-45, sheet 60) Counties

645. Clay (cont'd: ED 45, sheet 61-end), Coahoma, and Copiah (part: ED 22, sheet 44) Counties

646. Copiah (cont'd: ED 22, sheet 45-end), Covington, and De Soto Counties

647. Franklin, Greene, and Grenada (part: EDs 1-67, sheet 8) Counties

648. Grenada (cont'd: ED 67, sheet 9-end), Hancock, Harrison, and Hinds (part: EDs 1-10, sheet 16) Counties

649. Hinds (cont'd: ED 10, sheet 17-end) and Holmes (part: ED 7, sheet 50) Counties

650. Holmes (cont'd: ED 7, sheet 51-end), Issaquena, Itawamba, Jackson, and Jasper (part: ED 108, sheet 1-ED 112, sheet 4, ED 158, sheets 1-4) Counties

651. Jasper (cont'd: ED 158, sheet 5-end), Jefferson, and Jones Counties

652. Kemper and Lafayette Counties

653. Lauderdale, Lawrence, and Leake Counties

654. Lee and Leflore Counties

655. Lincoln and Lowndes (part: EDs 1-107, sheet 26) Counties

656. Lowndes (cont'd: ED 107, sheet 27-end), Madison, and Marion (part: EDs 1-133, sheet 6) Counties

657. Marion (cont'd: ED 133, sheet 7-end) and Marshall Counties

658. Monroe and Montgomery (part: beginning-ED 145, sheet 2) Counties

659. Montgomery (cont'd: ED 145, sheet 3-end), Neshoba, Newton, and Noxubee (part: EDs 1-27, sheet 62) Counties

660. Noxubee (cont'd: ED 27, sheet 63-end) and Oktibbeha Counties

661. Panola and Perry (part: EDs 1-134, sheet 12) Counties

662. Perry (cont'd: ED 134, sheet 13-end), Pike, Pontotoc, and Prentiss (part: EDs 1-170, sheet 14) Counties

663. Prentiss (cont'd: ED 170, sheet 15-end), Quitman, Rankin, and Scott Counties

664. Sharkey, Simpson, Smith, and Sumner Counties

665. Sunflower, Tallahatchie, Tate, and Tippah (part: EDs 1-191, sheet 8) Counties

666. Tippah (cont'd: ED 191, sheet 9-end), Tishomingo, Tunica, and Union Counties

667. Warren and Washington (part: EDs 1-89, sheet 19) Counties

668. Washington (cont'd: ED 89, sheet 19-end), Wayne, and Wilkinson (part: EDs 1-150, sheet 26) Counties

669. Wilkinson (cont'd: ED 150, sheet 27-end), Winston, Yalobusha, and Yazoo (part: EDs 1-119, sheet 24) Counties

670. Yazoo County (cont'd: ED 119, sheet 25-end)

Missouri.

671. Adair, Andrew, and Atchison (part: EDs 1-11, sheet 12) Counties

672. Atchison (cont'd: ED 11, sheet 13-end), Audrain, and Barry (part: EDs 1-6, sheet 22) Counties

673. Barry (cont'd: ED 6, sheet 23-end), Barton, and Bates (part: EDs 1-161, sheet 2) Counties

674. Bates (cont'd: ED 161, sheet 3-end), Benton, Bollinger, and Buchanan (part: EDs 1-53, sheet 34) Counties

675. Buchanan County (cont'd: ED 53, sheet 35-ED 79, sheet 6)

676. Buchanan (cont'd: ED 79, sheet 7-end), Butler, Boone, and

Caldwell (part: EDs 1-178, sheet 6) Counties

677. Caldwell (cont'd: ED 178, sheet 7-end) and Callaway
Counties

678. Camden, Cape Girardeau, and Carroll (part: EDs 142-146,
sheet 8) Counties

679. Carroll (cont'd: ED 146, sheet 9-end), Carter, and Cass
(part: EDs 1-89, sheet 10) Counties

680. Cass (cont'd: ED 89, sheet 11-end), Cedar, and Chariton
Counties

681. Christian, Clark, and Clay (part: EDs 1-125, sheet 4)
Counties

682. Clay (cont'd: ED 125, sheet 5-end), Clinton, Cole, and
Cooper (part: EDs 1-130, sheet 20) Counties

683. Cooper (cont'd: ED 130, sheet 21-end), Crawford, and
Dade (part: EDs 1-15, sheet 40) Counties

684. Dade (cont'd: ED 15, sheet 41-end), Dallas, and Daviess
Counties

685. DeKalb, Dent, Douglas, and Dunklin Counties

686. Franklin and Gasconade (part: EDs 1-82, sheet 24) Counties

687. Gasconade (cont'd: ED 82, sheet 25-end), Gentry, and
Greene (part: EDs 1-39, sheet 21) Counties

688. Greene (cont'd: ED 40, sheet 1-end), Grundy, and Harrison
(part: EDs 1-293, sheet 4) Counties

689. Harrison (cont'd: ED 293, sheet 5-end) and Henry (part:
EDs 1-180, sheet 4) Counties

690. Henry (cont'd: ED 180, sheet 5-end), Hickory, Holt, and
Howard (part: EDs 1-98, sheet 18) Counties

691. Howard (cont'd: ED 98, sheet 19-end), Howell, and Iron
Counties

692. Kansas City, wards 1-3 (part: EDs 1-9, sheet 70)

693. Kansas City, wards 3-6 (cont'd: ED 9, sheet 71-end) and
Jackson County (excluding Kansas City) (part: EDs 1-28,
sheet 4)

694. Jackson (excluding Kansas City) (cont'd: ED 28, sheet 5-
end) and Jasper (part: EDs 1-67, sheet 18) Counties

695. Jasper (cont'd: ED 67, sheet 19-end) and Jefferson (part:
EDs 1-194, sheet 24) Counties

696. Jefferson (cont'd: ED 194, sheet 25-end), Johnson, and
Knox (part: EDs 1-69, sheet 15) Counties

697. Knox (cont'd: ED 69, sheet 16-end), Laclede, and Lafayette
(part: EDs 1-49, sheet 12) Counties

698. Lafayette (cont'd: ED 49, sheet 13-end) and Lawrence
Counties

699. Lewis, Lincoln, and Linn (part: beginning-ED 178, sheet 24)
Counties

700. Linn (cont'd: ED 179, sheet 1-end) and Livingston Counties

701. McDonald and Macon Counties

702. Madison, Maries, and Marion Counties

703. Mercer, Miller, and Mississippi (part: EDs 1-73, sheet 8)
Counties

704. Mississippi (cont'd: ED 73, sheet 9-end), Moniteau, and

Monroe Counties

705. Montgomery, Morgan, New Madrid, and Newton (part: EDs
1-102, sheet 4) Counties

706. Newton (cont'd: ED 102, sheet 5-end) and Nodaway (part:
EDs 1-262, sheet 4) Counties

707. Nodaway (cont'd: ED 262, sheet 5-end), Oregon, Osage,
Ozark, Pemiscot, and Perry (part: EDs 1-94, sheet 4)
Counties

708. Perry (cont'd: ED 94, sheet 5-end), Pettis, and Phelps (part:
EDs 1-123, sheet 2) Counties

709. Phelps (cont'd: ED 123, sheet 3-end) and Pike Counties

710. Platte, Polk, and Pulaski (part: EDs 1-146, sheet 18)
Counties

711. Pulaski (cont'd: ED 146, sheet 19-end), Putnam, and Ralls
Counties

712. Randolph and Ray (part: EDs 1-127, sheet 14) Counties

713. Ray (cont'd: ED 127, sheet 15-end), Reynolds, and Ripley
Counties

714. St. Charles, St. Clair, and St. Francois (part: EDs 1-123,
sheet 14) Counties

715. St. Francois (cont'd: ED 123, sheet 15-end), Ste. Genevieve,
and St. Louis (excluding the city of St. Louis) (part: EDs
1-180, sheet 32) Counties

716. St. Louis (excluding the city of St. Louis) (cont'd: ED 180,
sheet 33-end) and Saline (part: EDs 1-72, sheet 24)
Counties

717. Saline County (cont'd: ED 72, sheet 25-end) and City of St.
Louis (first enumeration), wards 1-3 (part: EDs 1-17,
sheet 39)

718. City of St. Louis (first enumeration), ward 4 (cont'd: ED 18,
sheet 1-ED 37, sheet 36)

719. City of St. Louis (first enumeration), wards 5-7 (cont'd: ED
38, sheet 1-ED 60, sheet 26)

720. City of St. Louis (first enumeration), wards 7-10 (cont'd: ED
60, sheet 27-ED 79, sheet 40)

721. City of St. Louis (first enumeration), wards 10-13 (cont'd:
ED 79, sheet 41-ED 100, sheet 23)

722. City of St. Louis (first enumeration), wards 13-16 (cont'd:
ED 100, sheet 23-ED 120, sheet 28)

723. City of St. Louis (first enumeration), wards 16-18 (cont'd:
ED 120, sheet 29-ED 137, sheet 33)

724. City of St. Louis (first enumeration), wards 18-23 (cont'd:
ED 137, sheet 137-ED 157, sheet 10)

725. City of St. Louis (first enumeration), wards 23-28 (cont'd:
ED 157, sheet 11-ED 168, sheet 67)

726. City of St. Louis (second enumeration), wards 1 and 2 (part:
ED 1, sheet 1-ED 29, sheet 14)

727. City of St. Louis (second enumeration), wards 2-4 (cont'd:
ED 29, sheet 15-ED 80, sheet 14)

728. City of St. Louis (second enumeration), wards 4-6 (cont'd:
ED 80, sheet 15-ED 126, sheet 20)

729. City of St. Louis (second enumeration), wards 6-9 (cont'd: ED 126, sheet 21-ED 166, sheet 25)

730. City of St. Louis (second enumeration), wards 10-12 (cont'd: ED 167, sheet 1-ED 229, sheet 7)

731. City of St. Louis (second enumeration), ward 12 (cont'd: ED 229, sheet 8-ED 247, sheet 17)

732. City of St. Louis (second enumeration), wards 13-15 (cont'd: ED 248, sheet 1-ED 295, sheet 16)

733. City of St. Louis (second enumeration), wards 15-18 (cont'd: ED 296, sheet 1-ED 343, sheet 19)

734. City of St. Louis (second enumeration), wards 18-20 (cont'd: ED 344, sheet 1-ED 395, sheet 2)

735. City of St. Louis (second enumeration), wards 20-26 (cont'd: ED 395, sheet 3-ED 433 sheet 20)

736. City of St. Louis (second enumeration), wards 27-28 (cont'd: ED 434, sheet 1-end), and Schuyler and Scotland (part: EDs 1-88, sheet 12) Counties

737. Scotland (cont'd: ED 88, sheet 13-end), Scott, Shannon, Shelby, and Stoddard (part: EDs 1-163, sheet 16) Counties

738. Stoddard (cont'd: ED 163, sheet 17-end), Stone, Sullivan, and Taney (part: EDs 1-124, sheet 6) Counties

739. Taney (cont'd: ED 124, sheet 7-end), Texas, Vernon, and Warren (part: EDs 1-150, sheet 21) Counties

740. Warren (cont'd: ED 151, sheet 1-end), Washington, Wayne, and Webster (part: EDs 1-136, sheet 48) Counties

741. Webster (cont'd: ED 136, sheet 49-end), Worth, and Wright Counties

Montana.

742. Entire territory

Nebraska.

743. Adams, Antelope, Blackbird, Boone, Buffalo, and Burt Counties

744. Butler, Cass, Cedar, Chase, and Cheyenne Counties

745. Clay, Colfax, Cuming, and Custer (part: EDs 1-170, sheet 10) Counties

746. Custer (cont'd: ED 170, sheet 11-end), Dakota, Dawson, Dixon, and Dodge Counties

747. Douglas County (part: EDs 1-18, sheet 36)

748. Douglas (cont'd: ED 18, sheet 37-end), Dundy, Fillmore, and Franklin (part: EDs 1-43, sheet 7) Counties

749. Franklin (cont'd: ED 44, sheet 1-end), Frontier, Furnas, Gage, Gosper, Greeley, and Hall Counties

750. Hamilton, Harlan, Hayes, Hitchcock, Holt, Howard, and Jefferson (part: EDs 1-292, sheet 30) Counties

751. Jefferson (cont'd: ED 292, sheet 31-end), Johnson, Kearney, Keith, Knox, and Lancaster (part: EDs 1-240, sheet 10) Counties

752. Lancaster (cont'd: ED 240, sheet 11-end), Lincoln, Madison, Merrick, Nance, and Nemaha (part: EDs 1-209, sheet 4)

Counties

753. Nemaha (cont'd: ED 209, sheet 5-end), Nuckolls, Otoe, Pawnee, and Phelps Counties

754. Pierce, Platte, Polk, Redwillow, and Richardson Counties

755. Saline, Sarpy, and Saunders (part: EDs 1-181, sheet 8) Counties

756. Saunders (cont'd: ED 181, sheet 9-end), Seward, Sherman, Sioux, Stanton, Thayer, Valley, and Washington (part: EDs 1-33, sheet 27) Counties

757. Washington (cont'd: ED 33, sheet 28-end), Wayne, Webster, Wheeler, and York Counties and unorganized territory approximately what is now Cherry County

Nevada.

758. Churchill, Douglas, Elko, Esmeralda, Eureka, Humboldt, Lander, Lincoln, and Lyon Counties

759. Nye, Ormsby, Roop, Storey, Washoe, and White Pine Counties

New Hampshire.

760. Belknap and Carroll Counties

761. Cheshire County

762. Coos and Hillsboro (part: ED 1-120, sheet 14) Counties

763. Hillsboro County (cont'd: ED 121, sheet 1-ED 143, sheet 24)

764. Hillsboro (cont'd: ED 143, sheet 25-end) and Grafton (part: EDs 1-81, sheet 18) Counties

765. Grafton (cont'd: ED 81, sheet 19-end) and Merrimack (part: EDs 1-165, sheet 15) Counties

766. Merrimack County (cont'd: ED 165, sheet 16-end)

767. Rockingham County (part: EDs 1-223, sheet 22)

768. Rockingham (cont'd: ED 224, sheet 1-end) and Sullivan Counties

769. Strafford County

New Jersey.

770. Atlantic and Bergen (part: EDs 1-2, sheet 2) Counties

771. Bergen County (cont'd: ED 2, sheet 3-end)

772. Burlington County (part: EDs 1-28, sheet 14)

773. Burlington (cont'd: ED 28, sheet 15-end) and Camden (part: EDs 1-46, sheet 20) Counties

774. Camden County (cont'd: ED 46, sheet 21-ED 64, sheet 12)

775. Camden (cont'd: ED 64, sheet 13-end), Cape May, and Cumberland (part: ED 82, sheet 30) Counties

776. Cumberland County (cont'd: ED 82, sheet 31-end) and city of Newark, wards 1-4 (part: EDs 1-35, sheet 40)

777. City of Newark, wards 4-8 (cont'd: ED 35, sheet 41-ED 54, sheet 24)

778. City of Newark, wards 8-12 (cont'd: ED 54, sheet 25-ED 74, sheet 33)

779. City of Newark, wards 12-15 (cont'd: ED 75, sheet 1-end)

and Essex County (excluding the city of Newark) (part: EDs 1-92, sheet 32)

780. Essex County (excluding the city of Newark) (cont'd: ED 92, sheet 33-ED 110, sheet 16)

781. Essex (excluding the city of Newark) (cont'd: ED 110, sheet 17-end) and Gloucester Counties

782. Jersey City (part: EDs 1-15, sheet 36)

783. Jersey City (cont'd: ED 15, sheet 37-ED 27, sheet 58)

784. Jersey City (cont'd: ED 27, sheet 59-ED 39, sheet 14)

785. Jersey City (cont'd: ED 39, sheet 15-ED 40, sheet 51) and Hudson County (part: ED 53, sheet 1-ED 64, sheet 57)

786. Hudson County (excluding Jersey City) (cont'd: ED 41, sheet 1-ED 52, sheet 25)

787. Hunterdon County

788. Mercer County (part: EDs 1-108, sheet 15)

789. Mercer (cont'd: ED 108, sheet 15-end) and Middlesex (part: EDs 1-122, sheet 40) Counties

790. Middlesex County (cont'd: ED 122, sheet 41-ED 144, sheet 10)

791. Middlesex (cont'd: ED 144, sheet 11-end) and Monmouth (part: EDs 1-117, sheet 78) Counties

792. Monmouth (cont'd: ED 117, sheet 79-end) and Morris (part: EDs 1-119, sheet 40) Counties

793. Morris County (cont'd: ED 119, sheet 41-end)

794. Ocean and Passaic (part: EDs 1-149, sheet 25) Counties

795. Passaic County (cont'd: ED 150, sheet 1-ED 155, sheet 18)

796. Passaic County (cont'd: ED 155, sheet 19-end)

797. Salem and Somerset (part: EDs 1-151, sheet 8) Counties

798. Somerset (cont'd: ED 151, sheet 9-end) and Sussex (part: EDs 1-185, sheet 2) Counties

799. Sussex (cont'd: ED 185, sheet 3-end) and Warren (part: EDs 1-206, sheet 38) Counties

800. Warren (cont'd: ED 206, sheet 30-end) and Union (part: EDs 1-175, sheet 30) Counties

801. Union County (cont'd: ED 175, sheet 31-end)

New Mexico.

802. Bernalillo, Colfax, Dona Ana, Grant, and Lincoln Counties

803. Mora, Rio Arriba, and San Miguel Counties

804. Santa Fe, Socorro, Taos, Valencia Counties

New York.

805. City of Albany, wards 1-9 (part: EDs 1-18, sheet 46)

806. City of Albany wards 10-16 (cont'd: ED 19, sheet 1-ED 34, sheet 48)

807. City of Albany, wards 16-17 (cont'd: ED 34, sheet 49-end) and Albany County (excluding the city of Albany) (part: EDs 1-52, sheet 26)

808. Albany County (excluding the city of Albany) (cont'd: ED 52, sheet 27-end)

809. Allegany County (part: EDs 1-26, sheet 36)

810. Allegany (cont'd: ED 26, sheet 37-end) and Broome (part: EDs 1-47, sheet 14) Counties

811. Broome (cont'd: ED 47, sheet 15-end) and Cattaraugus (part: EDs 1-10, sheet 18) Counties

812. Cattaraugus County (cont'd: ED 10, sheet 19-ED 35, sheet 14)

813. Cattaraugus (cont'd: ED 35, sheet 15-end) and Cayuga (part: EDs 1-19, sheet 10) Counties

814. Cayuga County (cont'd: ED 19, sheet 11-end)

815. Chautauqua County (part: EDs 1-58, sheet 12)

816. Chautauqua (cont'd: ED 58, sheet 13-end) and Chemung (part: EDs 1-67, sheet 10) Counties

817. Chemung County (cont'd: ED 67, sheet 11-end)

818. Chenango County (part: EDs 1-113, sheet 30)

819. Chenango (cont'd: ED 113, sheet 31-end) and Clinton (part: EDs 1-23, sheet 37) Counties

820. Clinton (cont'd: ED 24, sheet 1-end) and Columbia (part: EDs 1-8, sheet 12) Counties

821. Columbia County (cont'd: ED 8, sheet 13-end)

822. Cortland and Delaware (part: EDs 1-67, sheet 21) Counties

823. Delaware County (cont'd: ED 67, sheet 22-end)

824. Dutchess County (part: EDs 1-48, sheet 46)

825. Dutchess County (cont'd: ED 49, sheet 1-ED 271, sheet 20)

826. Dutchess (cont'd: ED 271, sheet 21-end) and Erie (excluding the city of Buffalo) (part: EDs 1-90, sheet 27)

827. Erie County (excluding the city of Buffalo) (cont'd: ED 90, sheet 28-end) and city of Buffalo, ward 1 (part: EDs 1-112, sheet 14)

828. City of Buffalo, wards 1-5 (cont'd: ED 112, sheet 15-ED 127, sheet 2)

829. City of Buffalo, wards 5 and 6 (cont'd: ED 127, sheet 3-ED 142, sheet 4)

830. City of Buffalo, wards 6-8 (cont'd: ED 142, sheet 5-ED 157, sheet 51)

831. City of Buffalo, wards 9-12 (cont'd: ED 158, sheet 1-ED 172, sheet 44)

832. City of Buffalo, wards 12-13 (cont'd: ED 172, sheet 45-end) and Essex County (part: EDs 1-51, sheet 37)

833. Essex (cont'd: ED 52, sheet 1-end) and Franklin (part: EDs 1-82, sheet 6) Counties

834. Franklin (cont'd: ED 82, sheet 7-end) and Fulton (part: EDs 1-14, sheet 4) Counties

835. Fulton (cont'd: ED 14, sheet 5-end) and Genesee Counties

836. Greene County (part: EDs 1-89, sheet 12)

837. Greene (cont'd: ED 89, sheet 13-end), Hamilton, and Herkimer (part: EDs 1-33, sheet 28) Counties

838. Herkimer (cont'd: ED 33, sheet 29-end) and Jefferson (part: EDs 1-116, sheet 2) Counties

839. Jefferson (cont'd: ED 116, sheet 3-end) and St. Lawrence (part: EDs 1-148, sheet 46) Counties

840. Jefferson County (part: ED 148, sheet 47-end) and city of

Brooklyn, wards 1 and 2 (part: EDs 1-12, sheet 42)

841. City of Brooklyn, wards 2-4 (cont'd: ED 12, sheet 43-ED 26, sheet 27)

842. City of Brooklyn, wards 5 and 6 (cont'd: ED 27, sheet -ED 40, sheet 48)

843. City of Brooklyn, wards 6 & 7 (cont'd: ED 40, sheet 49-ED 54, sheet 42)

844. City of Brooklyn, wards 7-9 (cont'd: ED 54, sheet 43-ED 72, sheet 44)

845. City of Brooklyn, wards 9-11 (cont'd: ED 72, sheet 45-ED 88, sheet 28)

846. City of Brooklyn, wards 11 and 12 (cont'd: ED 88, sheet 29-ED 102, sheet 14)

847. City of Brooklyn, wards 12-14 (cont'd: ED 102, sheet 14-ED 120, sheet 2)

848. City of Brooklyn, wards 14 and 15 (cont'd: ED 120, sheet 3-ED 136, sheet 46)

849. City of Brooklyn, ward 16 (cont'd: ED 137, sheet 1-ED 141, sheet 40)

850. City of Brooklyn, wards 16 and 17 (cont'd: ED 141, sheet 41-ED 157, sheet 32)

851. City of Brooklyn, ward 17 (cont'd: ED 157, sheet 33-ED 170, sheet 42)

852. City of Brooklyn, wards 18 and 19 (cont'd: ED 171, sheet 1-ED 184, sheet 30)

853. City of Brooklyn, wards 19 and 20 (cont'd: ED 184, sheet 31-ED 204, sheet 22)

854. City of Brooklyn, wards 20 and 21 (cont'd: ED 204, sheet 23-ED 220, sheet 46)

855. City of Brooklyn, wards 22 and 23 (cont'd: ED 221, sheet 1-ED 238, sheet 4)

856. City of Brooklyn, wards 23-25 (cont'd: ED 238, sheet 5-end) and Kings County (excluding the city of Brooklyn) (part: EDs 1-253, sheet 45)

857. Kings (excluding the city of Brooklyn) (cont'd: ED 253, sheet 46-end) and Lewis (part: EDs 1-163, sheet 20)

858. Lewis (cont'd: ED 163, sheet 21-end) and Livingston (part: EDs 1-25, sheet 32) Counties

859. Livingston (cont'd: ED 25, sheet 33-end) and Madison (part: EDs 1-51, sheet 6) Counties

860. Madison County (cont'd: ED 51, sheet 7-end)

861. Monroe County (part: EDs 1-60, sheet 2)

862. Monroe County (cont'd: ED 60, sheet 3-ED 79, sheet 38)

863. Monroe County (cont'd: ED 79, sheet 3-ED 95, sheet 32)

864. Monroe County (cont'd: ED 95, sheet 33-end)

865. Montgomery County

866. New York City, ward 1 (part: ED 1, sheet 1-ED 6, sheet 41)

867. New York City, wards 1-5 (cont'd: ED 6, sheet 43-ED 30, sheet 30)

868. New York City, wards 4, 6, and 14 (cont'd: ED 30, sheet 31-ED 50, sheet 30)

869. New York City, wards 14, 15, and 17 (cont'd: ED 50, sheet 31-ED 68, sheet 24)

870. New York City, wards 7 and 18 (cont'd: ED 69, sheet 1-ED 88, sheet 9)

871. New York City, wards 7 and 8 (cont'd: ED 88, sheet 10-ED 112, sheet 33)

872. New York City, wards 8, 15, 7, and 13 (cont'd: ED 113, sheet 1-ED 136, sheet 34)

873. New York City, wards 13 and 11 (cont'd: ED 137, sheet 1-ED 156, sheet 2)

874. New York City, wards 11, 15, 9, and 18 (cont'd: ED 156, sheet 3-ED 182, sheet 14)

875. New York City, wards 18, 16, 13, and 10 (cont'd: ED 182, sheet 15-ED 200, sheet 33)

876. New York City, wards 10, 17, and 9 (cont'd: ED 200, sheet 34-ED 218, sheet 4)

877. New York City, ward 9 (cont'd: ED 218, sheet 5-ED 241, sheet 32)

878. New York City, wards 9, 16, 17 (cont'd: ED 241, sheet 33-ED 262, sheet 4)

879. New York City, ward 17 (cont'd: ED 262, sheet 5-ED 274, sheet 30)

880. New York City, wards 17, 18, 21, 16, and 20 (cont'd: ED 274, sheet 31-ED 297, sheet 4)

881. New York City, wards 21, 20, and 11 (cont'd: ED 297, sheet 5-ED 313, sheet 34)

882. New York City, wards 11 and 16 (cont'd: ED 313, sheet 35-ED 336, sheet 32)

883. New York City, ward 16 (cont'd: ED 336, sheet 33-ED 348, sheet 33)

884. New York City, wards 16, 20, 17, and 11 (cont'd: ED 348, sheet 34-ED 374, sheet 47)

885. New York City, wards 11 and 20 (cont'd: ED 375, sheet 1-ED 392, sheet 32)

886. New York City, wards 20 and 18 (cont'd: ED 392, sheet 33-ED 412, sheet 14)

887. New York City, ward 18 (cont'd: ED 412, sheet 15-ED 433, sheet 20)

888. New York City, wards 18 and 22 (cont'd: ED 433, sheet 21-ED 452, sheet 26)

889. New York City, wards 22, 18, and 21 (cont'd: ED 452, sheet 27-ED 476, sheet 26)

890. New York City, wards 21 and 19 (cont'd: ED 477, sheet 1-ED 496, sheet 24)

891. New York City, wards 21 and 22 (cont'd: ED 496, sheet 25-ED 518, sheet 10)

892. New York City (ED 518, sheet 11-ED 539, sheet 36)

893. New York City, ward 19 (cont'd: ED 540, sheet 1-ED 561, sheet 52)

894. New York City, wards 19 and 22 (cont'd: ED 540, sheet

1-ED 576, sheet 30)

895. New York City, wards 19 and 22 (cont'd: ED 576, sheet 31-ED 591, sheet 33)

896. New York City, wards 19 and 12 (cont'd: ED 592, sheet 1-ED 612, sheet 50)

897. New York City, wards 19 and 12 (cont'd: ED 613, sheet 1-ED 627, sheet 12)

898. New York City, ward 12 (cont'd: ED 627, sheet 13-ED 646, sheet 34)

899. New York City, wards 12 and 23 (cont'd: ED 647, sheet 1-ED 670, sheet 12)

900. New York City, wards 23 and 24 (cont'd: ED 670, sheet 13-end) and Niagara County (part: EDs 1-186, sheet 20)

901. Niagara County (cont'd: ED 186, sheet 21-end)

902. Oneida County (excluding the city of Utica) (part: EDs 1-107, sheet 38)

903. Oneida County (excluding the city of Utica) (cont'd: ED 108, sheet 1-ED 150, sheet 16)

904. Oneida County (excluding the city of Utica) (cont'd: ED 150, sheet 17-ED 160, sheet 26) and city of Utica, wards 1-9 (part: ED 124, sheet 1-ED 139, sheet 14)

905. City of Utica, ward 9 (cont'd: ED 139, sheet 15-ED 143, sheet 34) and Onondaga County (excluding City of Syracuse) (part: EDs 1-179, sheet 23)

906. Onondaga County (excluding the city of Syracuse) (cont'd: ED 180, sheet 1-end)

907. City of Syracuse, wards 1-6 (part: EDs 1-216, sheet 12)

908. City of Syracuse, wards 6-8 (cont'd: ED 216, sheet 13-end) and Ontario County (part: EDs 1-123, sheet 17)

909. Ontario County (cont'd: ED 123, sheet 18-end)

910. Orange County (part: EDs 1-25, sheet 28)

911. Orange County (cont'd: ED 25, sheet 29-ED 41, sheet 8)

912. Orange (cont'd: ED 41, sheet 9-end) and Orleans Counties

913. Oswego County (excluding the city of Oswego) (part: ED 227, sheet 1-ED 243, sheet 32) and city of Oswego, ward 1 (ED 244, sheet 1-ED 247, sheet 32)

914. City of Oswego, wards 1-8 (cont'd: ED 247, sheet 33-ED 258, sheet 25)

915. Oswego (excluding the city of Oswego) (cont'd: ED 259, sheet 1-end) and Otsego (part: EDs 1-102, sheet 40) Counties

916. Otsego County (cont'd: ED 102, sheet 41-end)

917. Putnam and Queens (part: EDs 1-270, sheet 64) Counties

918. Queens County (cont'd: ED 270, sheet 65-ED 284, sheet 50)

919. Queens County (cont'd: ED 284, sheet 51-end)

920. City of Troy, wards 1-10 (part: EDs 1-144, sheet 52)

921. City of Troy, wards 10-13, and Rensselaer County (excluding the city of Troy) (part: ED 144, sheet 53-ED 159, sheet 78)

922. Rensselaer County (excluding the city of Troy) (cont'd: ED

159, sheet 79-end)

923. Richmond County

924. Rockland County

925. St. Lawrence County (part: EDs 1-227, sheet 25)

926. St. Lawrence County (cont'd: ED 228, sheet 1-ED 240, sheet 39)

927. St. Lawrence County (cont'd: ED 241, sheet 1-end)

928. Saratoga County (part: EDs 1-85, sheet 12)

929. Saratoga (cont'd: ED 85, sheet 13-end) and Schenectady (part: EDs 1-107, sheet 32)

930. Schenectady (cont'd: ED 108, sheet 1-end) Schuyler, and Schoharie (part: EDs 1-185, sheet 16) Counties

931. Schoharie (cont'd: ED 185, sheet 17-end) and Seneca (part: EDs 1-160, sheet 74) Counties

932. Seneca (cont'd: ED 160, sheet 75-end) and Steuben (part: EDs 1-163, sheet 17) Counties

933. Steuben County (cont'd: ED 164, sheet 1-ED 184, sheet 10)

934. Steuben (cont'd: ED 184, sheet 11-end) and Suffolk (part: EDs 1-315, sheet 50) Counties

935. Suffolk County (cont'd: ED 315, sheet 51-end)

936. Sullivan County

937. Tioga County

938. Tompkins County

939. Ulster County (part: EDs 1-140, sheet 45)

940. Ulster County (cont'd: ED 141, sheet 1-ED 162, sheet 24)

941. Ulster (cont'd: ED 162, sheet 25-end) and Warren Counties

942. Washington County (part: EDs 1-154, sheet 21)

943. Washington (cont'd: ED 154, sheet 22-end) and Wayne (part: EDs 1-177, sheet 18) Counties

944. Wayne County (cont'd: ED 177, sheet 19-end)

945. Westchester County (part: EDs 1-104, sheet 8)

946. Westchester County (cont'd: ED 104, sheet 9-ED 123, sheet 30)

947. Westchester County (cont'd: ED 123, sheet 31-end)

948. Wyoming County

949. Yates County

North Carolina.

950. Alamance County (part: EDs 1-2, sheet 12)

951. Alamance (cont'd: ED 2, sheet 13-end), Alexander, Alleghany, Anson, and Ashe (part: EDs 1-15, sheet 24) Counties

952. Ashe (cont'd: ED 15, sheet 25-end) and Beaufort Counties

953. Bertie, Bladen, and Brunswick Counties

954. Buncombe and Burke Counties

955. Cabarrus and Caldwell Counties

956. Camden, Carteret, and Caswell (part: EDs 1-17, sheet 2)

957. Caswell (cont'd: ED 17, sheet 3-end), Catawba, and Chatham (part: EDs 1-29, sheet 26) Counties

958. Chatham (cont'd: ED 29, sheet 27-end), Cherokee, Chowan, Clay, and Cleveland (part: EDs 1-74 sheet 38) Counties

959. Cleveland (cont'd: ED 70, sheet 39-end), Columbus, and Craven (part: EDs 1-43, sheet 52) Counties

960. Craven (cont'd: ED 43, sheet 53-end) and Cumberland Counties

961. Currituck, Dare, Davidson, Davie, and Duplin (part: EDs 1-74, sheet 2) Counties

962. Duplin (cont'd: ED 74, sheet 3-end) and Edgecombe (part: EDs 1-70, sheet 26) Counties

963. Edgecomb (cont'd: ED 70, sheet 27-end), Forsyth, and Franklin Counties

964. Gaston, Gates, Graham, and Granville (part: EDs 1-104, sheet 30) Counties

965. Granville (cont'd: ED 104, sheet 31-end), Greene, and Guilford (part: EDs 1-122, sheet 6) Counties

966. Guilford (cont'd: ED 122, sheet 7-end) and Halifax Counties

967. Harnett, Haywood, Henderson, and Hertford (part: EDs 1-69, sheet 10) Counties

968. Hertford (cont'd: ED 69, sheet 11-end), Hyde, and Iredell (part: EDs 1-153, sheet 19) Counties

969. Iredell (cont'd: ED 154, sheet 1-end), Jackson, and Johnston Counties

970. Jones, Lenoir, Lincoln, and McDowell (part: EDs 1-140, sheet 2) Counties

971. McDowell (cont'd: ED 140, sheet 3-end), Macon, Madison, Martin, and Mecklenburg (part: EDs 1-105, sheet 30) Counties

972. Mecklenburg County (cont'd: ED 105, sheet 31-end)

973. Mitchell, Montgomery, Moore, and Nash (part: EDs 1-173, sheet 24) Counties

974. Nash (cont'd: ED 173, sheet 25-end), New Hanover, and Northampton (part: EDs 1-182, sheet 40) Counties

975. Northampton (cont'd: ED 182, sheet 41-end), Onslow, and Orange (part: EDs 1-195, sheet 34) Counties

976. Orange (cont'd: ED 195, sheet 35-end), Pamlico, Pasquotank, and Pender Counties

977. Perquimans, Person, and Pitt (part: EDs 1-127, sheet 32)

978. Pitt (cont'd: ED 127, sheet 33-end), Polk, Randolph, and Richmond (part: EDs 1-167, sheet 2) Counties

979. Richmond (cont'd: ED 167, sheet 3-end) and Robeson Counties

980. Rockingham and Rowan (part: EDs 1-244, sheet 16) Counties

981. Rowan (cont'd: ED 244, sheet 17-end), Rutherford, and Sampson (part: EDs 1-197, sheet 2) Counties

982. Sampson (cont'd: ED 197, sheet 3-end), Stanly, Stokes, and Surry (part: EDs 1-172, sheet 16) Counties

983. Surry (cont'd: ED 172, sheet 17-end), Swain, Transylvania, Tyrrell, and Union (part: EDs 1-215, sheet 4) Counties

984. Union (cont'd: ED 215, sheet 5-end) and Wake (part: EDs 1-270, sheet 2)

985. Wake (cont'd: ED 270, sheet 3-end) and Warren (part: EDs 1-289, sheet 58) Counties

986. Warren (cont'd: ED 289, sheet 59-end), Washington, Watauga, and Wayne Counties

987. Wilkes and Wilson (part: EDs 1-310, sheet 36) Counties

988. Wilson (cont'd: ED 310, sheet 37-end), Yadkin, and Yancey Counties

Ohio.

989. Adams County (part: EDs 1-9, sheet 18)

990. Adams (cont'd: ED 9, sheet 19-end) and Allen Counties

991. Ashland and Ashtabula (part: EDs 1-4, sheet 21) Counties

992. Ashtabula (cont'd: ED 4, sheet 22-end) and Athens (part: EDs 1-4, sheet 50) Counties

993. Athens (cont'd: ED 4, sheet 51-end) and Auglaize (part: EDs 1-10, sheet 18)

994. Auglaize (cont'd: ED 10, sheet 19-end) and Belmont (part: EDs 1-28, sheet 58) Counties

995. Belmont (cont'd: ED 28, sheet 59-end) and Brown (part: EDs 1-10, sheet 42) Counties

996. Brown (cont'd: ED 10, sheet 43-end) and Butler (part: EDs 1-27, sheet 12) Counties

997. Butler (cont'd: ED 27, sheet 13-end) and Carroll (part: EDs 1-41, sheet 8) Counties

998. Carroll (cont'd: ED 41, sheet 9-end), Champaign, and Clark (part: EDs 1-36, sheet 26) Counties

999. Clark County (cont'd: ED 36, sheet 27-end)

1000. Clermont County

1001. Clinton and Columbiana (part: EDs 1-49, sheet 36) Counties

1002. Columbiana County (cont'd: ED 49, sheet 37-end)

1003. Coshocton and Crawford (part: EDs 1-103, sheet 52) Counties

1004. Crawford County (cont'd: ED 103, sheet 53-end) and city of Cleveland, wards 1-4 (part: EDs 1-10, sheet 38)

1005. City of Cleveland, wards 4 and 5 (cont'd: ED 10, sheet 39-ED 16, sheet 77)

1006. City of Cleveland, wards 6-8 (cont'd: ED 17, sheet 1-ED 28, sheet 55)

1007. City of Cleveland, wards 9-12 (cont'd: ED 29, sheet 1-ED 40, sheet 24)

1008. City of Cleveland, wards 12-18 (cont'd: ED 40, sheet 25-ED 53, sheet 6)

1009. City of Cleveland, ward 18 (cont'd: ED 53, sheet 7-end), and Cuyahoga County (excluding the the city of Cleveland) (part: EDs 1-73, sheet 18)

1010. Cuyahoga (excluding the city of Cleveland) (cont'd: ED 73, sheet 19-end) and Darke (part: EDs 1-70, sheet 10) Counties

1011. Darke (cont'd: ED 70, sheet 11-end) and Defiance (part: EDs 1-242, sheet 14) Counties

1012. Defiance (cont'd: ED 242, sheet 15-end), Delaware, and

Erie (part: EDs 1-115, sheet 24) Counties

1013. Erie (cont'd: ED 115, sheet 24-end) and Fayette (part: EDs 1-51, sheet 34) Counties

1014. Fayette (cont'd: ED 51, sheet 35-end) and Fairfield (part: EDs 1-210, sheet 12) Counties

1015. Fairfield (cont'd: ED 210, sheet 13-end) and Franklin (part: EDs 1-16, sheet 30) Counties

1016. Franklin County (cont'd: ED 16, sheet 31-ED 35, sheet 8)

1017. Franklin (cont'd: ED 35, sheet 9-end) and Fulton (part: EDs 1-24, sheet 34) Counties

1018. Fulton (cont'd: ED 24, sheet 35-end), Gallia, and Geauga (part: EDs 1-68, sheet 35) Counties

1019. Geauga (cont'd: ED 69, sheet 1-end) and Greene (part: EDs 1-92, sheet 14) Counties

1020. Greene (cont'd: ED 92, sheet 15-end) and Guernsey (part: EDs 1-82, sheet 22) Counties

1021. Guernsey (cont'd: ED 82, sheet 23-end) and Hancock Counties

1022. Hamilton County (excluding the city of Cincinnati) (part: EDs 1-95, sheet 40)

1023. Hamilton County (excluding the city of Cincinnati) (cont'd: ED 95, sheet 41-end) and city of Cincinnati, ward 1 (part: EDs 1-111, sheet 40)

1024. City of Cincinnati, wards 1-5 (cont'd: ED 111, sheet 41-ED 125, sheet 44)

1025. City of Cincinnati, ward 5 (cont'd: ED 125, sheet 45-ED 140, sheet 30)

1026. City of Cincinnati, wards 6-12 (cont'd: ED 140, sheet 31-ED 152, sheet 22)

1027. City of Cincinnati, wards 12-16 (cont'd: ED 152, sheet 23-ED 165, sheet 43)

1028. City of Cincinnati, wards 17-20 (cont'd: ED 166, sheet 1-ED 180, sheet 76)

1029. City of Cincinnati, wards 21-23 (cont'd: ED 180, sheet 77-ED 193, sheet 32)

1030. City of Cincinnati, wards 24-25 (cont'd: ED 193, sheet 33-end) and Hardin County (part: EDs 1-101, sheet 28)

1031. Hardin (cont'd: ED 101, sheet 29-end) and Harrison Counties

1032. Henry and Highland (part: EDs 1-42, sheet 40) Counties

1033. Highland (cont'd: ED 42, sheet 41-end) and Hocking (part: EDs 1-65, sheet 18) Counties

1034. Hocking (cont'd: ED 65, sheet 19-end) and Holmes Counties

1035. Huron County

1036. Jackson County (part: EDs 1-80, sheet 2)

1037. Jackson (cont'd: ED 80, sheet 3-end) and Jefferson Counties

1038. Knox and Lake Counties

1039. Lawrence County

1040. Licking County

1041. Logan and Lorain (part ED 1-162, sheet 14) Counties

1042. Lorain (cont'd: ED 162, sheet 15-end) and Lucas (part: EDs 1-29, sheet 38) Counties

1043. Lucas (cont'd: ED 29, sheet 39-ED 46, sheet 29)

1044. Lucas (cont'd: ED 46, sheet 30-end) and Madison (part: EDs 65, sheet 2) Counties

1045. Madison (cont'd: ED 65, sheet 3-end) and Mahoning (part: EDs 1-106, sheet 2) Counties

1046. Mahoning (cont'd: ED 106, sheet 3-end) and Marion Counties

1047. Medina and Meigs (part: EDs 1-111, sheet 6) Counties

1048. Meigs (cont'd: ED 111, sheet 7-end) and Mercer (part: EDs 1-191, sheet 36) Counties

1049. Mercer (cont'd: ED 191, sheet 37-end) and Miami (part: EDs 1-146, sheet 26) Counties

1050. Miami (cont'd: ED 146, sheet 27-end), Monroe, and Morgan (part: EDs 1-137, sheet 19) Counties

1051. Montgomery County (part: EDs 1-163, sheet 18)

1052. Montgomery County (cont'd: ED 163, sheet 19-end)

1053. Morgan (cont'd: ED 138, sheet 1-end) and Morrow Counties

1054. Muskingum County (part: EDs 1-178, sheet 46)

1055. Muskingum (cont'd: ED 179, sheet 1-end), Noble, and Ottawa (part: EDs 1-62, sheet 22) Counties

1056. Ottawa (cont'd: ED 62, sheet 23-end) and Paulding Counties

1057. Perry and Pickaway (part: EDs 1-218, sheet 20) Counties

1058. Pickaway (cont'd: ED 218, sheet 21-end) and Pike (part: EDs 1-132, sheet 14) Counties

1059. Pike (cont'd: ED 132, sheet 15-end), Portage, and Preble (part: EDs 1-196, sheet 42) Counties

1060. Preble (cont'd: ED 196, sheet 43-end) and Putnam (part: EDs 1-141, sheet 4) Counties

1061. Putnam (cont'd: ED 141, sheet 5-end) and Richland (part: EDs 1-221, sheet 8) Counties

1062. Richland (cont'd: ED 221, sheet 9-end) and Ross (part: EDs 1-152, sheet 10) Counties

1063. Ross (cont'd: ED 152, sheet 11-end) and Sandusky (part: EDs 1-84, sheet 15) Counties

1064. Sandusky (cont'd: ED 84, sheet 16-end) and Scioto Counties

1065. Seneca County (part: EDs 1-210, sheet 32)

1066. Seneca (cont'd: ED 210, sheet 33-end), Shelby, and Stark (part: EDs 1-136, sheet 52) Counties

1067. Stark County (cont'd: ED 136, sheet 53-ED 151, sheet 6)

1068. Stark (cont'd: ED 151, sheet 7-end) and Summit (part: EDs 1-167, sheet 14) Counties

1069. Summit County (cont'd: ED 167, sheet 15-end)

1070. Trumbull County (part: EDs 1-209, sheet 23)

1071. Trumbull (cont'd: ED 210, sheet 1-end) and Tuscarawas (part: EDs 1-217, sheet 4) Counties

1072. Tuscarawas County (cont'd: ED 217, sheet 5-ED 236, sheet 22)

1073. Tuscarawas (cont'd: ED 243, sheet 1-ED 243, sheet 8), Union, and Van Wert (part: EDs 1-153, sheet 36) Counties

1074. Van Wert (cont'd: ED 153, sheet 37-end), Vinton, and Warren (part: EDs 1-71, sheet 14) Counties

1075. Warren (cont'd: ED 71, sheet 15-end) and Washington (part: EDs 1-228, sheet 2) Counties

1076. Washington (cont'd: ED 228, sheet 3-end) and Wayne (part: ED 231, sheet 4) Counties

1077. Wayne (cont'd: ED 231, sheet 5-end) and Williams (part: EDs 1-8, sheet 36) Counties

1078. Williams (cont'd: ED 8, sheet 37-end) and Wood (part: EDs 1-102, sheet 20) Counties

1079. Wood (cont'd: ED 102, sheet 21-end) and Wyandot Counties

Oregon.

1080. Baker, Benton, Clackamas, Clatsop, Columbia, Coos, Curry, and Douglas (part: EDs 1-36, sheet 6) Counties

1081. Douglas (cont'd: ED 36, sheet 7-end), Grant, Jackson, Josephine, Lake, and Lane (part: EDs 1-67, sheet 7) Counties

1082. Lane (cont'd: ED 67, sheet 8-end), Linn, Marion, and Multnomah (part: EDs 1-92, sheet 8) Counties

1083. Multnomah (cont'd: ED 92, sheet 9-end), Polk, and Tillamook Counties

1084. Umatilla, Union, Wasco, Washington, and Yamhill Counties

Pennsylvania.

1085. Adams County

1086. City of Allegheny, wards 1-4 (part: EDs 1-14, sheet 24)

1087. City of Allegheny, wards 4-7 (cont'd: ED 14, sheet 25-ED 24, sheet 80)

1088. City of Allegheny, wards 8-13 (cont'd: ED 25, sheet 1-end) and Allegheny County (excluding the cities of Allegheny and Pittsburgh) (part: EDs 1-45, sheet 27)

1089. Allegheny County (excluding the cities of Allegheny and Pittsburgh) (cont'd: ED 46, sheet 1-ED 67, sheet 10)

1090. Allegheny County (excluding the cities of Allegheny and Pittsburgh) (cont'd: ED 67, sheet 11-ED 85, sheet 2)

1091. Allegheny County (excluding the cities of Allegheny and Pittsburgh) (cont'd: ED 85, sheet 3-end) and city of Pittsburgh, wards 1-5 (part: EDs 1-106, sheet 30)

1092. City of Pittsburgh, wards 5-12 (cont'd: ED 106, sheet 31-ED 125, sheet 58)

1093. City of Pittsburgh, wards 13-19 (cont'd: ED 126, sheet 1-ED 142, sheet 8)

1094. City of Pittsburgh, wards 19-27 (cont'd: ED 142, sheet 9-ED 160, sheet 72)

1095. City of Pittsburgh, ward 27 (cont'd: ED 160, sheet 73-end) and Armstrong County (part: EDs 1-4, sheet 53)

1096. Armstrong County (cont'd: ED 5, sheet 1-end)

1097. Beaver County

1098. Bedford County

1099. Berks County (part: EDs 1-26, sheet 39)

1100. Berks County (cont'd: ED 27, sheet 1-ED 37, sheet 23; ED 60, sheet 1-ED 69, sheet 10)

1101. Berks County (cont'd: ED 69, sheet 11-ED 73, sheet 41; ED 38, sheet 1-ED 53, sheet 22)

1102. Berks (cont'd: ED 53, sheet 23-ED 59, sheet 47) and Blair (part: EDs 1-160, sheet 12) Counties

1103. Blair County (cont'd: ED 160, sheet 13-end)

1104. Bradford County (part: EDs 1-26, sheet 34)

1105. Bradford (cont'd: ED 26, sheet 34-end) and Bucks (part: EDs 1-135, sheet 24) Counties

1106. Bucks County (cont'd: ED 135, sheet 25-ED 159, sheet 59)

1107. Bucks (cont'd: ED 160, sheet 1-end) and Carbon (part: EDs 1-115, sheet 24) Counties

1108. Carbon (cont'd: ED 115, sheet 25-end) and Butler (part: ED 39, sheet 10) Counties

1109. Butler County (cont'd: ED 39, sheet 11-end)

1110. Cambria County (part: EDs 1-201, sheet 8)

1111. Cambria (cont'd: ED 201, sheet 9-end) and Cameron Counties

1112. Centre County (part: EDs 1-235, sheet 54)

1113. Centre (cont'd: ED 235, sheet 55-end), Clinton, and Chester (part: EDs 1-47, sheet 4) Counties

1114. Chester County (cont'd: ED 47, sheet 5-ED 75, sheet 28)

1115. Chester County (cont'd: ED 75, sheet 29-end)

1116. Clearfield County (part: EDs 1-274, sheet 43)

1117. Clearfield (cont'd: ED 275, sheet 1-end) and Clarion (part: EDs 77, sheet 30) Counties

1118. Clarion (cont'd: ED 77, sheet 31-end) and Columbia (part: EDs 1-178, sheet 4) Counties

1119. Columbia (cont'd: ED 178, sheet 5-end) and Crawford (part: EDs 1-105, sheet 4) Counties

1120. Crawford County (cont'd: ED 105, sheet 3-ED 115, sheet 24)

1121. Crawford (cont'd: ED 115, sheet 25-end) and Cumberland (part: EDs 1-69, sheet 6) Counties

1122. Cumberland County (cont'd: ED 69, sheet 7-end)

1123. Dauphin County (part: EDs 1-96, sheet 32)

1124. Dauphin County (cont'd: ED 96, sheet 33-ED 119, sheet 14)

1125. Dauphin (cont'd: ED 119, sheet 15-end), Elk, and Delaware (part: EDs 1-12, sheet 6) Counties

1126. Delaware County (cont'd: ED 12, sheet 7-end)

1127. Erie County (part: EDs 1-152, sheet 6)

1128. Erie County (cont'd: ED 152, sheet 7-ED 172, sheet 10)

1129. Erie (cont'd: ED 172, sheet 11-end) and Fayette (part: EDs

1-41, sheet 26) Counties

1130. Fayette County (cont'd: ED 41, sheet 27-end)

1131. Forest and Franklin (part: EDs 1-101, sheet 4) Counties

1132. Franklin County (cont'd: ED 101, sheet 5-end)

1133. Fulton and Greene Counties

1134. Huntingdon County

1135. Indiana County

1136. Jefferson and Juniata (part: EDs 1-132, sheet 16) Counties

1137. Juniata (cont'd: ED 132, sheet 17-end) and Lackawanna (part: EDs 1-33, sheet 16) Counties

1138. Lackawanna County (cont'd: ED 33, sheet 17-ED 57, sheet 15)

1139. Lackawanna County (cont'd: ED 57, sheet 16-end)

1140. Lancaster County (excluding the city of Lancaster) (part: EDs 1-121, sheet 49)

1141. Lancaster County (excluding the city of Lancaster) (cont'd: ED 122, sheet 1-ED 142, sheet 2)

1142. City of Lancaster, wards 1-6 (part: ED 142, sheet 3-ED 155, sheet 34)

1143. City of Lancaster, ward 6 (cont'd: ED 155, sheet 35-ED 176, sheet 14)

1144. Lancaster (excluding the city of Lancaster) (cont'd: ED 176, sheet 15-end) and Lawrence (part: EDs 1-226, sheet 4) Counties

1145. Lawrence (cont'd: ED 226, sheet 5-end) and Lebanon (part: EDs 1-135, sheet 2) Counties

1146. Lebanon (cont'd: ED 135, sheet 3-end) and Lehigh (part: EDs 1-189, sheet 4) Counties

1147. Lehigh County (cont'd: ED 189, sheet 5-ED 209, sheet 12)

1148. Lehigh (cont'd: ED 209, sheet 13-end) and Luzerne (excluding the city of Wilkes-Barre) (part: EDs 1-102, sheet 19) Counties

1149. Luzerne County (excluding the city of Wilkes-Barre) (cont'd: ED 102, sheet 20-ED 112, sheet 49) and city of Wilkes-Barre, wards 1-12, and 15 (part: ED 113, sheet 1-ED 123, sheet 44)

1150. City of Wilkes-Barre, wards 13-14 (cont'd: ED 124, sheet 1-ED 127, sheet 37) and Luzerne County (excluding the city of Wilkes-Barre) (cont'd: ED 128, sheet 1-ED 146, sheet 8)

1151. Luzerne County (excluding the city of Wilkes-Barre) (cont'd: ED 146, sheet 9-end)

1152. Lycoming County (part: EDs 1-65, sheet 14)

1153. Lycoming (cont'd: ED 65, sheet 15-end) and McKean (part: EDs 1-81, sheet 4) Counties

1154. McKean (cont'd: ED 81, sheet 5-end), Mifflin (part: ED 168, sheet 1-ED 168, sheet 2), and Mercer (part: EDs 1-207, sheet 18) Counties

1155. Mercer County (cont'd: ED 207, sheet 19-ED 227, sheet 37; ED East, sheet 1-ED East, sheet 34)

1156. Mercer (cont'd: ED East, sheet 35-ED East, sheet 46; ED 229, sheet 1-ED 236, sheet 13), Mifflin (cont'd: ED 168, sheet 3-end), and Monroe (part: EDs 1-215, sheet 12) Counties

1157. Monroe (cont'd: ED 215, sheet 13-end) and Montgomery (part: EDs 1-10, sheet 18) Counties

1158. Montgomery County (cont'd: ED 10, sheet 19-ED 30, sheet 22)

1159. Montgomery County (cont'd: ED 30, sheet 23-ED 52, sheet 14)

1160. Montgomery (cont'd: ED 52, sheet 15-end), Montour, and Northampton (part: EDs 1-66, sheet 2) Counties

1161. Northampton County (cont'd: ED 66, sheet 3-ED 77, sheet 39)

1162. Northampton County (cont'd: ED 78, sheet 1-ED 91, sheet 26)

1163. Northampton (cont'd: ED 91, sheet 27-end) and Northumberland (part: EDs 1-146, sheet 50) Counties

1164. Northumberland County (cont'd: ED 146, sheet 51-end)

1165. Perry, Pike, and Potter (part: EDs 1-105, sheet 12) Counties

1166. Potter County (cont'd: ED 105, sheet 13-end) and city of Philadelphia, ward 1 (part: EDs 1-20, sheet 10)

1167. City of Philadelphia, wards 1 and 2 (cont'd: ED 20, sheet 11-ED 44, sheet 8)

1168. City of Philadelphia, wards 2 and 3 (cont'd: ED 44, sheet 9-ED 69, sheet 28)

1169. City of Philadelphia, wards 4-6 (cont'd: ED 70, sheet 1-ED 107, sheet 4)

1170. City of Philadelphia, wards 6 and 7 (cont'd: ED 107, sheet 5-ED 135, sheet 10)

1171. City of Philadelphia, wards 7-9 (cont'd: ED 135, sheet 11-ED 164, sheet 16)

1172. City of Philadelphia, wards 9-11 (cont'd: ED 164, sheet 17-ED 196, sheet 27)

1173. City of Philadelphia, wards 12 and 13 (cont'd: ED 197, sheet 1-ED 224, sheet 12)

1174. City of Philadelphia, wards 13-15 (cont'd: ED 224, sheet 13-ED 256, sheet 14)

1175. City of Philadelphia, ward 15 (cont'd: ED 256, sheet 15-ED 287, sheet 34)

1176. City of Philadelphia, wards 16 and 17 (cont'd: ED 288, sheet 1-ED 316, sheet 8)

1177. City of Philadelphia, wards 17 and 18 (cont'd: ED 316, sheet 9-ED 349, sheet 28)

1178. City of Philadelphia, ward 19 (cont'd: ED 350, sheet 1-ED 376, sheet 14)

1179. City of Philadelphia, ward 19 (cont'd: ED 376, sheet 15-ED 404, sheet 14)

1180. City of Philadelphia, wards 20 and 21 (cont'd: ED 404, sheet 15-ED 433, sheet 6)

1181. City of Philadelphia, wards 21 and 22 (cont'd: ED 433, sheet 7-ED 459, sheet 32)

1182. City of Philadelphia, wards 23 and 24 (cont'd: ED 460, sheet 1-ED 489, sheet 8)

1183. City of Philadelphia, ward 24 (cont'd: ED 489, sheet 9-ED 516, sheet 25)

1184. City of Philadelphia, ward 25 (cont'd: ED 517, sheet 1-ED 542, sheet 4)

1185. City of Philadelphia, wards 25 and 26 (cont'd: ED 542, sheet 5-ED 567, sheet 25)

1186. City of Philadelphia, wards 27 and 28 (cont'd: ED 568, sheet 1-ED 589, sheet 26)

1187. City of Philadelphia, ward 28 (cont'd: ED 590, sheet 1-ED 609, sheet 28)

1188. City of Philadelphia, ward 29 (cont'd: ED 610, sheet 1-ED 642, sheet 383

1189. City of Philadelphia, wards 30 and 31 (cont'd: ED 643, sheet 1-ED 670, sheet 4)

1190. City of Philadelphia, ward 31 (cont'd: ED 670, sheet 5-end), and Schuylkill County (part: EDs 1-176, sheet 62)

1191. Schuylkill County (cont'd: ED 176, sheet 63-ED 192, sheet 64)

1192. Schuylkill County (cont'd: ED 192, sheet 65-ED 215, sheet 32)

1193. Schuylkill County (cont'd: ED 215, sheet 33-ED 238, sheet 6)

1194. Schuylkill (cont'd: ED 238, sheet 7-end), Snyder, and Somerset (part: ED 1, sheet 6) Counties

1195. Somerset (cont'd: ED 1, sheet 7-end) and Sullivan Counties

1196. Susquehanna County (part: EDs 1-136, sheet 6)

1197. Susquehanna (cont'd: ED 136, sheet 7-end), Union, and Tioga (part: EDs 1-148, sheet 14) Counties

1198. Tioga County (cont'd: ED 148, sheet 15-end)

1199. Venango County

1200. Warren County

1201. Washington County (part: EDs 1-264, sheet 4)

1202. Washington (cont'd: ED 264, sheet 5-end) and Wayne (part: EDs 1-18, sheet 16) Counties

1203. Wayne (cont'd: ED 18, sheet 17-end) and Westmoreland (part: EDs 1-104, sheet 32) Counties

1204. Westmoreland County (cont'd: ED 104, sheet 33-ED 121, sheet 6)

1205. Westmoreland (cont'd: ED 121, sheet 7-end), Wyoming, and York (part: EDs 1-4, sheet 34) Counties

1206. York County (cont'd: ED 4, sheet 35-ED 20, sheet 15)

1207. York County (cont'd: ED 20, sheet 16-ED 38, sheet 30)

1208. York County (cont'd: ED 38, sheet 31-end)

Rhode Island.

1209. Bristol and Kent Counties

1210. Newport and Washington (part: EDs 1-158, sheet 12) Counties

1211. Washington County (cont'd: ED 158, sheet 13-end) and city of Providence (part: EDs 1-18, sheet 2)

1212. City of Providence (cont'd: ED 18, sheet 3-ED 42, sheet 22)

1213. City of Providence (cont'd: ED 42, sheet 23-end)

1214. Providence County (excluding the city of Providence) (part: EDs 1-119, sheet 46)

1215. Providence County (excluding the city of Providence) (cont'd: ED 119, sheet 47-ED 142, sheet 8)

1216. Providence County (excluding the city of Providence) (cont'd: ED 142, sheet 9-end)

South Carolina.

1217. Abbeville County

1218. Aiken County

1219. Anderson County

1220. Barnwell County

1221. Beaufort County and city of Charleston, wards 1 and 2 (part: EDs 1-56, sheet 18)

1222. City of Charleston, wards 2-8 (cont'd: ED 56, sheet 19-ED 77, sheet 44)

1223. Charleston County (excluding the city of Charleston) (part: EDs 1-91, sheet 20)

1224. Charleston (excluding the city of Charleston) (cont'd: ED 91, sheet 21-end) and Chester (part: EDs 1-42, sheet 2) Counties

1225. Chester (cont'd: ED 42, sheet 3-end), Chesterfield, and Clarendon (part: EDs 1-25, sheet 28) Counties

1226. Clarendon (cont'd: ED 25, sheet 29-end) and Colleton Counties

1227. Darlington County

1228. Edgefield County

1229. Fairfield and Georgetown (part: EDs 1-53, sheet 6) Counties

1230. Georgetown (cont'd: ED 53, sheet 7-end) and Greenville (part: EDs 1-90, sheet 44) Counties

1231. Greenville (cont'd: ED 90, sheet 46-end), Hampton, and Horry (part: EDs 1-64, sheet 2) Counties

1232. Horry (cont'd: ED 64, sheet 3-end), Kershaw, and Lancaster (part: EDs 1-80, sheet 58) Counties

1233. Lancaster (cont'd: ED 81, sheet 1-end), Laurens, and Lexington (part: EDs 1-125, sheet 16) Counties

1234. Lexington (cont'd: ED 125, sheet 17-end) and Marion (part: EDs 1-96, sheet 4) Counties

1235. Marion (cont'd: ED 96, sheet 5-end), Marlboro, and Newberry (part: EDs 1-110, sheet 31) Counties

1236. Newberry (cont'd: ED 110, sheet 32-end) and Oconee Counties

1237. Orangeburg County

1238. Pickens and Richland (part: EDs 1-169, sheet 26) Counties

1239. Richland County (cont'd: ED 169, sheet 27-end)

1240. Spartanburg County

1241. Sumter County (part: EDs 1-127, sheet 18)

1242. Sumter (cont'd: ED 127, sheet 19-end), Union, and Williamsburg (part: EDs 1-134, sheet 8) Counties

1243. Williamsburg (cont'd: ED 134, sheet 9-end) and York Counties

Tennessee.

1244. Anderson, Bedford, and Benton Counties

1245. Bledsoe, Blount, and Bradley Counties

1246. Cambell, Cannon, and Carroll (part: EDs 1-17, sheet 24) Counties

1247. Carroll (cont'd: ED 17, sheet 25-end), Carter, Cheatham, and Claiborne (part: EDs 1-108, sheet 16) Counties

1248. Claiborne (cont'd: ED 108, sheet 17-end), Clay, Cooke, and Coffee (part: EDs 1-20, sheet 34) Counties

1249. Coffee (cont'd: ED 20, sheet 35-end), Crockett, Cumberland, and Davidson (part: EDs 1-43, sheet 32) Counties

1250. Davidson County (cont'd: ED 43, sheet 33-ED 61, sheet 52)

1251. Davidson County (cont'd: ED 62, sheet 1-end)

1252. Decatur, De Kalb, and Dickson Counties

1253. Dyer and Fayette (part: EDs 1-26, sheet 26) Counties

1254. Fayette (cont'd: ED 26, sheet 27-end), Fentress, Franklin, and Gibson (part: EDs 1-33, sheet 6) Counties

1255. Gibson County (cont'd: ED 33, sheet 7-end)

1256. Giles County (part: EDs 1-105, sheet 34)

1257. Giles (cont'd: ED 105, sheet 35-end) and Grainger Counties

1258. Greene, Grundy, and Hamblen Counties

1259. Hamilton, Hancock, and Hardeman (part: EDs 1-55, sheet 18) Counties

1260. Hardeman (cont'd: ED 55, sheet 19-end) Hardin, and Hawkins (part: EDs 1-78, sheet 12) Counties

1261. Hawkins (cont'd: ED 78, sheet 13-end) and Haywood (part: EDs 1-74, sheet 2) Counties

1262. Haywood (cont'd: ED 74, sheet 3-end) Henderson, and Henry (part: EDs 1-74, sheet 18) Counties

1263. Henry (cont'd: ED 74, sheet 19-end), Hickman, Houston, and Humphreys (part: EDs 1-102, sheet 35) Counties

1264. Humphreys (cont'd: ED 103, sheet 1-end), Jackson, James, and Jefferson Counties

1265. Johnson and Knox (part: EDs 1-163, sheet 2) Counties

1266. Knox (cont'd: ED 163, sheet 3-end), Lake, Lauderdale, and Lawrence (part: EDs 1-112, sheet 10) Counties

1267. Lawrence (cont'd: ED 112, sheet 11-end), Lewis, Loudon, and Lincoln (part: EDs 1-130, sheet 14) Counties

1268. Lincoln (cont'd: ED 130, sheet 15-end), McMinn, McNairy, and Marion (part: EDs 75, sheet 1-27) Counties

1269. Marion (cont'd: ED 75, sheet 28-end) and Marshall Counties

1270. Macon and Madison Counties

1271. Maury and Meigs (cont'd: ED 1-82, sheet 6) Counties

1272. Meigs (cont'd: ED 82, sheet 7-end), Monroe, and Montgomery (part: EDs 1-138, sheet 18) Counties

1273. Montgomery (cont'd: ED 138, sheet 19-end), Moore, Morgan, and Obion (part: EDs 1-110, sheet 20) Counties

1274. Obion (cont'd: ED 110, sheet 21-end), Overton, and Perry Counties

1275. Polk, Putnam, Rhea, and Roane Counties

1276. Rutherford County

1277. Robertson, Scott, Sequatchie, and Sevier (part: EDs 1-184, sheet 8) Counties

1278. Sevier (cont'd: ED 184, sheet 9-end) and Shelby (part: EDs 1-126, sheet 14) Counties

1279. Shelby County (cont'd: ED 126, sheet 15-ED 146, sheet 2)

1280. Shelby (cont'd: ED 146, sheet 3-end), Smith, and Stewart (part: EDs 1-155, sheet 20) Counties

1281. Stewart (cont'd: ED 155, sheet 21-end), Sullivan, and Sumner (part: EDs 1-213, sheet 4) Counties

1282. Sumner (cont'd: ED 213, sheet 5-end) and Tipton Counties

1283. Trousdale, Unicoi, Union, Van Buren, and Warren (part: EDs 1-136, sheet 10) Counties

1284. Warren (cont'd: ED 136, sheet 11-end), Washington, Wayne, and Weakley (part: EDs 1-169, sheet 9) Counties

1285. Weakley (cont'd: ED 169, sheet 10-end), White, and Williamson (part: EDs 1-232, sheet 30) Counties

1286. Williamson (cont'd: ED 232, sheet 31-end) and Wilson (part: EDs 1-257, sheet 20) Counties

1287. Wilson County (cont'd: ED 257, sheet 21-end)

Texas.

1288. Anderson County (part: EDs 1-16, sheet 57)

1289. Anderson (cont'd: ED 7, sheet 1-end), Angelina, Aransas, Archer, Atascosa, Austin, Armstrong, Briscoe, Randall, and Swisher Counties

1290. Bandera, Bastrop, Baylor, Bee, and Bell Counties

1291. Bexar, Blanco, Borden, and Bosque Counties

1292. Bowie, Brazoria, Brazos, and Brown Counties

1293. Burleson, Burnet, and Caldwell (part: EDs 1-28, sheet 46) Counties

1294. Caldwell (cont'd: ED 28, sheet 47-end), Calhoun, Callahan, and Cameron Counties

1295. Camp, Cass, Chambers, Cherokee, Childress (part: EDs 184, sheet 2 only), and Clay (part: EDs 1-163, sheet 10) Counties

1296. Clay (cont'd: ED 163, sheet 11-end), Coleman, Collin, and Collingsworth Counties

1297. Colorado, Comal, Comanche, Concho, and Cooke (part: EDs 1-111, sheet 28) Counties

1298. Cooke (cont'd: ED 111, sheet 29-end), Coryell, Cottle,

Crockett, Crosby, Dickens, Floyd, Garza, King, Lynn, and Motley Counties

1299. Dallas, De Witt, and Gaines Counties

1300. Dawson, Deaf Smith, Delta, Denton, Dimmitt, Donley, Duval, and Eastland (part: EDs 1-174, sheet 14) Counties

1301. Eastland (cont'd: ED 174, sheet 15-end), Edwards, Ellis, El Paso, and Encinal Counties

1302. Erath, Falls, and Fannin (part: EDs 1-27, sheet 22) Counties

1303. Fannin (cont'd: ED 27, sheet 23-end) and Fayette (part: EDs 1-164, sheet 61) Counties

1304. Fayette (cont'd: ED 165, sheet 1-end), Fisher, Fort Bend, Franklin, Freestone, Frio, and Scurry Counties

1305. Galveston, Gillespie, and Goliad Counties

1306. Gonzales, Gray, Hutchinson, Roberts, and Grayson (part: EDs 1-9, sheet 64) Counties

1307. Grayson (cont'd: ED 9, sheet 65-end), Gregg, and Grimes (part: EDs 1-63, sheet 22) Counties

1308. Grimes (cont'd: ED 63, sheet 23-end), Guadalupe, Hall, Hamilton, Hansford, Hardeman, Hardin, Wilbarger, and Harris (part: EDs 1-74, sheet 18) Counties

1309. Harris (cont'd: ED 74, sheet 19-end) and Harrison (part: EDs 1-48, sheet 14) Counties

1310. Harrison (cont'd: ED 48, sheet 15-end), Hartley, Haskell, Hays, Hemphill, Henderson, Knox, Oldham, Wheeler, and Hidalgo (part: EDs 1-81, sheet 52) Counties

1311. Hidalgo (cont'd: ED 81, sheet 53-end), Hill, Hood, and Hopkins (part: EDs 1-61, sheet 32) Counties

1312. Hopkins (cont'd: ED 61, sheet 33-end), Houston, Howard, and Hunt Counties

1313. Jack, Jackson, Jasper, Jefferson, Johnson, and Jones Counties

1314. Karnes, Kaufman, Kendall, Kent, Kerr, and Stonewall Counties

1315. Kimble, Kinney, La Salle, Lamar, and Lampasas (part: EDs 1-87, sheet 2) Counties

1316. Lampasas (cont'd: ED 87, sheet 3-end), Lavaca, Lee, and Leon (part: EDs 1-90, sheet 14) Counties

1317. Leon (cont'd: ED 90, sheet 15-end), Liberty, Limestone, Live Oak, Llano, Lubbock, McCulloch, and Lipscomb Counties

1318. McLennan, McMullen, Madison, and Marion (part: EDs 1-88, sheet 2) Counties

1319. Marion (cont'd: ED 88, sheet 3-end), Martin, Mason, Matagorda, Maverick, Medina, Menard, and Milam (part: EDs 1-104, sheet 64) Counties

1320. Milam (cont'd: ED 104, sheet 65-end), Mitchell, Montague, Montgomery, Morris, and Nacogdoches (part: EDs 1-48, sheet 18) Counties

1321. Nacogdoches (cont'd: ED 48, sheet 19-end), Navarro, Newton, and Nolan Counties

1322. Neuces, Orange, Palo Pinto, Panola, and Parker (part: EDs 1-136, sheet 36) Counties

1323. Parker (cont'd: ED 136, sheet 37-end) Pecos, Polk, Potter, Presidio, Tains, and Red River (part: EDs 1-103, sheet 46)

1324. Red River (cont'd: ED 103, sheet 47-end), Refugio, Robertson, Rockwell, and Runnels Counties

1325. Rusk, Sabine, San Augustine, San Jacinto, San Patricio, and San Saba (part: EDs 1-113, sheet 8) Counties

1326. San Saba (cont'd: ED 113, sheet 9-end), Shackelford, Shelby, and Smith (part: EDs 1-102, sheet 60) Counties

1327. Smith (cont'd: ED 102, sheet 61-end), Somervell, Starr, and Stephens Counties

1328. Tarrant, Taylor, Throckmorton, Titus, and Tom Green Counties

1329. Travis, Trinity, and Tyler (part: EDs 1-105, sheet 18) Counties

1330. Tyler (cont'd: ED 105, sheet 19-end), Upshur, Uvalde, Van Zandt, and Victoria Counties

1331. Walker, Waller, and Washington (part: EDs 1-145, sheet 46) Counties

1332. Washington (cont'd: ED 145, sheet 47-end), Webb, Wharton, Wichita, and Williamson (part: EDs 1-160, sheet 42) Counties

1333. Williamson (cont'd: ED 160, sheet 43-end), Wilson, Wise, and Wood (part ED 1-127, sheet 10) Counties

1334. Wood (cont'd: ED 127 sheet 11-end), Young, Zapata, and Zavala Counties

Utah.

1335. Beaver, Box Elder, and Cache (part: EDs 1-10, sheet 50) Counties

1336. Cache (cont'd: ED 10, sheet 51-end), Davis, Emery, Iron, Juab, Kane, Millard, Morgan, Piute, and Rich Counties

1337. Salt Lake, San Juan, and Sanpete (part: EDs 1-65, sheet 20) Counties

1338. Sanpete (cont'd: ED 65, sheet 21-end), Sevier, Summit, Toole, Uintah, and Utah (part: EDs 1-88, sheet 14) Counties

1339. Utah (cont'd: ED 88, sheet 15-end), Wasatch, Washington, and Weber Counties

Vermont.

1340. Addison County (part: EDs 1-10, sheet 28)

1341. Addison (cont'd: ED 11, sheet 1-end) and Bennington Counties

1342. Caledonia and Essex Counties

1343. Chittenden County

1344. Franklin, Grand Isle, and Lamoille (part: EDs 1-124, sheet 12) Counties

1345. Lamoille (cont'd: ED 124, sheet 13-end) and Orange (part: EDs 1-141, sheet 36) Counties

1346. Orange (cont'd: ED 141, sheet 37-end) and Orleans
    Counties
1347. Rutland County (part: EDs 1-190; sheet 12)
1348. Rutland (cont'd: ED 190, sheet 13-end) and Washington
    (part: EDs 1-218, sheet 6) Counties
1349. Washington (cont'd: ED 218, sheet 7-end) and Windham
    Counties
1350. Windsor County

Virginia.
1351. Accomack and Alexandria Counties
1352. Albermarle and Alleghany (part: EDs 1-2, sheet 22)
    Counties
1353. Alleghany (cont'd: ED 2, sheet 23-end). Amelia, Amherst,
    and Appomattox (part: EDs 1-7, sheet 50) Counties
1354. Appomattox (cont'd: ED 7, sheet 51-end) and Augusta
    (part: EDs 1-22, sheet 18) Counties
1355. Augusta (cont'd: ED 22, sheet 19-end), Bath, and Bedford
    (part: EDs 1-20, sheet 28) Counties
1356. Bedford (cont'd: ED 20, sheet 29-end), Bland, and
    Botetourt (part: EDs 1-13, sheet 26) Counties
1357. Botetourt (cont'd: ED 13, sheet 27-end), Brunswick,
    Buchanan, and Buckingham Counties
1358. Campbell County (part: EDs 1-50, sheet 52)
1359. Campbell (cont'd: ED 50, sheet 53-end) and Caroline
    Counties
1360. Carroll, Charles City, Charlotte, and Clarke Counties
1361. Chesterfield (part: EDs 63, sheet 1-ED 75, sheet 26),
    Craig, and Culpeper Counties
1362. Cumberland and Dinwiddie (part: EDs 1-88, sheet 16)
    Counties
1363. Dinwiddie (cont'd: ED 88, sheet 17-ED 88, sheet 24),
    Chesterfield (cont'd: ED 89, sheet 1-ED 89, sheet 15),
    Dinwiddie (cont'd: ED 89, sheet 16-ED 99, sheet 25),
    Elizabeth City, and Essex (part: EDs 1-18, sheet 27)
    Counties
1364. Essex (cont'd: ED 18, sheet 27-end), Fairfax, and Fauquier
    (part: EDs 1-43, sheet 25) Counties
1365. Fauquier (cont'd: ED 43, sheet 26-end), Floyd, and
    Fluvanna Counties
1366. Franklin and Frederick (part: EDs 1-43, sheet 34) Counties
1367. Frederick (cont'd: ED 43, sheet 35-end), Giles, Gloucester,
    and Goochland (part: EDs 1-56, sheet 20) Counties
1368. Goochland (cont'd: ED 56, sheet 21-end), Grayson,
    Greene, and Greensville Counties
1369. Halifax County
1370. Hanover and Henrico (part: EDs 1-76, sheet 22) Counties
1371. Henrico County (cont'd: ED 76, sheet 23-ED 88, sheet 52)
1372. Henrico County (cont'd: ED 88, sheet 53-end)
1373. Henry, Highland, Isle of Wight, and James City (part: EDs
    1-34, sheet 36) Counties

1374. James City (cont'd: ED 34, sheet 37-end), King and
    Queen, and King George Counties
1375. King William, Lancaster, Lee, and Loudoun (part: EDs
    1-53, sheet 71) Counties
1376. Loudoun (cont'd: ED 54, sheet 1-end), Louisa, and
    Lunenburg (part: EDs 1-134, sheet 54) Counties
1377. Lunenburg (cont'd: ED 135, sheet 1-end), Madison,
    Mathews, and Mecklenburg (part: EDs 1-143, sheet 38)
    Counties
1378. Mecklenburg (cont'd: ED 143, sheet 39-end), Middlesex,
    and Montgomery Counties
1379. Nansemond, Nelson, New Kent, and Northampton
    Counties
1380. Norfolk County (part: EDs 1-62, sheet 6) Counties
1381. Norfolk County (cont'd: ED 62, sheet 7-ED 75, sheet 12)
1382. Norfolk (cont'd: ED 75, sheet 13-end), Northumberland,
    Nottoway, and Orange (part: EDs 1-120, sheet 24)
    Counties
1383. Orange (cont'd: ED 120, sheet 25-end), Page, Patrick, and
    Powhatan Counties
1384. Prince Edward, Prince George, and Pittsylvania (part: EDs
    1-170, sheet 62) Counties
1385. Pittsylvania (cont'd: ED 170, sheet 63-end) and Prince
    William (part: EDs 1-128, sheet 17) Counties
1386. Prince William (cont'd: ED 128, sheet 18-end), Princess
    Anne, Pulaski, Rappahannock, Richmond, and Roanoke
    (part: EDs 1-60, sheet 64) Counties
1387. Roanoke (cont'd: ED 60, sheet 65-end) and Rockbridge
    (part: EDs 1-68, sheet 30) Counties
1388. Rockbridge (cont'd: ED 68, sheet 31-end) and Rockingham
    (part: EDs 1-81, sheet 30) Counties
1389. Rockingham (cont'd: ED 81, sheet 31-end), Russell, and
    Scott Counties
1390. Shenandoah, Smyth, and Southampton (part: EDs 1-101,
    sheet 4) Counties
1391. Southampton (cont'd: ED 101, sheet 5-end), Spotsylvania,
    and Stafford Counties
1392. Surry and Sussex (part: EDs 1-113, sheet 46) Counties
1393. Sussex (cont'd: ED 113, sheet 47-end), Tazewell, Warren,
    Warwick, Westmoreland, and Washington (part: EDs
    1-93, sheet 32) Counties
1394. Washington (cont'd: ED 93, sheet 33-end), Wise, and
    Wythe (part: EDs 1-109, sheet 16) Counties
1395. Wythe (cont'd: ED 109, sheet 17-end) and York Counties

Washington.
1396. Chehalis, Clallam, Clark, Columbia, Cowlitz, Island,
    Jefferson, and King (part: EDs 1-8, sheet 12) Counties
1397. King (cont'd: ED 8, sheet 13-end), Kitsap, Klickitat, Lewis,
    Mason, Pacific, Pierce, San Juan, Skamania, Snohomish,
    Spokane, Stevens, Thurston, and Wahkiakum (part: EDs

1-26, sheet 30) Counties

1398. Wahkiakum (cont'd: ED 26, sheet 31-end), Walla Walla, Whatcom, Whitman, and Yakima Counties

West Virginia.

1399. Barbour County (part: EDs 1-75, sheet 14)

1400. Barbour (cont'd: ED 75, sheet 15-end), Berkeley, Boone, and Braxton Counties

1401. Brooke, Cabell, Calhoun, Clay, and Doddridge Counties

1402. Fayette, Gilmer, Grant, and Greenbrier (part: EDs 1-36, sheet 38) Counties

1403. Greenbrier (cont'd: ED 36, sheet 39-end), Hampshire, Hancock, Hardy, and Harrison (part: EDs 1-111, sheet 30) Counties

1404. Harrison (cont'd: ED 111, sheet 31-end), Jackson, and Jefferson (part: EDs 1-4, sheet 22) Counties

1405. Jefferson (cont'd: ED 4, sheet 23-end) and Kanawha (part: EDs 1-61, sheet 26) Counties

1406. Kanawha (cont'd: ED 61, sheet 27-end), Lewis, Lincoln, and Logan Counties

1407. McDowell, Marion, Marshall, and Mason (part: EDs 1-91, sheet 14) Counties

1408. Mason (cont'd: ED 91, sheet 15-end), Mercer, and Mineral (part: EDs 1-34, sheet 18) Counties

1409. Mineral (cont'd: ED 34, sheet 19-end), Monongalia, Monroe, Morgan, and Nicholas (part: EDs 1-103, sheet 19) Counties

1410. Nicholas (cont'd: ED 104, sheet 1-end) and Ohio (part: EDs 1-212, sheet 14) Counties

1411. Ohio (cont'd: ED 212, sheet 15-end), Pendleton, Pleasants, Pocahontas, and Preston (part: EDs 1-62, sheet 32) Counties

1412. Preston (cont'd: ED 62, sheet 33-end), Putnam, Raleigh, and Randolph (part: EDs 1-57, sheet 6) Counties

1413. Randolph (cont'd: ED 57, sheet 7-end), Ritchie, Roane, and Summers Counties

1414. Taylor, Tucker, Tyler, Upshur, and Wayne (part: EDs 1-139, sheet 14) Counties

1415. Wayne (cont'd: ED 139, sheet 15-end), Webster, Wetzel, and Wirt (part: EDs 1-158, sheet 32) Counties

1416. Wirt (cont'd: ED 158, sheet 33-end), Wood, and Wyoming Counties

Wisconsin.

1417. Adams, Ashland, Barron, Bayfield, Buffalo, and Burnett Counties

1418. Brown and Calumet (part: EDs 1-30, sheet 12) Counties

1419. Calumet (cont'd: ED 30, sheet 13-end), Chippewa, and Clark Counties

1420. Columbia and Crawford (part: EDs 1-48, sheet 6) Counties

1421. Crawford (cont'd: ED 48, sheet 7-end) and Dane (part:

EDs 1-77, sheet 2) Counties

1422. Dane (cont'd: ED 77, sheet 3-end) and Dodge (part: EDs 1-9, sheet 4) Counties

1423. Dodge County (cont'd: ED 9, sheet 5-end)

1424. Door, Douglas, Dunn, and Eau Claire (part: EDs 1-129, sheet 16) Counties

1425. Eau Claire (cont'd: ED 129, sheet 17-end) and Fond du Lac (part: EDs 1-42, sheet 32) Counties

1426. Fond du Lac (cont'd: ED 42, sheet 33-end) and Grant (part: EDs 1-106, sheet 4) Counties

1427. Grant County (cont'd: ED 106, sheet 5-end)

1428. Green and Green Lake Counties

1429. Iowa and Jackson Counties

1430. Jefferson and Juneau (part: EDs 1-192, sheet 8) Counties

1431. Juneau (cont'd: ED 193, sheet 1-end), Kenosha, and Kewaunee (part: EDs 1-56, sheet 32) Counties

1432. Kewaunee (cont'd: ED 56, sheet 33-end) and La Crosse Counties

1433. Lafayette, Langlade, Lincoln, and Marathon Counties

1434. Manitowoc County (part: EDs 1-79, sheet 38)

1435. Manitowoc (cont'd: ED 79, sheet 39-end), Marinette, and Marquette Counties, and city of Milwaukee, ward 1 (part: EDs 1-93, sheet 14)

1436. City of Milwaukee, wards 1-4 (cont'd: ED 93, sheet 15-ED 110, sheet 6)

1437. City of Milwaukee, wards 4-8 (cont'd: ED 110, sheet 7-ED 127, sheet 57)

1438. City of Milwaukee, wards 8-12 (cont'd: ED 128, sheet 1-ED 140, sheet 15)

1439. City of Milwaukee, wards 12 and 13 (cont'd: ED 140, sheet 16-end) and Milwaukee (excluding the city of Milwaukee), Monroe, and Oconto (part: EDs 1-103, sheet 6) Counties

1440. Oconto (cont'd: ED 103, sheet 7-end) and Outagamie (part: EDs 1-129, sheet 10) Counties

1441. Outagamie (cont'd: ED 129, sheet 11-end), Ozaukee, Pepin, and Pierce (part: EDs 1-118, sheet 6) Counties

1442. Pierce (cont'd: ED 118, sheet 7-end), Polk, and Portage Counties

1443. Price and Racine Counties

1444. Rock County

1445. Richland and St. Croix (part: EDs 1-237, sheet 2) Counties

1446. St. Croix (cont'd: ED 237, sheet 3-end), Sauk, and Shawano (part: EDs 1-149, sheet 16) Counties

1447. Shawano (cont'd: ED 149, sheet 17-end) and Sheboygan (part: EDs 1-216, sheet 33) Counties

1448. Sheboygan (cont'd: ED 217, sheet 1-end), Taylor, Trempealeau, and Vernon (part: EDs 1-6, sheet 13) Counties

1449. Vernon (cont'd: ED 6, sheet 14-end) and Walworth (part: EDs 1-234, sheet 12) Counties

Wyoming.

ELEVENTH CENSUS OF THE UNITED STATES, 1890. M407. 3 ROLLS.

Most of the 1890 population schedules were badly damaged by fire in the Commerce Department Building in January 1921. The extant schedules are numbered and noted at the end of rolls 1-3 below.

INDEX TO THE ELEVENTH CENSUS OF THE UNITED STATES, 1890. M496. 2ROLLS. 16-MM.

This name index covers the few extant 1890 population schedules. Numbers on the cards match those listed at the end of rolls 1-3 of M407 above.

SPECIAL SCHEDULES OF THE ELEVENTH CENSUS (1890) ENUMERATING UNION VETERANS AND WIDOWS OF UNION VETERANS OF THE CIVIL WAR. M123. 118 ROLLS.

An act of March 1, 1889, provided that the Superintendent of Census in taking the Eleventh Census should "cause to be taken on a special schedule of inquiry, according to such form as he may prescribe, the names, organizations, and length of service of those who had served in the Army, Navy, or Marine Corps of the United States in the war of the rebellion, and who are survivors at the time of said inquiry, and the widows of soldiers, sailors, or marines." Each schedule calls for the following information: name of the veteran (or if he did not survive, the names of both the widow and her deceased husband); the veteran's rank, company, regiment or vessel, date of enlistment, date of discharge, and length of service in years, months, and days; post office and address of each person listed; disability incurred by the veteran; and remarks necessary to a complete statement of his term of service. Practically all of the schedules for the States Alabama through Kansas and approximately half of those for Kentucky appear to have been destroyed, possibly by fire, before the transfer of the remaining schedules to the National Archives in 1943.

Kentucky.

Louisiana.

Cameron, Iberia, Iberville, and Lafayette Parishes

Maine.

6. Androscoggin, Cumberland, Franklin, Kennebec, Oxford, Sagadahoc, Somerset, and York Counties
7. Aroostook, Hancock, Knox, Lincoln, Penobscot, Piscataquis, Waldo, and Washington Counties

Maryland.

8. Baltimore City and Baltimore County
9. Caroline, Cecil, Dorchester, Harford, Kent, Queen Annes, Somerset, Talbot, Wicomico, and Worcester Counties
10. Allegany, Anne Arundel, Calvert, Carroll, Charles, Frederick, Garrett, Howard, Montgomery, Prince Georges, St. Mary's, and Washington Counties

Massachusetts.

11. Hampshire, Norfolk, and Plymouth Counties
12. Middlesex County
13. Barnstable, Berkshire, Bristol, Dukes, Franklin, and Nantucket Counties
14. Hampden County
15. Essex County
16. Suffolk County

Michigan.

17. Branch, Calhoun, Hillsdale, Jackson, Lenawee, Monroe, Washtenaw, and Wayne Counties
18. Genesee, Huron, Lapeer, Macomb, Oakland, Saginaw, St. Clair, Sanilac, and Tuscola Counties
19. Clinton, Eaton, Gratiot, Ingham, Ionia, Isabella, Livingston, Mecosta, Midland, Montcalm, and Shiawassee Counties
20. Allegan, Barry, Berrien, Cass, Kalamazoo, Kent, Muskegon, Newaygo, Oceana, Ottawa, St. Joseph, and Van Buren Counties
21. Alcona, Alger, Alpena, Antrim, Arenac, Baraga, Bay, Benzie, Charlevoix, Cheboygan, Chippewa, Clare, Crawford, Delta, Emmet, Gladwin, Gogebic, Grand Traverse, Houghton, Iosco, Iron, Isle Royale, Kalkaska, Keweenaw, Lake, Leelanau, Luce, Mackinac, Manistee, Manitou, Marquette, Mason, Menominee, Missaukee, Montgomery, Ogemaw, Ontonagon, Osceola, Oscoda, Otsego, Presque Isle, Roscommon, Schoolcraft, and Wexford Counties

Minnesota.

22. Blue Earth, Brown, Cottonwood, Dodge, Fairbault, Fillmore, Freeborn, Houston, Jackson, Lac qui Parle, Lincoln, Lyon, Martin, Mower, Murray, Nicollet, Nobles, Olmsted, Pipestone, Redwood, Rock, Steele, Waseca, Watonwan, Winona, and Yellow Medicine Counties, and certain Federal, State, local, and private institutions
23. Big Stone, Carver, Chippewa, Dakota, Goodhue, Hennepin, Kandiyohi, Le Sueur, McLeod, Meeker, Renville, Rice, Scott, Sibley, Swift, Wabasha, and Wright Counties
24. Aitkin, Anoka, Benton, Carlton, Cass, Chisago, Cook, Crow Wing, Isanti, Itasca, Kanabec, Lake, Mille Lacs, Morrison, Pine, Ramsey, St. Louis, Sherburne, and Washington Counties
25. Becker, Beltrami, Clay, Douglas, Grant, Hubbard, Kittson, Marshall, Norman, Otter Tail, Polk, Pope, Stearns, Stevens, Todd, Traverse, Wadena, and Wilkin Counties

Mississippi.

26. Entire state

Missouri.

27. Jefferson, St. Charles, and St. Louis Counties, and certain Federal, State, local, and private institutions
28. Bollinger, Butler, Cape Girardeau, Carter, Dunklin, Iron, Madison, Mississippi, New Madrid, Oregon, Pemiscot, Perry, Reynolds, Ripley, St. Francois, St. Genevieve, Scott, Shannon, Stoddard, Washington, and Wayne Counties
29. Audrain, Boone, Callaway, Camden, Cole, Crawford, Dent, Franklin, Gasconade, Lincoln, Maries, Miller, Montgomery, Osage, Phelps, Pike, Pulaski, and Warren Counties
30. Barry, Christian, Dade, Dallas, Douglas, Greene, Howell, Jasper, Laclede, Lawrence, McDonald, Newton, Ozark, Polk, Stone, Taney, Texas, Webster, and Wright Counties
31. Adair, Chariton, Clark, Howard, Knox, Lewis, Linn, Macon, Marion, Monroe, Putnam, Ralls, Randolph, Schuyler, Scotland, Shelby, and Sullivan Counties
32. Barton, Bates, Benton, Cass, Cedar, Cooper, Henry, Hickory, Johnson, Lafayette, Moniteau, Morgan, Pettis, St. Clair, Saline, and Vernon Counties
33. Andrew, Atchison, Caldwell, Carroll, Clinton, Grundy, Harrison, Holt, Livingston, Mercer, Nodaway, Ray, and Worth Counties
34. Buchanan, Clay, Jackson, and Platte Counties

Montana.

35. Entire state

Nebraska.

36. Adams, Butler, Chase, Clay, Dundy, Fillmore, Franklin, Frontier, Furnas, Gosper, Hamilton, Harlan, Hayes, Hitchcock, Jefferson, Kearney, Nuckolls, Phelps, Polk, Red Willow, Saline, Seward, Thayer, Webster, and York Counties
37. Antelope, Arthur, Banner, Blaine, Boone, Box Butte, Brown, Buffalo, Burt, Cedar, Cherry, Cheyenne, Colfax, Cuming, Custer, Dakota, Dawes, Dawson, Deuel, Dixon, Dodge, Garfield, Grant, Greeley, Hall, Holt, Hooker, Howard, Keith, Keya Paha, Kimball, Knox, Lincoln, Logan, Loup,

McPherson, Madison, Merrick, Nance, Perkins, Pierce, Platte, Rock, Scotts Bluff, Sheridan, Sherman, Sioux, Stanton, Thomas, Thurston, Valley, Washington, Wayne, and Wheeler Counties

38. Cass, Douglas, Gage, Johnson, Lancaster, Nemaha, Otoe, Pawnee, Richardson, Sarpy, and Saunders Counties

Nevada.
39. Entire state

New Hampshire.
40. Entire state

New Jersey.
41. Bergen, Essex, Morris, Passaic, Sussex, and Warren Counties
42. Hudson, Hunterdon, Mercer, Middlesex, Somerset, and Union Counties
43. Atlantic, Burlington, Camden, Cape May, Cumberland, Gloucester, Monmouth, Ocean, and Salem Counties

New Mexico.
44. Entire territory

New York.
46. New York County (part)
46. New York County (part)
47. Kings, Queens, Richmond, and Suffolk Counties
48. Columbia, Dutchess, Putnam, and Westchester Counties
49. Delaware, Orange, Rockland, Sullivan, and Ulster Counties
50. Albany, Greene, Otsego, Rensselaer, and Schoharie Counties
51. Fulton, Hamilton, Herkimer, Montgomery, Saratoga, Schenectady, Warren, and Washington Counties
52. Clinton, Essex, Franklin, Jefferson, Lewis, and St. Lawrence Counties
53. Cayuga, Madison, Oneida, Onondaga, and Oswego Counties
54. Allegany, Broome, Chemung, Chenango, Cortland, Schuyler, Steuben, Tioga, and Tompkins Counties
55. Genesee, Livingston, Monroe, Ontario, Orleans, Seneca, Wayne, Wyoming, and Yates Counties
56. Cattaraugus, Chautauqua, Erie, and Niagara Counties
57. Certain Federal, State, local, and private institutions throughout New York State

North Carolina.
58. Entire state

North Dakota.
59. Entire state

Ohio.
60. Allen, Crawford, Defiance, Fulton, Henry, and Paulding Counties

61. Putnam, Sandusky, Seneca, Van Wert, Williams, and Wyandot Counties
62. Hancock, Lucas, Ottawa, and Wood Counties
63. Auglaize, Champaign, Clark, Drake, Greene, and Hardin Counties
64. Logan, Mercer, Miami, Montgomery, Preble, and Shelby Counties
65. Butler, Clermont, Clinton, and Warren Counties
66. Hamilton County
67. Adams, Brown, and Gallia Counties
68. Highland, Hocking, Jackson, Lawrence, Pike, Ross, Scioto, and Vinton Counties
69. Delaware, Fairfield, Fayette, and Franklin Counties
70. Knox, Licking, Madison, Marion, Morrow, Perry, Pickaway, and Union Counties
71. Ashland and Cuyahoga Counties
72. Erie, Holmes, Huron, Lorain, Medina, Richland, and Wayne Counties
73. Athens, Belmont, Coshocton, Guernsey, Harrison, Meigs, Monroe, Morgan, Muskingum, Noble, and Washington Counties
74. Ashtabula, Carroll, Columbiana. Geauga, Jefferson, Lake, Mahoning, Portage, Stark, Summit, Trumbull, and Tuscarawas Counties
75. Federal, State, local, and private institutions throughout Ohio

Oklahoma and Indian Territories.
76. Entire territory

Oregon.
77. Entire state

Pennsylvania.
78. Philadelphia County (part)
79. Philadelphia County (part)
80. Philadelphia County (part)
81. Chester, Delaware, Lancaster, and York Counties
82. Berks, Bucks, Lehigh, Montgomery, and Northampton Counties
83. Columbia, Dauphin, Lebanon, Montour, Northumberland, and Schuylkill Counties
84. Carbon, Lackawanna, Luzerne, Monroe, Pike, Susquehanna, Wayne, and Wyoming Counties
85. Bradford, Cameron, Center, Clearfield, Clinton, Elk, Lycoming, McKean, Potter, Sullivan, and Tioga Counties
86. Adams, Bedford, Blair, Cumberland, Franklin, Fulton, Huntingdon, Juniata, Mifflin, Perry, Snyder, and Union Counties
87. Armstrong, Cambria, Clarion, Indiana, Jefferson, and Westmoreland Counties

88. Allegheny County
89. Butler, Crawford, Erie, Forest, Lawrence, Mercer, Venango, and Warren Counties
90. Beaver, Fayette, and Greene Counties
91. Somerset and Washington Counties and certain Federal, State, local, and private institutions throughout Pennsylvania

Rhode Island.
92. Entire state

South Carolina.
93. Entire state

South Dakota.
94. Entire state

Tennessee.
95. Anderson, Blount, Campbell, Carter, Claiborne, Cocke, Grainger, Greene, Hamblen, Hancock, Hawkins, Jefferson, Johnson, Knox, Loudon, Morgan, Roane, Scott, Sevier, Sullivan, Unicoi, Union, and Washington Counties
96. Bledsoe, Bradley, Cannon, Clay, Cumberland, DeKalb, Fentress, Grundy, Hamilton, Jackson, James, McMinn, Macon, Marion, Meigs, Monroe, Overton, Pickett, Polk, Putnam, Rhea, Sequatchie, Smith, Van Buren, Warren, and White Counties
97. Bedford, Cheatham, Coffee, Davidson, Franklin, Giles, Lincoln, Marshall, Maury, Moore, Robertson, Rutherford, Sumner, Trousdale, Williamson, and Wilson Counties
98. Benton, Carroll, Chester, Crockett, Decatur, Dickson, Dyer, Fayette, Gibson, Hardin, Hardeman, Haywood, Henry, Henderson, Hickman, Houston, Humphreys, Lake, Lauderdale, Lawrence, Lewis, Madison, McNairy, Montgomery, Obion, Perry, Shelby, Stewart, Tipton, Wayne, and Weakley Counties

Texas.
99. Anderson, Angelina, Bowie, Camp, Cass, Chambers, Cherokee, Delta, Fannin, Franklin, Galveston, Gregg, Harris, Harrison, Henderson, Hopkins, Houston, Hunt, Jefferson, Lamar, Liberty, Marion, Montgomery, Morris, Nacogdoches, Newton, Orange, Panola, Polk, Rains, Red River, Rusk, Sabine, San Jacinto, Shelby, Smith, Titus, Trinity, Tyler, Upshur, Van Zandt, Walker, and Wood Counties
100. Collin, Cooke, Dallas, Denton, Ellis, Grayson, Hill, Johnson, Kaufman, McLennan, Navarro, Rockwall, and Tarrant Counties
101. Austin, Bexar, Brazoria, Brazos, Burleson, Calhoun, Caldwell, Cameron, Colorado, Comal, DeWitt, Dimmit, Duval, Falls, Fayette, Fort Bend, Frio, Freestone, Goliad, Gonzales, Grimes, Guadalupe, Hays, Hidalgo, Jackson, Karnes, Kinney, La Salle, Lavaca, Lee, Leon, Live Oak, Limestone, Madison, Matagorda, Maverick, Medina, Milam, Nueces, Robertson, San Patricio, Starr, Travis, Uvalde, Victoria, Waller, Washington, Webb, Wilson, Wharton, Zapata, and Zavala Counties
102. Archer, Armstrong, Bandera, Baylor, Bell, Blanco, Bosque, Brewster, Briscoe, Brown, Buchel, Burnet, Callahan, Carson, Childress, Clay, Coleman, Collingsworth, Comanche, Coryell, Cottle, Dallam, Deaf Smith, Dickens, Donley, Eastland, Ector, Edwards, El Paso, Erath, Fisher, Foley, Gillespie, Gray, Hale, Hall, Hamilton, Hardeman, Hartley, Haskell, Hemphill, Hood, Harvard, Jack, Jeff Davis, Jones, Kendell, Kent, Kerr, Kimble, King, Knox, Lampasas, Lipscomb, Llano, McCulloch, Martin, Mason, Menard, Midland, Mills, Mitchell, Montague, Nolan, Ochiltree, Oldham, Palo Pinto, Parker, Pecos, Potter, Randall, Reeves, Roberts, Runnels, San Saba, Scurry, Shackelford, Sherman, Somervell, Stephens, Stonewall, Sutton, Swisher, Taylor, Throckmorton, Tom Green, Val Verde, Wheeler, Wichita, Wilbarger, Williamson, Wise, and Young Counties

Utah.
103. Entire state

United States Vessels and Navy Yards.
104.

Vermont.
105. Entire state

Virginia.
106. Accomack, Charles City, Elizabeth City, Essex, Gloucester, Greensville, Isle of Wight, James City, King and Queen, King William, Lancaster, Mathews, Middlesex, Nansemond, New Kent, Norfolk, Northampton, Northumberland, Prince George, Princess Anne, Richmond, Southampton, Surry, Sussex, Warwick, Westmoreland, York, Amelia Appomattox, Brunswick, Buckingham, Charlotte, Chesterfield, Cumberland, Dinwiddie, Fluvanna, Goochland, Halifax, Henrico, Lunenburg, Mecklenburg, Nottoway, Powhatan, Prince Edward, Alexandria, Caroline, Clarke, Culpeper, Fairfax, Fauquier, Frederick, Hanover, King George, Loudoun, Louisa, Madison, Orange, Page, Prince William, Rappahannock, Rockingham, Shenandoah, Spotsylvania, Stafford, and Warren Counties
107. Albemarle, Allegheny, Amherst, Augusta, Bath, Bedford, Botetourt, Campbell, Franklin, Henry, Highland, Nelson, Patrick, Pittsylvania, Rockbridge, Buchanan, Carroll,

Craig, Dickenson, Floyd, Grayson, Lee, Montgomery, Pulaski, Roanoke, Russell, Scott, Smyth, Tazewell, Washington, Wise, and Wythe Counties, Hampton Normal and Agricultural Institute, and two Federal institutions in Elizabeth City County

Washington.
108. Entire state

West Virginia.
109. Barbour, Berkeley, Brooke, Calhoun, Doddridge, Gilmer Grant, Hampshire, Hancock, Hardy, Harrison, Jefferson, Lewis, Marion, Marshall, Mineral, Monongalia, Morgan, Ohio, Pendleton, Pleasants, Preston, Randolph, Ritchie, Taylor, Tucker, Tyler, Upshur, Wetzel, Wirt, and Wood Counties
110. Boone, Braxton, Cabell, Clay, Fayette, Greenbrier, Jackson, Kanawha, Lincoln, Logan, McDowell, Mason, Mercer, Monroe, Nicholas, Pocahontas, Putnam, Raleigh, Roane, Summers, Wayne, Webster, and Wyoming Counties

Wisconsin.
111. Milwaukee and Walworth Counties
112. Dodge, Jefferson, Kenosha, Ozaukee, Racine, Washington, and Waukesha Counties
113. Crawford, Dane, Grant, Green, Iowa, Juneau, Lafayette, Richland, Rock, Sauk, and Vernon Counties
114. Adams, Brown, Calumet, Columbia, Door, Fond du Lac, Green Lake, Kewaunee, Manitowoc, Marquette, Outagamie, Sheboygan, Waushara, and Winnebago Counties
115. Ashland, Clark, Florence, Forest, Langlade, Lincoln, Marathon, Marinette, Oconto, Oneida, Portage, Price, Shawano, Taylor, Waupaca, and Wood Counties
116. Barron, Bayfield, Buffalo, Burnett, Chippewa, Douglas, Dunn, Eau Claire, Jackson, La Crosse, Monroe, Pepin, Pierce, Polk, St. Croix, Sawyer, Trempealeau, and Washburn Counties

Wyoming.
117. Entire state

Washington, DC, and miscellaneous.
118. Entire district

First Territorial Census for Oklahoma, 1890. N1811. 1 roll
These schedules were on one negative roll of microfilm given to the National Archives many years ago and placed in the Microfilm Reading Room. It was assigned the number GR24, by which it is referred to in the *Guide to Genealogical Research in the National Archives* (National Archives and Records Administration, revised 1985). In 1994, GR24 was assigned a new number, M1811, in order to issue it as an official National Archives Microfilm Publication. The territorial census was taken on and after June 1, 1890. The name of the county and city or township (often given by township number and range number) is given at the top of each schedule. The county name is often left blank or indicated as "none."

MICROFILM ORDER

Microfilm publication numbers (preceded by an "M" or "T") are assigned to each microfilm publication. Please enter the microfilm publication number and roll number(s) in the proper columns. Because we accept orders for individual rolls, as well as for complete microfilm publications, we must know which rolls you wish to purchase.

Effective May 15, 1996, the price for each roll of microfilm is $34 for U.S. orders. The price is $39 per roll for foreign orders. Shipping is included. These prices are subject to change without notice. For current price information, write to National Archives Customer Service Center (NWCC2), 8601 Adelphi Road, College Park, MD 20740; or call 1-800-234-8861 (in the Washington, DC, metropolitan area, 301-713-6800).

Sample of correctly completed form.

MICRO. PUB. NUMBER	ROLL NUMBER(S)	PRICE
T624	1138	$34.
T1270	88 - 89	$68.

Additional order forms are available upon request.

ORDERED BY *(Include organization if shipping to a business address.)*

Name	
Organization *(if applicable)*	
Address *(Number and Street)*	
City, State & ZIP Code	
Daytime Telephone Number *(Include area code)*	

PAYMENT TYPE

SEND YOUR ORDER TO:

CREDIT CARD

Check one and enter card number below. ☐ VISA ☐ MasterCard ☐ American Express ☐ Discover

Exp. Date

Signature

National Archives Trust Fund Cashier (NAT)
8601 Adelphi Road
College Park, MD 20740
(Credit card orders may be faxed to 301-713-6169)

OTHER

☐ Check ☐ Money Order
Make payable to: National Archives Trust Fund.

Amount Enclosed $

National Archives Trust Fund
P.O. Box 100793
Atlanta, GA 30384-0793

IDENTIFY THE ROLLS YOU WISH TO ORDER

MICRO. PUB. NUMBER	ROLL NUMBER(S)	PRICE		MICRO. PUB. NUMBER	ROLL NUMBER(S)	PRICE
					Subtotal (this column)	
					Subtotal from first column	
Subtotal (this column)					**TOTAL PRICE**	

NATIONAL ARCHIVES TRUST FUND BOARD   NATF Form 36 (rev. 2-2001)

Privacy Act and Paperwork Reduction Act Public Burden statements are on the back of this page.

NATIONAL ARCHIVES TRUST FUND BOARD   NATF Form 36 (rev. 2-2001)

OMB Control No. 3095-0046 Expires 02-29-2004

MICROFILM ORDER

Microfilm publication numbers (preceded by an "M" or "T") are assigned to each microfilm publication. Please enter the microfilm publication number and roll number(s) in the proper columns. Because we accept orders for individual rolls, as well as for complete microfilm publications, we must know which rolls you wish to purchase.

Effective May 15, 1996, the price for each roll of microfilm is $34 for U.S. orders. The price is $39 per roll for foreign orders. Shipping is included. These prices are subject to change without notice. For current price information, write to National Archives Customer Service Center (NWCC2), 8601 Adelphi Road, College Park, MD 20740; or call 1-800-234-8861 (in the Washington, DC, metropolitan area, 301-713-6800).

Sample of correctly completed form.

MICRO. PUB. NUMBER	ROLL NUMBER(S)	PRICE
T624	1138	$34.
T1270	88 - 89	$68.

Additional order forms are available upon request.

ORDERED BY *(Include organization if shipping to a business address.)*	Name
	Organization *(if applicable)*
	Address *(Number and Street)*
	City, State & ZIP Code
	Daytime Telephone Number *(Include area code)*

PAYMENT TYPE

SEND YOUR ORDER TO:

CREDIT CARD

Check one and enter card number below. ☐ VISA ☐ MasterCard ☐ American Express ☐ Discover

Exp. Date

Signature

National Archives Trust Fund
Cashier (NAT)
8601 Adelphi Road
College Park, MD 20740
(Credit card orders may be faxed to 301-713-6169)

OTHER

☐ Check ☐ Money Order

Make payable to: National Archives Trust Fund.

Amount Enclosed $

National Archives Trust Fund
P.O. Box 100793
Atlanta, GA 30384-0793

IDENTIFY THE ROLLS YOU WISH TO ORDER

MICRO. PUB. NUMBER	ROLL NUMBER(S)	PRICE		MICRO. PUB. NUMBER	ROLL NUMBER(S)	PRICE
					Subtotal (this column)	
					Subtotal from first column	
	Subtotal (this column)				**TOTAL PRICE**	

NATIONAL ARCHIVES TRUST FUND BOARD   NATF Form 36 (rev. 2-2001)

Privacy Act and Paperwork Reduction Act Public Burden statements
are on the back of this page.